Income Support for the Poorest

DIRECTIONS IN DEVELOPMENT

Human Development

Income Support for the Poorest

A Review of Experience in Eastern Europe and Central Asia

Emil Tesliuc, Lucian Pop, Margaret Grosh, and Ruslan Yemtsov

THE WORLD BANK
Washington, D.C.

Contents

Boxes

Figures

Tables

Preface

As countries weigh how best to reform their social protection systems—especially social assistance, or those noncontributory programs that aim to target the poor—one of the most vexing questions they face is how to determine who is eligible for the programs.

The conceptual, moral, and political discussions around the issue are often heated, and their resolutions vary across countries, programs, and time. Even when broad-stroke decisions are taken about who should be eligible, implementing those decisions with respect to particular individuals or households is technically complex and administratively demanding. Errors are inevitable, and they both undermine the effectiveness of the programs and risk upsetting their often delicate political support. Thus, targeting and eligibility determination are staple themes in the social assistance literature.

This book adds to that literature, reviewing the role and working of last-resort income support (LRIS) programs in Eastern Europe and Central Asia. The programs are narrowly targeted to the poorest, mostly with means testing or hybrid means testing, and commonly provide a minimum income guarantee. The programs were mainly put in place as part of the transition from central planning to market economies. They have been evolving and maturing since. Their experience is rich and varied and yet is relatively little documented or analyzed in the global literature.

The detailed cases discussed in this book go beyond examinations of the technical feasibility or efficiency of poverty-targeted programs in the region. The focus is on how these programs can improve their coverage, how they can control error and fraud, and how they can be implemented effectively in decentralized settings. The study breaks particularly new and important ground in (a) its treatment of administrative costs and (b) its dissection of income by sources according to the difficulty of verification and in quantifying the importance of the different sources to different groups in the economy.

Many of the themes treated are persistent subjects essential for any practitioner in the world of social assistance. These include the importance and affordability of the provision of adequate administrative capacity, the clear and consistent definitions of roles among agencies and levels of government, and the utility of developing and enhancing good management information systems. Perhaps especially important, the book shows that with good administrative capacity, means testing can be accomplished in settings with sizeable informal sectors.

Importantly, in terms of overall strategy for such programs, the authors suggest that currently, the role of LRIS programs within the overall social protection systems of the region is often too small. Therefore, LRIS programs need to revise and index their eligibility thresholds. If this is done, the authors submit that the programs can continue to serve a meaningful segment of the low-income households in each country—and can be used as the nexus to weave together a variety of income supports and services for these households.

This book fits within the larger strategic stream of work on social protection and labor systems, a direction strongly endorsed by *Resilience, Equity, and Opportunity* (the World Bank's 2012 Social Protection and Labor Strategy). Accordingly, for the World Bank Group, this book marks an important contribution to its mission to help countries across the world develop and improve their social protection and labor systems.

Arup Banerji
Director
Social Protection and Labor
The World Bank

Acknowledgments

This study was prepared by a team led by Emil Tesliuc (senior economist, Social Protection team for Europe and Central Asia) and comprising Lucian Pop (senior economist, Social Protection team for South Asia), Margaret Grosh (lead economist, Human Development Department for Latin America and the Caribbean), and Ruslan Yemtsov (lead economist, global Social Protection team).

The study has had a long history and gestation, and the authors owe many thanks to many people. In particular, it draws on extensive data and documentation built by many others. The team thanks David Coady (International Monetary Fund) for the conceptual framework for the analysis of social assistance programs and the methodology for collecting and analyzing administrative costs for social assistance programs. Most of the comparative information in chapter 2 is drawn from the Europe and Central Asia Social Protection Database, World Bank, developed and maintained by Ramya Sundaram, Victoria Strokova, and Tomas Damerau. The analysis of the dynamics of the targeting performance of selected last-resort income support (LRIS) programs was carried out by Vlad Grigoras (University of Bucharest and World Bank). The comparative poverty data were generously provided by Victor Sulla, who also maintained the comparative Eastern Europe and Central Asia poverty database. All our social protection colleagues in the Europe and Central Asia Region have helped the team at various stages, notably by compiling a first set of administrative data and program design parameters for LRIS programs in that region, and many were involved in the teams that generated many of the sources of country-specific work. They are too numerous to mention in the acknowledgments; rather, their work is found in the reference lists in the chapters. The six background reports (country case studies) from which this study draws were prepared by Vilma Kolpeja (Albania), Lyudmila Harutyunian (Armenia), Georgi Shopov (Bulgaria), CASE Kyrgyzstan (the Kyrgyz Republic), Laimute Zalimiene (Lithuania), and Lucian Pop (Romania). The background papers were first presented and discussed in a regional workshop in Bucharest, Romania. The team is very grateful to its counterparts from the governments of Albania, Armenia, Bulgaria, the Kyrgyz Republic, Lithuania, and Romania for sharing their ideas and feedback before and during the workshop, as well as for their commitment to participating in further discussions and for their support to the data collection for the administrative cost surveys carried out in the six countries. Some of the case studies used in this study were financed by the Bank-Netherlands Partnership Program (BNPP) on scaling up poverty work, administered by Asad Alam (presently country director, South Africa).

The task was completed under the general guidance of Arup Banerji, Anush Bezhanyan, Robert Holzmann, Bassam Ramadan, and Sandor Sipos. Phillippe Leite, Kathy Lindert, and Carlo del Ninno provided substantive inputs at early stages. The report benefited from peer review by Aline Couduel, Boryana Gotcheva, and Philip O'Keefe.

About the Authors

Emil Tesliuc is a senior economist in the World Bank's Europe and Central Asia Region. He has extensive operational, research, and policy experience in the areas of social assistance and social risk management. He has written a number of papers on poverty, vulnerability, and social protection. He is currently leading client engagements focused on improving targeting and the control of error and fraud in social protection programs in several Eastern European countries. He holds a PhD in economics from the Academy of Economic Studies in Bucharest, 1999, and a master of public policy degree from Princeton University, 2001.

Lucian Pop is a senior economist in the World Bank's South Asia Region, having served in prior assignments in the global Social Protection Department and in the Europe and Central Asia Region. He has been involved in investment projects, policy-development lending, and analytical work. Before joining the Bank, he was a lecturer at the University of Bucharest. His expertise includes the design and implementation of social assistance programs, poverty analysis, and the evaluation of social programs. He holds a PhD in sociology from the University of Bucharest, 2007.

Margaret Grosh is the lead economist for the World Bank's Latin America and the Caribbean Region Human Development Department. She has written, lectured, and advised extensively on social assistance programs, especially on targeting and cash transfer programs, globally and for Latin America. She has extensive experience with social protection both for crisis response and for improvement of equality of opportunity. Earlier, she led the team for social assistance in the World Bank's global Social Protection Department and, before that, the Living Standard Measurement Study in the Research Department. She holds a PhD in economics from Cornell University, 1986.

Ruslan Yemtsov is a lead economist and team leader for social assistance in the World Bank's global Social Protection Department. He has worked as a poverty economist in the Middle East and North Africa Region and in the Europe and Central Asia Region. His experience includes preparing poverty assessments (Bosnia and Herzegovina, Croatia, the Arab Republic of Egypt, Georgia, the former Yugoslav Republic of Macedonia, Serbia, and others); working on targeting and social assistance reviews (Croatia, Morocco, and the Russian Federation); and leading regional flagship reports on poverty, subsidy reforms, and statistical capacity. He has published journal articles, research papers, and chapters in monographs on labor markets, inequality, public policy, and wealth and income distribution. He holds a PhD in economics from Moscow State University, 1991.

Abbreviations

ASPIRE	Atlas of Social Protection: Indicators of Resilience and Equity
CIS	Commonwealth of Independent States
CTR	cost-transfer ratio
DMI	differentiated minimum income (Bulgaria)
EFC	error, fraud, and corruption
EU	European Union
EU10	new member states of the European Union
EU10+	Bulgaria, Croatia, the Czech Republic, Estonia, Hungary, Latvia, Lithuania, Poland, Romania, the Slovak Republic, and Slovenia
FBP	Family Benefit Program (Armenia)
GDP	gross domestic product
GMI	guaranteed minimum income (Bulgaria)
HBS	Household Budget Survey
HMT	hybrid means test
ICT	information and communication technology
LRIS	last-resort income support
LRSA	last-resort social assistance
LSMS	Living Standards Measurement Study (World Bank)
MIS	management information system
MoLFSP	Ministry of Labor, Family, and Social Protection (Romania)
MoLSA	Ministry of Labor, Social Affairs, and Equal Opportunities (Albania)
MT	means test
MTR	marginal tax rate
NASB	National Agency for Social Benefits (Romania)
NASBI	National Agency for Social Benefits and Inspection (Romania)
NE	Ndihma Ekonomike (Albania)
NEETD	not in employment, education, training, or disabled
NSSI	National Social Security Institute (Bulgaria)
OECD	Organisation for Economic Co-operation and Development

PES	public employment service
PMT	proxy means test
PPP	purchasing power parity
RSAD	regional social assistance directorate (Bulgaria)
RSSA	regional social services agency (Armenia)
SA	social assistance
SAD	social assistance directorate (Bulgaria)
SB	social benefit
SPeeD	Social Protection Expenditure and Evaluation Database
SSI	state-supported income
SSS	State Social Service (Albania)
SWB	social welfare benefits
TSA	targeted social assistance
UMB	Unified Monthly Benefit (Kyrgyz Republic)

CHAPTER 1

Introduction

Motivation

Most countries in the world aspire to protect their poorest and most vulnerable families from destitution and thus provide some type of income support to those who are very poor. These programs are often layered into social policy along with other transfers, subsidies, or services. The way to best provide such last-resort income support (LRIS) and its role in wider social policy is a matter of some complexity, much experimentation, and much study.

In Eastern Europe and Central Asia, 28 of 30 countries operate LRIS programs. Means tests and minimum income guarantees are the most common ways of determining eligibility and benefit levels, respectively. Despite the formidable challenges inherent in LRIS programs, the experience in Eastern Europe and Central Asia is on balance rather favorable. Most countries have at least one program that has operated on a continuous basis over a decade or more. The programs are all progressively targeted—all those reviewed deliver at least 40 percent of their benefits to the poorest quintile, two-thirds deliver 60 percent of their benefits to the poorest quintile, and a few deliver 80 percent of their benefits to the poorest quintile. Targeting performance has been sustained over time. Administrative costs are on average quite tolerable; they are 7–10 percent of total program costs for most mature programs of reasonable scale. In addition, work disincentives seem to have been held in check through a combination of means such as paying benefits that rarely exceed one-third of the income of the beneficiaries in the poorest quintile; sometimes tweaking the eligibility or benefit formula to encourage work; or requiring beneficiaries to register with employment services or work in exchange for benefits.

Means tests have been effective in Eastern Europe and Central Asia, but the "how to" and case knowledge for means testing has been less well documented than in the case for other targeting methods. This is unfortunate, because many countries both within Eastern Europe and Central Asia and beyond could use elements of this knowledge to improve their programs. The context of high informality and relatively low capacity and governance is common to Eastern Europe and Central Asia and many lower- to upper-middle-income countries. Moreover, some secular trends will make means testing increasingly feasible as the technology revolution makes for easier creation and sharing of databases across government agencies (including information on formal incomes, family size, and family assets) and as growth and changes in regulation gradually increase the size of formal sectors.

This study examines the experience of LRIS programs in Eastern Europe and Central Asia. It documents the outcomes of such programs throughout the region in terms of expenditure, coverage, targeting, and simulated effects on poverty and inequality. For a subset of countries, the study documents and draws lessons from the design and implementation arrangements—institutional frameworks and administrative structures, eligibility determination, benefits and conditions, governance mechanisms, and administrative costs—on the basis of information gleaned during in-depth country engagements that have extended a decade or more (Albania, Armenia, Bulgaria, the Kyrgyz Republic, Lithuania, and Romania) and other detailed work available from newer or more specific engagements (Croatia, the Russian Federation, Serbia, Ukraine, and Uzbekistan). The very granular detail available is highly unusual and conveys well the challenges and range of solutions possible in running these complex programs.

The findings have implications for three sets of policy action. First, the study can inform improvements of LRIS programs in the region. Many countries have been making reforms—some incremental, some sweeping—over the past two decades, and there is still an active policy agenda in this area. Second, these programs have features of interest to other similar programs outside the region. The experience with means testing and complex benefit formulas in middle-income countries with significant informal sectors may be helpful to countries in other regions. Brazil, Chile, and China, for example, have recently adapted elements of minimum income guarantees in their social assistance programming. Third, the study can inform the role of LRIS in the wider social assistance and social protection systems in Eastern Europe and Central Asia. That role has been diminishing over the past decade, but it may be sensible for it to expand again as fiscal constraints and demographic aging of the population put pressure on social protection systems.

Road Map of the Study

Chapter 2 provides an overview of the role of LRIS in the wider social assistance policies of Eastern Europe and Central Asia. It then reports on the program's coverage (the number of beneficiaries), generosity (the size of the transfer received by the beneficiaries), and incidence (the distribution of benefits across the income distribution), which are easily and widely available proxies for understanding final impacts. For a small set of countries, the chapter traces this information over time.

Chapter 3 looks into the institutional and financing arrangements of the LRIS programs in the case study countries. These arrangements are important because program performance is not only a matter of design but also implementation, and implementation depends on the institutional actors involved, the allocation of various functions and responsibilities, and their administrative capacity. The chapter distills lessons from the diverse experiences with different approaches to decentralization and provides background to the other chapters that handle the most difficult topics in program design and implementation.

Chapter 4 covers one of the two most charged issues in narrowly targeted LRIS programs—how eligibility is determined. The chapter starts by parsing household income by sources, describing both how income from some sources is harder or easier to verify and how the patterns differ across countries, income distribution, and sources of data. It provides significant detail on how select countries handle the intricacies of applications, formulas for eligibility, verification, and recertifications. The chapter discusses how to reduce the gap between the economic and administrative definitions of income used for determining eligibility, how to reduce the gap between reported and true income through cost-efficient documentation and verification, whether and how to complement income testing with asset testing, and how to combine means testing with other targeting as appropriate.

Chapter 5 takes up the other charged issue in these programs—the benefit formula and how labor disincentives can be held in check with the guaranteed minimum income design. In these programs, paying low benefits (which in turn implies low coverage and adequacy) has been an important mechanism. However, there are also a number of wrinkles in the benefit formula to encourage work, such as earnings disregards and the like, as well as links or requirements to register with employment offices and to provide community service and recently, in a few places, links with schooling requirements for children in the family.

Chapter 6 focuses on two key elements of control and accountability systems in LRIS programs—modern management information systems and strategies to reduce error, fraud, and corruption. Only a few programs in the region have addressed these issues by taking up the challenge of fully modernizing their programs. These recent experiences may provide inspiration to other programs.

Chapter 7 examines the administrative costs of the LRIS programs in the case study countries. The issue of the expense of operating narrowly targeted and highly complex programs and whether the marginal costs associated with means testing pay off in improved targeting accuracy is one of the most polemical in the social assistance field. This chapter illustrates the way to think about the issue, and annex 7A provides an instrument to delineate the functions and activities of different levels of government and to measure their costs. The data reported provide solid evidence that the programs produced very progressive distribution of benefits, sustained over time and for tolerable administrative costs—7–10 percent of total program costs for mature programs of reasonable scale.

Chapter 8 highlights and summarizes the lessons embedded in the earlier chapters and shows how they can help strengthen the LRIS programs in the Eastern Europe and Central Asia region, can provide lessons for poverty-targeted programs in other regions, and can inform thinking about the role of LRIS programs in larger social assistance systems.

Data Sources

This is a comparative study across many countries, and thus, as in all such studies, comparability of data matters enormously. We draw as much of the information as possible from four databases designed to be comparable. We supplement this with more individual, but rich, information gleaned from a variety of reports from World Bank staff or country governments in the course of policy dialogue in the respective countries. The need for comparable data means some specific figures will be different from what national observers of the same programs might expect. These figures may be produced with data or methods somewhat different from local time series to keep comparable methods across countries, or they may not be the most recent year, often in preference to looking at the bigger picture, which always implies time lags.

Source 1: Regional Archive of Household Surveys: Eastern Europe and Central Asia Databank and ECAPOV

The Eastern Europe and Central Asia household survey data archive (Eastern Europe and Central Asia Databank) with harmonized key variables was created in the early 2000s with a specific objective in mind: regional monitoring of poverty and inequality trends (ECAPOV [database of household surveys for Eastern Europe and Central Asia]; see Alam et al. 2005). The data archive originally contained the main official household surveys used to produce poverty assessments from 1995 to 2005 (as many rounds as was available at that time) for 22 countries. Over time, it grew to include more countries (28) and more years and is maintained by the poverty analysis and monitoring network of the World Bank.[1]

The main objective of harmonized key variables is to produce standardized consumption aggregates and key sociodemographic characteristics of household members that would allow comparisons of poverty profiles across countries and time, as well as comparisons of inequality levels and decompositions. This approach did not attempt to look at individual income sources, such as social protection transfers.

Source 2: Eastern Europe and Central Asia Social Protection Expenditure and Evaluation Database

The Eastern Europe and Central Asia Social Protection Expenditure and Evaluation Database (SPeeD) was established in 2005 at the same time as the ECAPOV database, to provide additional harmonization of social protection variables for surveys in the ECAPOV database and to complement data from household surveys by administrative statistics. Its design was greatly influenced by the use of comparative assessments of targeting for various programs. For 23 countries (of 30 countries in the region), it contains a full, regularly updated inventory of social protection programs from about 2000 onward, comprising program rules, budgets, and number of beneficiaries and benefits, which are linked with all available (typically annual) official household surveys with social protection modules.[2]

This unique data set (Latin America has recently started a similar linked administrative and survey database) can be used to assess the performance of social protection systems as a whole and the individual components, of which LRIS constitutes an important part. Because data on welfare (consumption) and programs are harmonized across countries, the data set can provide comparative assessment of key performance measures: coverage of the population and the poor, targeting accuracy, adequacy of benefits, and cost-benefit ratios. The data set also provides a useful description of trends in spending and evolution of caseloads across all programs.

Source 3: World Bank Atlas of Social Protection: Indicators of Resilience and Equity

A global effort to compile program level information from administrative and household survey sources is under way by the Human Development Network of the World Bank through the Atlas of Social Protection: Indicators of Resilience and Equity (ASPIRE) database. The effort is designed to mimic the Eastern Europe and Central Asia region approach and to a large extent was inspired by Eastern Europe and Central Asia databases, using similar channels. For each region, it relies on poverty-focused official household survey archives and databases that are harmonized by the poverty analysis and monitoring network of the World Bank. This effort is complemented by the social protection network in each region, which harmonizes social transfer data in the survey data sets and compiles program-level information from the administrative sources. The global database is a compilation of these regional depositories and now covers 56 countries (of which 17 countries are in Eastern Europe and Central Asia), with data spanning 1995–2012. Data for Eastern Europe and Central Asia in the ASPIRE database are the same as in the SPeeD database. The data from the other regions provide useful benchmarks to contrast the experience of Eastern Europe and Central Asia with that of other regions.

Source 4: Country Reports for Selected Countries

To obtain the level of detail needed to draw lessons from, and for, the design and implementation of LRIS programs, we rely on many reports generated by World Bank staff or government program officials over the years of policy dialogue. Many of these reports are unique, focusing on specific issues of interest in a particular country at a particular point in time. These reports provide great depth of information, albeit sometimes in a fragmented way. Thus, we also make extensive use of more comparable case studies of the LRIS programs in six countries that were prepared for a workshop titled "Program Implementation Matters for Targeting Performance: Evidence and Lessons from the ECA Region," which was held in Bucharest in 2005. The data collection methods for the country studies were (a) open interviews with the staff of the agencies formulating policy or implementing the respective program; (b) focus groups or one-to-one discussions with program administrators, program applicants, or beneficiaries; and (c) a literature review (laws and regulations, policy documents, administrative manuals, budget documents, and monitoring and evaluation reports).

The core countries of focus in this report are Albania, Armenia, Bulgaria, the Kyrgyz Republic, Lithuania, and Romania. These countries cover much of the spectrum from lower- to-upper-middle-income in Eastern Europe and Central Asia. Each LRIS program has been a mature (albeit constantly evolving) program for many years and has consistently performed well on at least one dimension of coverage, adequacy, and incidence. The World Bank and the core countries (and, in many cases, the study authors) have had a sustained dialogue that has produced a great deal of material from which to learn. A brief history of the LRIS programs in these six countries is provided in table 1.1. The study supplements the information and lessons from these six countries with lessons from other countries—Russian Federation, Ukraine, Uzbekistan, and the Western Balkans (Albania, Bosnia and Herzegovina, Kosovo, the former Yugoslav Republic of Macedonia, Montenegro, and Serbia)—where they illustrate interesting additional insights into the topics discussed.

Table 1.1 Summary Program Review

Country and program	Start year	Context and motivation for introducing the program	Target group, as stated in official documents or legislation	Reforms
Albania: Ndihma Ekonomike (NE)	1993	Social assistance was almost nonexistent in the past. The program was created to provide support to an increasing number of unemployed who were losing unemployment benefits because of long-term unemployment. When the program started to operate (June 1, 1993), there were about 150,000 unemployed people whose unemployment benefit had already expired. Another 240,000 unemployed people were expected to be in the same situation by the end of 1993. One-third of them were in households whose sole source of income was the unemployment benefit.	Households that have insufficient incomes or any other living means from economic activity, social protection or any other protection system, capital, or family members abroad	1995: introduction of "exclusion criteria" related to access to income-generating assets or a household member being employed Late 1990s and early 2000s: attempt to condition or complement the program with workfare 2005: right given to local governments to distribute NE (NE benefits also based on local criteria, which should not contradict rules defined by the program) 2005: delinking of the threshold from the unemployment benefit 2008, 2010: revisions of the methodology of funds allocation to local governments
Armenia: Family Benefit Program (FBP)	1999	There occurred very high poverty and unemployment (over 50 percent); inflation; humanitarian crises, including resettlement of large numbers of the population following the Nagorno-Karabakh conflict and 1998 earthquake; population aging; and budget constraints that required targeting of benefits. FBP was built starting from the Paros system, which was used to determine the level of poverty for distribution of humanitarian aid (1995; in 1996, about 71 percent of Armenian families were registered with Paros). The program consolidated 26 fragmented, categorically tested social assistance benefits into a single targeted family benefit.	Vulnerable families	2004: introduction of an oversight mechanism (Social Support Councils) 2007, 2008: adjustments of the eligibility threshold to increase coverage of the poor; introduction of gradual improvements to the eligibility formula

table continues next page

Table 1.1 Summary Program Review (*continued*)

Country and program	Start year	Context and motivation for introducing the program	Target group, as stated in official documents or legislation	Reforms
Bulgaria: guaranteed minimum income (GMI)	1992	Inflation, economy restructuring, and increase in long-term unemployment and poverty occurred. The introduction of a GMI was influenced by the Belgian Minimum Guaranteed Income and the French Minimum Social Inclusion Income programs.	Citizens, families, and cohabiting persons who, due to health, age, social, and other reasons independent of themselves, are unable alone (through labor or incomes realized from property), or with the help of persons obliged to support them according to the law, to satisfy their basic vital needs	2001: introduction of nationwide thresholds 2003: change from decentralized, cost-shared financing to centralized financing 2007: introduction of school attendance conditionality (reductions in the benefit level for children of school age who are not attending school) 2006: introduction of free hospital care for a subgroup of beneficiaries 2008: introduction of time limits (18 months) for beneficiaries able to work but unemployed; introduction of gradual improvements in eligibility criteria, verification controls, and recertification
Kyrgyz Republic: Unified Monthly Benefit (UMB)	1995	The country experienced increasing poverty. The social assistance system was reformed to provide targeted social assistance for the poor and to improve the system by consolidating the state benefits paid to families with children, social pensions, and compensation for bread and bakery products into one program (UMB).	Poor households with children, elderly, or disabled members	1998: introduction of the definition of guaranteed minimum level of consumption 1998: start of inclusion of imputed income from land in the aggregated household income
Lithuania: social benefit (SB)	1990	Restructuring of the Soviet social security system was carried out after independence. A new set of programs was introduced, consisting of a mix of categorical and means-tested benefits.	Low-income families or individuals: families or individuals by themselves who are unable to ensure sufficient earnings for subsistence	2004: introduction of asset test
Romania: GMI	1995	Inflation, economy restructuring, and an increase in long-term unemployment and poverty (over 25 percent) occurred. Only categorical social assistance programs were in place—mainly, child allowances and some compensatory benefits. The program was created to respond to the new context (including the need to rationalize the budget) and to fill in the gaps.	Low-income families or individuals	1997: fully decentralized financing 2002: introduction of cost-shared financing (central and local governments) 2006: introduction of unified methodology for imputing incomes from agriculture 2007: introduction of the Social Inspection as the main organization in charge of detecting error, fraud, and corruption and applying sanctions 2011: introduction of phased-out cost-shared financing; central government financing of 100 percent of benefits (through conditional grants)

Notes

1. Only two countries in Eastern Europe and Central Asia are not represented in the Eastern Europe and Central Asia Databank: the Czech Republic and Turkmenistan.
2. The 23 countries included in the full SPeeD data set are Albania, Armenia, Azerbaijan, Belarus, Bosnia and Herzegovina, Bulgaria, Croatia, Georgia, Kazakhstan, Kosovo, the Kyrgyz Republic, Latvia, Lithuania, the former Yugoslav Republic of Macedonia, Moldova, Montenegro, Romania, Russia, Serbia, the Slovak Republic, Tajikistan, Turkey, and Ukraine. Some data are also available for Estonia, Hungary, Poland, and Uzbekistan, but information is not complete or is not regularly updated.

Reference

Alam A., M. Murthi, R. Yemtsov, E. Murrugarra, N. Dudwick, E. Hamilton, and E. Tiongson. 2005. *Growth, Poverty, and Inequality: Eastern Europe and the Former Soviet Union.* Washington, DC: World Bank.

CHAPTER 2

The Role of Last-Resort Income Support in Eastern Europe and Central Asia

Almost all countries (28 of 30)[1] in the Eastern Europe and Central Asia region operate at least one last-resort income support (LRIS) program, albeit on different scales (table 2.1). These programs are a small part of the panoply of social assistance (noncontributory public transfers targeted in some way to the poor and vulnerable), which is in turn a small part of the overall social protection system in the region.

In most cases, the last-resort benefit is designed as a targeted program for those individuals who do not have access to other social assistance programs and who do not have much income from employment (for example, in Croatia, Montenegro, and Ukraine). Minimum income support programs may complement other public transfers, whether they are contributory (for instance, old-age pensions) or noncontributory (for instance, child allowances), as well as income from work that is insufficient to bring recipients to a defined minimum income standard (these are called guaranteed minimum income, or GMI, programs, as for example, in Bulgaria, Romania, Serbia, and the Slovak Republic), or to fill a specific expenditure gap (for example, Russian housing allowances). Finally, some countries run their LRIS program as a flat benefit system, not intending to bring all beneficiaries to a particular income level, but taking into consideration income from all sources (Estonia and Latvia) or actual welfare levels estimated by proxy means tests (Armenia and Georgia).

The roles of LRIS programs within the larger social protection system differ somewhat in Eastern Europe and Central Asia's middle- and low-income countries. In middle-income countries, LRIS programs typically occupy a small niche. Social insurance and universal transfers cover a wide swath of the population, and targeted LRIS assistance is directed to a comparatively smaller group. GMI programs in the Baltic countries, Central Europe, the Western Balkan countries, Bulgaria, and Romania are of this type.[2] In contrast, in low-income

Table 2.1 LRIS Programs in Eastern Europe and Central Asia and Number of Beneficiaries

Country	Number of beneficiaries (year)	Abbreviation of program name	Name or description of last-resort program
Albania[a]	100,300 (2009)	NE	Ndihma Ekonomike
Armenia[a]	105,000 (2010)	FBP	Family Benefit Program
Azerbaijan[a]	180,000 (2011)	TSA	Targeted social assistance
Belarus	287,000 (2008)	GASP	Public Targeted social assistance
Bosnia and Herzegovina[a]	9,000 (2008)	CSW	Child Social Welfare Benefits[b]
Bulgaria[a]	47,842 (2011)	GMI	Social monthly assistance/guaranteed minimum income
Croatia[a]	102,168 (2010)	SA	Social monthly assistance
Czech Republic[a]	71,153 (2008)	DPHN	Benefit in material need
Estonia[a]	38,000 (2008)	MT benefits	Subsistence benefit (means-tested benefit)
Georgia[a]	153,000 (2010)	TSA	Targeted social assistance
Hungary[a]	269,000 (2009)	RSA	Regular social assistance
Kazakhstan[a]	134,000 (2010)	TSA	Targeted social assistance
Kosovo	426,000 (2008)	SWB	Social welfare benefits
Kyrgyz Republic	356,000 (2010)	UMB	Unified Monthly Benefit
Latvia[a]	62,117 (2011)	GMI	Guaranteed minimum income
Lithuania[a]	74,433 (2009)	S. Benefit	Social benefit
Macedonia, FYR[a]	52,700 (2009)	SFA	Social financial assistance
Moldova[a]	27,000 (2010)	AS	Ajutor Social
Montenegro[a]	12,500 (2009)	FMS/MOP	Family material support and benefits based on social care
Poland[a]	444,615 (2011)	MPI	Temporary social assistance benefits (Pomoc Społeczna)
Romania[a,c]	232,300 (2010)	GMI	Social aid-guaranteed minimum income
Russian Federation[a,d]	2,344,494 (2009)	SZ	Various regional targeted cash assistance programs (social assistance for the poor)
Serbia[a]	167,000 (2009)	MOP	Material support for low-income households
Slovak Republic[a]	111,000 (2010)	BMN	Material need benefit
Slovenia[a]	48,700 (2010)	FSA	Financial social assistance
Tajikistan[a,e]	6,500 (2011)	TSA	Targeted social assistance (pilot)
Ukraine	76,300 (2010)	SA program	Targeted social assistance to low-income families
Uzbekistan	—	PB	Poverty benefit/targeted social assistance

Sources: General: Isik-Dikmelik 2012, Social Protection Expenditure and Evaluation Database (SPeeD), World Bank, Washington, DC. Country sources: Belarus—World Bank 2012c; Bulgaria—World Bank 2012a; Czech Republic (estimated monthly average of monthly beneficiaries count)—Ministry of Labour and Social Affairs http://www.mpsv.cz; Latvia—World Bank 2012b; Poland—Kozek, Zieleńska, and Kubisa 2013; Russian Federation—Roskomstat 2011; Slovenia—Ministry of Labour, Family and Social Affairs, http://www.mddsz.gov.si; Slovak Republic—Sundaram, Strokova, and Gotcheva 2012; Bosnia and Herzegovina, Kosovo—World Bank 2013.

Note: — = not available; LRIS = last-resort income support.

a. Number of households are included rather than individuals listed if households are units of assistance.
b. Including nonwar invalids' and disability benefits and civilian victims of war benefits.
c. Number of beneficiaries receiving GMI (as opposed to approved cases).
d. Russia's housing allowance (means-tested subsidy) covering about 5 million families is excluded.
e. Tajikistan is piloting LRIS programs in several regions.

countries, the LRIS programs are often the main social assistance instrument; the Unified Monthly Benefit in the Kyrgyz Republic, which was introduced in 1995 to replace a multitude of programs inherited from Soviet times, is an example. Armenia, Georgia, and Kosovo are other examples of countries using such poverty-targeted unified programs. The concentration of resources may help overcome significant capacity constraints and far greater demands in low-income countries.

Different models also exist in terms of links to other social assistance programs. In the European Union (EU), GMI schemes are usually combined with other support and activation measures and go beyond cash handouts. This approach recognizes that while the poor need cash assistance to help maintain minimum living standards, they also need other social and activation services to help them improve their basic situation, remove barriers to work, and connect them to gainful employment (Immervoll 2009). In Eastern Europe and Central Asia, this integrated approach is only recently gaining momentum, and most LRIS programs remain focused on cash assistance.

Most LRIS programs in the Eastern Europe and Central Asia region were introduced during the early or mid-1990s to cope with the rising unemployment and poverty that characterized the transitional period in Eastern Europe and countries of the former Soviet Union as they moved from centrally planned to market economies. At the start of the transition, poverty-targeted programs were almost nonexistent and, despite the presence of wide coverage of other social protection mechanisms (especially social insurance), a significant part of the population was falling through the systems' cracks.

Context for Last-Resort Programs in Eastern Europe and Central Asia: Poverty, Informality, and Inherited Social Protection Systems

All countries in Eastern Europe and Central Asia suffered what has come to be known as the "transition recession" in the 1990s. Output in Central and Eastern Europe fell by roughly 15 percent. The recession was much deeper and more protracted in the Commonwealth of Independent States (CIS), where output fell by 45 percent and the recovery had just started in 1997, only to be extinguished by the Russian financial crisis of 1998, before taking hold in 1999. Since then, the CIS has been among the fastest-growing developing regions, and by 2007 it had again attained the gross national product per capita level of 1990. However, the transition region was among the hardest hit by the global economic crisis in 2008. Gross domestic product (GDP) contracted by 5.2 percent, and registered unemployment increased in 2009. Although some countries, such as Poland, experienced slow but positive growth, several countries had severe output contractions (Latvia, for example, where real GDP fell by 18 percent).

The economic crisis hit households on multiple fronts: as workers lost their jobs, wage earnings were reduced, and remittances fell. The extent and severity of the effect on the welfare of citizens have varied, depending on the nature of the shocks experienced, the policy response, and the coping mechanisms available to households (Bidani and Sulla 2011).

In terms of GDP per capita levels in purchasing power parity (PPP), the income level ranges from about US$2,000 in 2005 PPP terms for the low-income CIS countries (the Kyrgyz Republic and Tajikistan) to almost US$20,000 for the EU10+ (in Croatia and Poland).[3] GDP per capita for low-income CIS countries is roughly comparable to levels observed in comparator countries (see table 2.2 for country data and selected benchmark country statistics). Countries selected for the in-depth analysis in this study—Albania, Armenia, Bosnia and Herzegovina, Bulgaria, Croatia, the Kyrgyz Republic, Lithuania, Romania, the Russian Federation, Serbia, and Ukraine—represent the full spectrum of economic structures and poverty rates in Eastern Europe and Central Asia.

The low-income CIS countries represent the poorest group in Eastern Europe and Central Asia. In this subregion, 25 percent of the population lives below the US$2.50-a-day poverty line, and another 40 percent between the US$2.50-a-day and US$5.00-a-day poverty lines. In this group, two countries selected for the study, Armenia and the Kyrgyz Republic, have high poverty rates, based on both national and international benchmarks.

Table 2.2 Country Contexts

Country	Population (millions) (1)	GDP per capita, PPP (US$) (2)	Poverty rate at US$2.50 per day, PPP (%) (3)	Poverty rate, national (%) (4)	Inequality (Gini) (5)	Employment in agriculture (% of total employment) (6)	Size of the unobserved economy (% of GDP) (7)
Eastern Europe and Central Asia countries							
Albania	3.14	7,293	13.3	12.4	0.304	58.0	34.3
Armenia	3.08	6,075	28.1	35.8	0.278	46.2	41.1
Bosnia and Herzegovina	3.77	8,095	1.5	14.0	0.356	—	32.8
Bulgaria	7.62	11,792	3.4	10.6	0.278	7.5	32.7
Croatia	4.43	17,663	0.2	11.1	0.303	12.8	30.4
Kyrgyz Republic	5.28	2,193	31.5	33.7	0.348	36.3	38.8
Lithuania	3.36	17,753	1.2	20.0	0.333	7.7	29.7
Romania	21.51	13,449	5.2	13.8	0.281	28.7	30.2
Russian Federation[a]	141.95	15,923	0.8	11.1	0.414	9.0	40.6
Serbia[a]	7.35	10,554	1.1	9.2	0.275	27.1	—
Ukraine[a]	46.26	7,277	0.2	25.3	0.255	16.7	46.8
Comparator countries							
Brazil[a]	191.9	9,500	14.8	21.4	0.547	17.0	36.6
Mexico[a]	110.4	12,900	11.7	51.3	0.477	13.0	28.8

Sources: World Development Indicators (database), World Bank, Washington, DC, http://data.worldbank.org/data-catalog/world-development -indicators, and ECAPOV (database), World Bank, Washington, DC, http://povertydata.worldbank.org/poverty/region/ECA.
Note: Most data are for 2007–08 or latest available year. — = not available; GDP = gross domestic product; PPP = purchasing power parity.
a. Data in column (7) are from Schneider, Buehn, and Montenegro (2010).

In the Western Balkans, poverty is moderate. Several countries in the study representing this group—Albania, Bosnia and Herzegovina, and Serbia—show significant differences inherent to this very heterogeneous region.

Among the new EU members and the middle-income CIS countries, poverty as defined by $2.50 a day is low, but these countries identify 10–20 percent of their population as poor or at risk of social exclusion. Bulgaria, Croatia, Lithuania, Romania, Russia, and Ukraine fit well into this range.

All the countries in Eastern Europe and the former Soviet Union experienced an increase in inequality. However, despite an apparent common legacy, these countries experienced very different paces in this increase. On the one hand, a rapid increase in inequality occurred in the middle- and low-income CIS countries, followed by some moderation in the 2000s. On the other hand, the new member states of the EU10, appear to have experienced a more gradual but steady increase in inequality. By the late 2000s, the region exhibited the full spectrum of inequality outcomes, ranging from fairly unequal (Russia, Gini of 0.414) to fairly equal distributions of income (Ukraine, Gini of 0.255). Nevertheless, economic inequality remains below what is observed in comparable economies of Latin America (see table 2.2).

Informality has important implications both for the financing of social protection and for the design of social policies. Informal workers tend to be poorly protected by the insurance mechanisms related to employment and therefore require special attention. They also tend to be much poorer than the rest of the population. At the same time, high informality of economy and employment makes targeting based on formal means tests difficult to carry out, thus hindering targeting to those who really need assistance. The degree of informality therefore is an important factor influencing social policy.

Columns (6) and (7) in table 2.2 provide some information on the size of the informal economy. The share of the working population employed in agriculture typically acts as a proxy for an employment-based definition of the informal sector because individuals employed in the agricultural sector are not well covered using traditional social insurance mechanisms. Column (7) provides macroeconomic estimates of the shadow economy, which have a number of limitations and contradictions with employment-based statistics.[4] The degree to which the informal economy is important does seem to resemble two comparator countries—Brazil and Mexico.

How Much Is Spent on LRIS Programs?

Total social protection spending is high in Eastern Europe and Central Asia, absorbing an average of 10 percent of GDP: 8 percent for social insurance (mostly pensions) and close to 2 percent for social assistance (LRIS programs constitute one part of this set). Weigand and Grosh (2008) show that worldwide, average social protection spending as a share of GDP in countries of Eastern Europe and Central Asia is the second highest after that of countries in the Organisation for Economic Co-operation and Development (OECD).[5]

Figure 2.1 Social Assistance Spending by Main Types of Programs, 2008–09

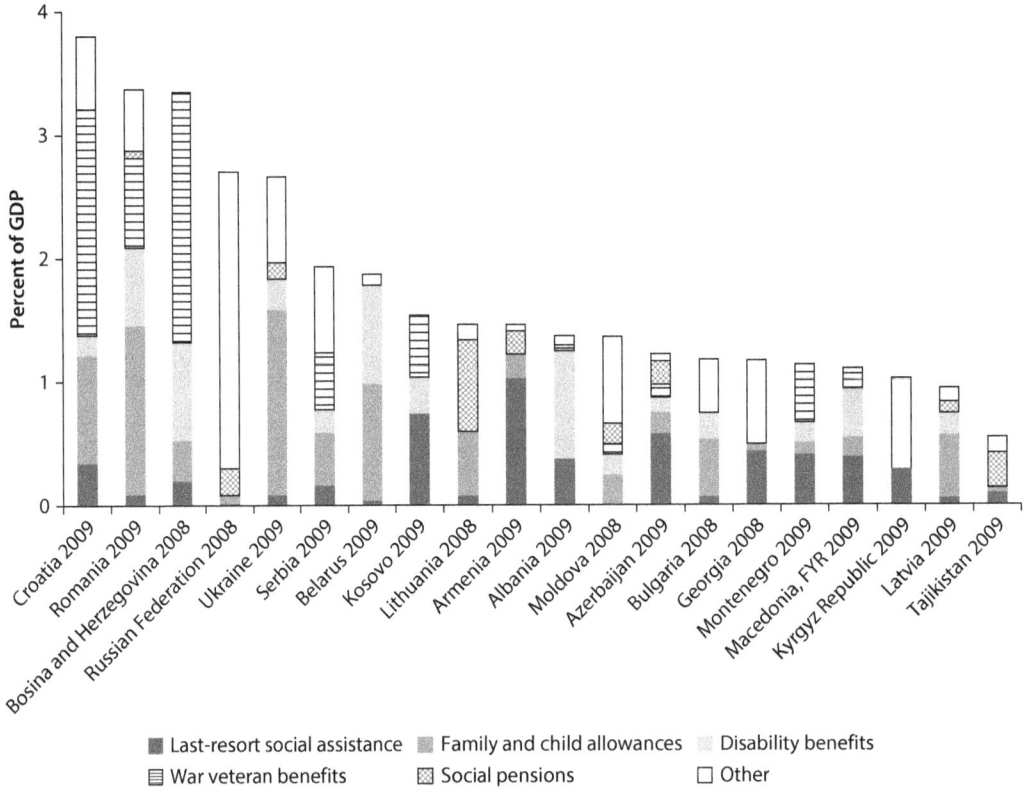

Legend:
- ■ Last-resort social assistance
- ▦ Family and child allowances
- ░ Disability benefits
- ▤ War veteran benefits
- ▨ Social pensions
- □ Other

Source: Europe and Central Asia Social Protection Expenditure and Evaluation Database (SPeeD), World Bank, Washington, DC, http://intranet .worldbank.org/WBSITE/INTRANET/INTCOUNTRIES/INTECA/INTOFFVICEPRE/0,,contentMDK:23170361~pagePK:64168332~piPK:64168299~theSite PK:4381828,00.html.
Note: Data from Russian regions cannot be disaggregated and are represented as "other," but last-resort income support constitutes a sizable share of this aggregate. GDP = gross domestic product.

Updated figures on budget spending (figure 2.1) show a similar level of spend-ing among countries of Eastern Europe and Central Asia and similar patterns: most countries spend 1–2 percent of GDP on social assistance; a few spend more—expenditure on social assistance exceeds 3 percent of GDP in Bosnia and Herzegovina, Croatia, and Romania. Conversely, in a few countries expen-ditures are quite low; indeed, they are considerably less than 1 percent of GDP in Latvia and Tajikistan.

Social Assistance: Spending by Type of Programs

In most countries, LRIS is accompanied by a panoply of interventions. The main categories of social assistance programs in Eastern European and Central Asian countries are as follows:

- *LRIS programs*, whose main objective is to alleviate poverty and provide income support to the poor and vulnerable.

- *Family and child support with services and allowances* that aim to protect families with children as well as to increase fertility rates, protect the jobs and incomes of mothers and parents more broadly, and promote the development of human capital.
- *Social pensions* that protect the elderly, who may not have a pension income or who have insufficient income.
- *Housing allowances (including energy subsidies)* that subsidize dwelling expenses and that are often means tested.
- *Disability allowances* that provide financial and in-kind support to people with disabilities who are not eligible for contributory disability benefits or pensions. Most Eastern European and Central Asian countries operate noncontributory disability benefits schemes as part of their social safety net.
- *War veteran benefits* that compensate the families of fallen soldiers for the loss of the breadwinner, protect disabled former soldiers and their families, and in certain instances, reward veterans of wars for their service.
- *Workfare and public work programs* remain relatively rare in countries of Eastern Europe and Central Asia, despite their reintroduction in some countries during the recent global crisis that began in 2008. Although some last-resort programs include workfare requirements for workable beneficiaries, these requirements are often not strictly enforced: the public employment services lack the funding or capacity to organize regular public work or training for the beneficiaries.
- *Other programs*, such as privileges given to certain groups of people or price and tariff subsidies, still remain in place as legacy programs in most CIS countries.

Some countries have more than one means- or income-tested program: Bulgaria and Romania have income-tested child and family allowances and heating allowances as well as LRIS; Lithuania has a minimum income guarantee alongside a means-tested utilities compensation program (for heating and other utility bills); a similar approach is taken by Russia, where most regions run both targeted cash transfers of last resort and means-tested housing subsidies. Only in rare cases do the other means-tested programs use exactly the same rules and criteria as the LRIS programs, but in general they are based on the same principles.

As can be seen from figure 2.1, LRIS spending varies significantly across countries in Eastern Europe and Central Asia: from significant (such as in Armenia, which spends 1.0 percent of GDP, and Albania, Azerbaijan, Georgia, Kosovo, Montenegro, and the former Yugoslav Republic of Macedonia, which spend around 0.5 percent of GDP) to almost negligible (Belarus, Bulgaria, Latvia, Lithuania, and Romania).

LRIS programs have a varied place in the social assistance systems of Eastern Europe and Central Asia. Where social protection evolved gradually over the transition from central planning to a market-based economy, social assistance is represented by a complex mix of different schemes (as in Bulgaria, Croatia, Latvia, Lithuania, or Ukraine), where LRIS constitutes a small fraction of the spending and a small fraction of GDP.

Systems that have undergone radical reforms are rather an exception (such as Albania, Armenia, Georgia, and Kosovo), and in these systems LRIS appears to occupy a more prominent place among other programs and as a share of GDP. For example, Armenia in 1999 merged 28 categorical programs into a single poverty-targeted program (Family Benefit Program), which now accounts for 80 percent of the country's social assistance spending. Albania operates one LRIS program and one noncontributory disability benefit program, whereas Kosovo has four social assistance schemes or programs, and LRIS accounts for close to half of all social assistance spending.

Last-Resort Programs in Eastern Europe and Central Asia: Adequacy of Spending Envelopes

Spending on LRIS programs can be judged adequate if it is commensurate with their objective of eliminating poverty. Poverty is eliminated when every poor person is lifted to at least the poverty line, in other words, when the total poverty gap (the aggregate distance between actual consumption and the poverty line) is filled by a transfer. A comparison of total expenditures on the programs compared with the poverty gap helps ascertain to what extent a program could in principle eliminate poverty, though of course targeting errors and administrative costs mean that expenditures will have to be somewhat higher than the value of the poverty gap to achieve the intended effects on poverty.

Different definitions of poverty exist, and figure 2.2 shows recent figures for three alternative measures, using the most recent survey data available (2008–09 in most cases) and calculating the poverty gaps as a percentage of GDP.

Figure 2.2 Cost of Filling the Poverty Gap (Various Poverty Lines) versus Spending on LRIS Programs, 2008–09

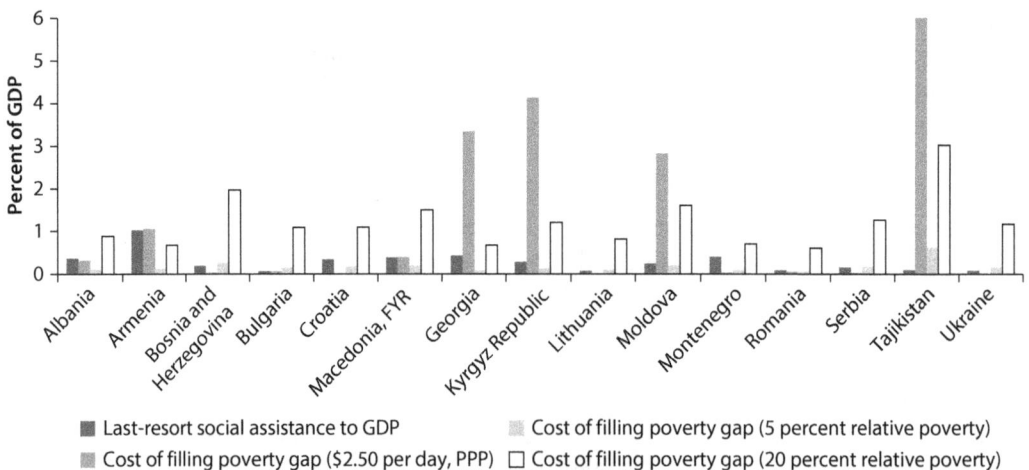

■ Last-resort social assistance to GDP   ▨ Cost of filling poverty gap (5 percent relative poverty)
▨ Cost of filling poverty gap ($2.50 per day, PPP) □ Cost of filling poverty gap (20 percent relative poverty)

Sources: Estimates based on Europe and Central Asia Social Protection observatory (see figure 2.1) and poverty data from ECAPOV (database), http://povertydata.worldbank.org/poverty/region/ECA.
Note: Years of poverty and budget data differ across countries, but closest survey year is used for each country. GDP = gross domestic product; LRIS = last-resort income support; PPP = purchasing power parity.

We use one absolute threshold of US$2.50 per day in PPP and two relative poverty thresholds—poverty defined as the bottom 5 percent or bottom 20 percent of the population. In fact, according to national poverty lines, all countries discussed here have a poverty rate well above 5 percent (see table 2.2), so one can take the lower relative poverty line (defining the poorest 5 percent of the population) to represent the extremely poor by any country's standards. Such a group would be regarded as clearly deserving to be a priority in terms of any LRIS targeting. In most countries, the cut-off at 20 percent of the poorest will capture both the poor and those "vulnerable" to extreme poverty.

In most countries, spending on LRIS is comparable to or exceeds the poverty gap at US$2.50 per day (Albania, Armenia, Bosnia and Herzegovina, Croatia, Lithuania, Romania, Serbia, and Ukraine; see figure 2.2). Only a few of the poorest countries with a large absolute poverty gap spend less on LRIS than the value of the poverty gap: Tajikistan spends only 0.1 percent of GDP on LRIS, too little to fill an absolute poverty gap as high as 6.0 percent of GDP; Moldova has LRIS spending of 0.25 percent of GDP but a poverty gap of 2.8 percent of GDP; the Kyrgyz Republic spends 0.3 percent, compared with its poverty gap of 4.1 percent; and Georgia spends 0.4 percent, while its poverty gap is 3.3 percent of GDP. But in these countries (with the exception of Tajikistan), spending on LRIS is at least comparable to the cost of completely eliminating extreme relative poverty (defined as the poorest 5 percent of the population).

The spending on LRIS is well below the poverty gap when the poverty line is defined as the poorest 20 percent of the population, even in middle-income countries; however, this does not mean that the bottom quintile is an irrelevant group to judge the performance of LRIS. First, this is a common measure universally used to compare how well different social programs target those at the bottom of income distribution. Even though poverty headcounts and target groups differ across countries and programs, to be effective in helping those who are poor and vulnerable (and not only those who are poor at the moment of a survey), programs need to target broadly those at the bottom of the distribution, be it 20 percent or 40 percent. For simplicity and to be close to the extreme poor, this study uses the 20 percent cutoff. Second, LRIS programs operate in the context of and complement other social assistance programs, and this combined effect on the poor and vulnerable population is the focus of this chapter.

Last-Resort Programs in Eastern Europe and Central Asia: What Do They Achieve?

The effectiveness of a transfer in reducing poverty depends on the following factors: (a) whether a significant part of the poor are covered by the program (*coverage*); (b) whether its funds go primarily to the poor (*incidence*); and (c) whether the transfer is adequate (*generosity*) to raise the income of recipients in a meaningful way (above the poverty line). Programs can be compared with each other in terms of how efficiently they reduce poverty, which is an ultimate measure of their effect.

In what follows, we look first at coverage, incidence, and generosity of selected LRIS programs and then discuss their effect on poverty. We use data from the data archive of the Eastern Europe and Central Asia Social Protection Expenditure and Evaluation Database (SPeeD) that harmonize available official household survey data.[6]

What Are the Limitations of the Data?

We use data from household surveys to assess the performance of social assistance programs. The inclusion of questions on specific transfers in the household survey questionnaire drives the extent to which we can measure the performance of these transfers.[7] A World Bank study (2010) looked in detail at social assistance transfers that are included in the household surveys alongside the social assistance transfers for which administrative data are available. Unfortunately, household surveys seem to capture a varying span of data, compared with the administrative data available, ranging from about 29 percent in Bosnia and Herzegovina to 59 percent in Montenegro to 95 percent in Latvia.[8]

How Well Are the Poor in Eastern Europe and Central Asia Covered by LRIS Programs?

The essential feature of LRIS programs is their targeting of the poor, and the number of beneficiaries of targeted social assistance (TSA) in principle should be comparable to the number of poor people. Countries differ in terms of how they define poverty, and typically the real value of the poverty line increases with income levels (Ravallion and Chen 2011). To get a sense of the scale of both nationally defined poverty and absolute poverty defined with a comparable international poverty line, table 2.3 presents headcount rates for (a) US$2.50 per day (in 2005 PPP), (b) poverty rates defined by national poverty lines, and (c) program coverage from administrative data (expressed as a percentage of the population).

Absolute poverty rates differ significantly across countries, as does the ability of LRIS programs to cover the poverty gap. In countries with low poverty incidence (Bulgaria, Croatia, Montenegro, Romania, and Serbia), the percentage of the population covered by social assistance and LRIS programs is above or close to the poverty headcount figures. Two poor countries (Albania and Kosovo) also serve a share of the population roughly in line with the percentage of population that is poor; but in other countries (either low or middle income), both social assistance and LRIS cover very small percentages of the population, well below the poverty rates, meaning that even with perfect targeting, most of the poor will not be covered. For example, in Georgia between 25 percent (national poverty line) and 50 percent of the population is poor (using US$2.50 a day as a benchmark), but the coverage of LRIS is only about 3 percent of the population (see table 2.3).

Even where the number of beneficiaries in a program may be commensurate with the number of poor, one must look at household survey data to see how

Table 2.3 Poverty Headcounts and Number of Beneficiaries of Social Assistance and LRIS Programs

Country	Poverty at US$2.50 per day 2005 PPP (% of population)[a]	National poverty rate (% of population)[b]	Social assistance beneficiaries Number of beneficiaries (thousands)	Maximum share of population (%)	LRIS direct and indirect beneficiaries[c] Number of beneficiaries (thousands)	Share of population (%)
Albania[c]	13.3	12.4	473	15.0	400	12.7
Armenia[c]	28.1	35.8	480	16.4	303	10.2
Bosnia and Herzegovina	1.5	14.0	181	4.8	9	0.25
Bulgaria	3.4	10.6	1,700	22.3	39	0.4
Croatia	0.2	11.1	330	7.4	100	2.3
Georgia	49.1	24.7	370	8.5	140	3.2
Kosovo	36.2	34.5	650	30.6	427	20.1
Kyrgyz Republic	31.5	33.7	610	11.7	387	7.5
Lithuania	1.2	20.0	100	3.0	37	1.1
Macedonia, FYR	9.0	19.0	31	1.5	11	0.5
Montenegro[c]	1.4	9.3	66	10.7	40	6.5
Romania	5.2	13.8	1,100	5.1	300	1.4
Serbia	1.1	9.2	568	7.7	139	1.9
Ukraine[c]	0.5	25.0	1,900	4.1	200	0.4

Sources: Based on World Bank data and staff calculations; data for all countries are for 2008–09.

Note: The total number of social assistance beneficiaries is a simple sum of all household members of social assistance program participants; therefore, it overestimates the actual coverage in cases where benefits overlap (that is, households receiving multiple benefits are counted several times). Counts of LRIS beneficiaries may differ from figures in table 2.1 due to differences in reference year. LRIS = last-resort income support; PPP = purchasing power parity.

a. Data are from the most recent poverty monitoring database by the World Bank, PovcalNet, http://iresearch.worldbank.org/PovcalNet/index.htm.
b. Most recent data with national poverty lines available to the World Bank, except for Ukraine, where national statistics office figures are used, and Lithuania, where the European Union relative poverty line is used.
c. For these countries the number of beneficiaries includes both direct (recipients) and indirect (household members).

well the poor are actually covered by programs. For such household survey data, see table 2.4 and figure 2.3.

In none of the countries do the LRIS programs achieve even 50 percent coverage of the poorest quintile, the best being Armenia with a coverage rate of close to 40 percent. Some groupings of countries are of interest: Armenia and Kosovo are at the top of the list as having LRIS programs with the widest coverage of the poorest quintile. This is clearly related to the role LRIS plays as the mainstay social assistance. Interestingly, a similar or slightly higher range of magnitudes is observed in some comparator countries in Latin America and the Caribbean: about one-half the bottom quintile is covered by Mexico's Oportunidades, Brazil's Bolsa Família, and the conditional cash transfer in the Dominican Republic.[9] In Bosnia and Herzegovina and Kazakhstan, in contrast, LRIS programs cover less than 5 percent of the bottom quintile. Bulgaria, Croatia, Romania, and Serbia, which have multiple programs, seem to have intermediate coverage rates for LRIS (around 15 percent). Coverage rates of 22 percent for Albania and Georgia, however, represent a worrying sign, because the LRIS program in these countries is the sole provider of targeted support to the poor and vulnerable.

The preceding discussion demonstrates that LRIS coverage rates in isolation from other social assistance programs are difficult to interpret. Comparing

Table 2.4 Share of the Poorest Quintile Covered by LRIS, Latest Data Available

Program and country	Year	Share of poorest quintile covered (%)	Program and country	Year	Share of poorest quintile covered (%)
Armenia: FBP (Family Benefit Program)	2010	38	Romania: GMI (social aid-guaranteed minimum income)	2009	13
Kosovo SWB (social welfare benefits)	2009	33	Croatia SA (social monthly assistance)	2008	12
Macedonia, FYR: SFA (social financial assistance)	2010	24	Latvia: GMI (Guaranteed minimum income) and dwelling	2010	10
Albania: NE (Ndihma Ekonomike)	2008	22	Estonia: MT benefits (subsistence benefit [means-tested benefit])	2004	7
Georgia: TSA (targeted social assistance)	2007	22	Hungary RSA (regular social assistance)	2004	7
Kyrgyz Republic: UMB (Unified Monthly Benefit)	2007	22	Lithuania: S. Benefit (social benefit)	2008	6
Poland MPI benefits (temporary social assistance benefits [Pomoc Społeczna])	2011	18	Ukraine SA program (targeted social assistance to low-income families)	2010	6
Bulgaria: GMI (social monthly assistance/guaranteed minimum income)	2007	15	Bosnia and Herzegovina: CSW (child social welfare benefit)	2007	4
Serbia: MOP (material support for low-income households)	2010	15	Kazakhstan: TSA (targeted social assistance)	2007	3
Montenegro: FMS/MOP (family material support and benefits based on social care)	2010	13	Tajikistan: TSA (targeted social assistance)	2011	0

Source: Calculations based on Social Protection Expenditure and Evaluation Database (SPeeD), World Bank, Washington, DC (see figure 2.1).
Note: LRIS = last-resort income support.

Figure 2.3 Share of Poorest Quintile Covered by All Social Assistance and by LRIS, Latest Data Available

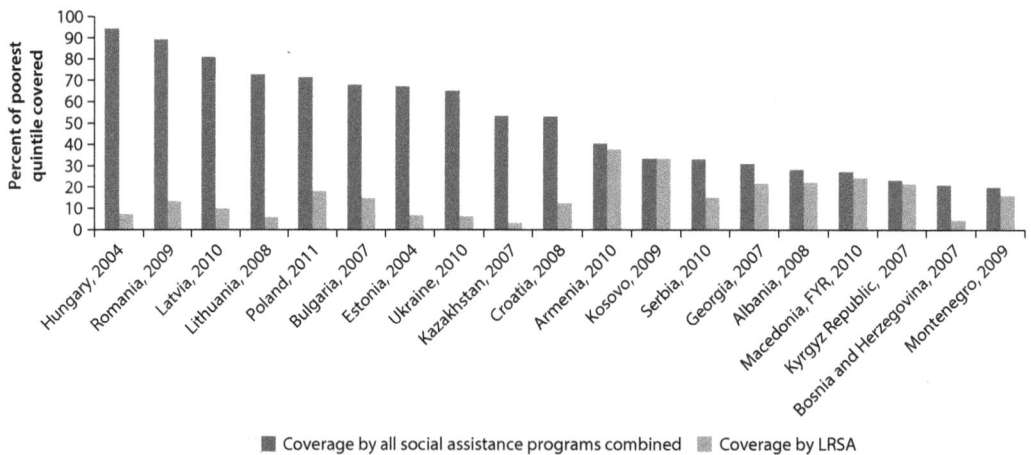

Source: Calculations based on Eastern Europe and Central Asia Social Protection Expenditure and Evaluation Database (SPeeD), World Bank, Washington, DC (see figure 2.1).
Note: For the list of program names see table 2.1. LRIS = last-resort income support; LRSA = last-resort social assistance.

coverage data of the poorest quintile by all social assistance programs with coverage by last-resort programs can be helpful (see figure 2.3).[10]

In richer countries, even though LRIS programs cover only a small fraction of the poorest quintile, 70–90 percent of the poor are covered by different forms of social assistance (Bulgaria, Hungary, Romania, Ukraine, and the Baltic countries); in poorer countries where LRIS programs have the highest coverage, the programs are not supplemented by other forms of assistance but are the sole form of support to poor families, and the gap remains large with more than half the poorest not receiving any form of social assistance (Albania, Armenia, Georgia, and Kosovo).

Thus, LRIS programs do not provide extensive coverage of the poor in most countries of Eastern Europe and Central Asia, where such programs tend to be small. In cases where absolute poverty affects a small fraction of the population or where by design LRIS aims only at those at the very bottom of the distribution—the extreme poor—such coverage may be intentional. But in other cases (Albania, Georgia, and the Kyrgyz Republic), it is a rather worrying sign to find that the majority of the poorest quintile (and the national poverty rates in these countries are in excess of or close to this mark) is not covered by social assistance.

How Well Does LRIS Focus Its Assistance on the Poorest?

The second factor that determines the effect of cash transfers on well-being is their incidence, or the percentage of benefits going to the poorest (10 percent, 20 percent, 40 percent—however poverty is measured). If the program can direct more resources to the poor while excluding the nonpoor, it will achieve greater effect in reducing poverty compared with a program of similar budget but less progressive incidence.

The data from household surveys consistently show that the incidence of LRIS programs is highly progressive. Over 70 percent of all funds go to the poorest quintile of population in about half the cases, and nowhere is it below 40 percent—a measure that is considered moderately progressive targeting (Coady, Grosh, and Hoddinott 2004). Lithuania achieves a 90 percent ratio to the poorest—one of the highest in the world (see figure 2.4). Only 3–8 percent of LRIS benefits go to the richest quintile (figure 2.5).[11]

Eastern Europe and Central Asia's LRIS programs are among the most progressively targeted in the world. Figure 2.5 compares the share of benefits going to each quintile across a number of social assistance programs in Eastern Europe and Central Asia among the best-targeted programs represented in the ASPIRE database.[12] In the figure, programs from Bulgaria, Moldova, Romania, and Ukraine appear above well-known conditional cash transfer programs in Latin America, transferring a higher share of their funds to the poorest 20 percent of the population. But at the same time, LRIS programs coexist in all countries in Eastern Europe and Central Asia with other social assistance programs that transfer lower shares of their budget to the poorest quintile—at times dramatically so (compare Moldovan and Romanian LRIS shares with child allowances in the same countries).

Figure 2.4 Share of LRIS Benefits Going to the Poorest Quintile in Eastern Europe and Central Asia, Latest Data Available

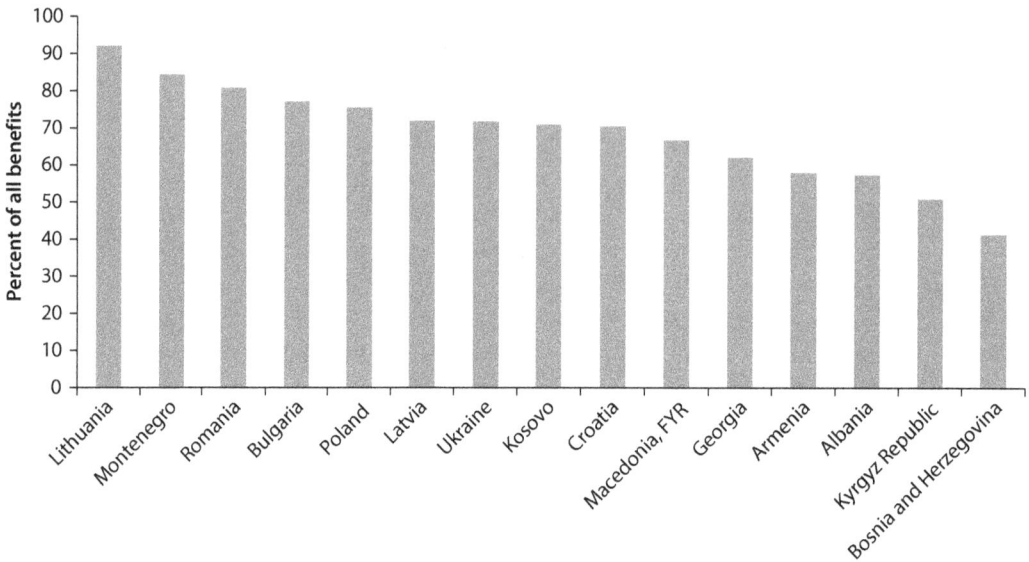

Source: Europe and Central Asia Social Protection Expenditure and Evaluation Database (SPeeD), World Bank, Washington, DC (see figure 2.1), latest year available.
Note: For the list of program names see table 2.1. LRIS = last-resort income support.

How Generous Are the LRIS Programs in Eastern Europe and Central Asia?

The third factor that determines performance of cash transfers in terms of poverty reduction is the size of benefits. Clearly, many considerations lie behind setting the benefit level, including need, fiscal space, and incentive effects (Grosh et al. 2008), but from a simple income supplement point of view, to reduce poverty, an LRIS transfer should be at least comparable to the poverty gap of the household it is helping.

In Eastern Europe and Central Asia, the TSA benefits vary greatly as a share of household expenditures (figure 2.6). For recipient households in the first quintile, benefits are on average equivalent to 25 percent of their consumption, an amount that is comparable to the poverty gap of an average poor household in these countries. In Georgia, Kosovo, and Lithuania, benefits exceed 40 percent of the poorest quintile's budget—exceeding as well the poverty gaps of recipients. Beneficiaries in the first quintile in most countries (Albania, Kazakhstan, the Kyrgyz Republic, Latvia, and Ukraine) receive less than 20 percent of their consumption as a transfer; in these countries, the LRIS transfer represents less than one-half of the absolute poverty line (see discussion in chapter 4).

The Effect of LRIS on Poverty in Eastern Europe and Central Asia

Given the typically restrained size of LRIS programs in Eastern Europe and Central Asia, one would expect to find that their effects on poverty are small in

Figure 2.5 Benefit Incidence of Selected Cash Transfer Programs around the World

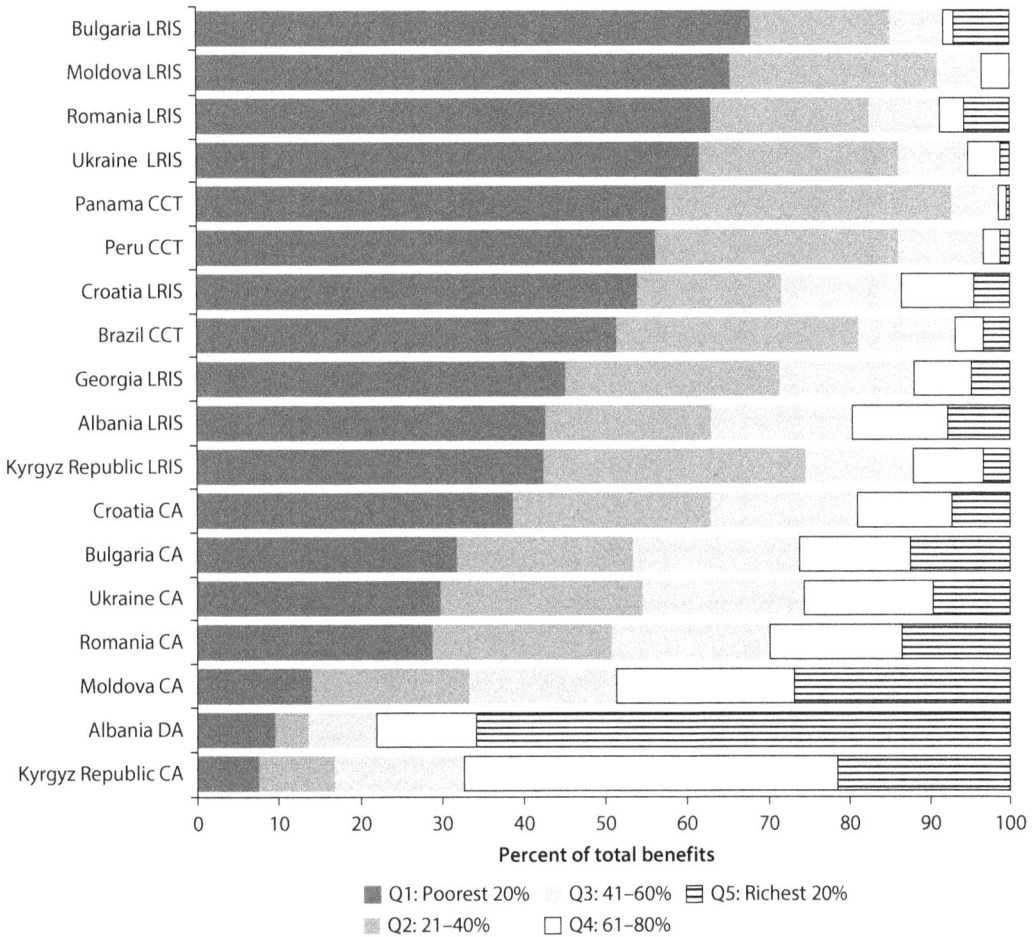

Source: Atlas of Social Protection: Indicators of Resilience and Equity (ASPIRE) (database), 2007–10, World Bank, Washington, DC, http://www
.worldbank.org/aspire.
Note: Percentage of social assistance transfers in each program received by the population in each quintile (Q) from poorest to richest. CA = child
and family allowance; CCT = conditional cash transfer; DA = disability allowance; LRIS = last-resort income support. Because of differences in
defining the welfare measure in a harmonized way globally, results are slightly different from those in figure 2.6, which uses definitions specific to
Eastern Europe and Central Asia.

most cases—despite their sharp targeting and efficiency in transferring resources
to the poor. Although the programs are highly progressive, their limited coverage and generosity would make the society-wide effect of the transfers rather
small.

Table 2.5 presents the most recent data on the poverty and inequality effects
of LRIS programs in the context of the overall social assistance systems assessment, using a relative poverty measure of the poorest quintile of consumption or
income in each country. It shows how LRIS programs affect the poverty headcount, the poverty gap, and overall inequality and how much they contribute to
total poverty reduction achieved by social assistance. In addition, comparing the

Figure 2.6 Benefits as a Share of Posttransfer Consumption of Beneficiary Households in the Poorest Quintile, Eastern Europe and Central Asia

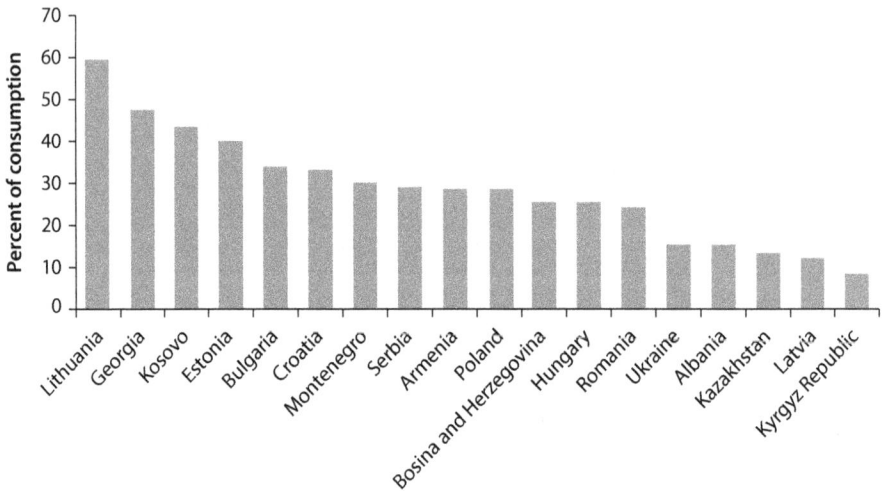

Source: Europe and Central Asia Social Protection Expenditure and Evaluation Database (SPeeD), World Bank, Washington, DC (see figure 2.1), latest available year.
Note: See table 2.1 for a list of programs.

reduction in the poverty gap with the cost of the program or total budget of transfers paid gives a measure of transfer efficiency.

Overall, social assistance systems in Eastern Europe and Central Asia have a sizable effect on poverty, especially on poverty gaps. In some countries, the pre-transfer poverty gap is almost halved. LRIS programs contribute a fraction to that, reflecting their small role in the system in some countries. But LRIS programs achieve notable reductions in the poverty gap of their beneficiaries given their budgets. Table 2.5 shows that in a simulated absence of the LRIS benefits, the *poverty gap* would rise by 10–50 percent across most countries. This indicates that the LRIS benefits reach a high proportion of the extremely poor and constitute a significant poverty alleviation instrument.

Thus, LRIS programs in Eastern Europe and Central Asia achieve remarkable results in terms of helping the poor even within limited budgets. They are cost-effective: for each monetary unit (dollar) spent on LRIS benefits in Eastern Europe and Central Asia, 40–70 percent (cents) goes directly to the poorest to reduce their poverty gap. This is one of the highest cost/benefit ratios in the world (comparable to some best-performing programs, such as conditional cash transfers in Latin America and the Caribbean). This cost/benefit calculation does not take into account administrative costs, which are on the order of 7–10 percent of total program costs (as seen in chapter 7); even with this caveat, however, LRIS programs remain among the most effective transfer programs for the poor.

Table 2.5 Effect of LRIS and Social Assistance as a Whole on Poverty and Inequality Indexes, Selected Countries of Eastern Europe and Central Asia and Latin America

Country	LRIS				All social assistance			
	Reduction in poverty headcount[a]	Reduction in poverty gap[a]	Reduction in Gini index[a]	Cost/benefit ratio	Reduction in poverty headcount[a]	Reduction in poverty gap[a]	Reduction in Gini index[a]	Cost/benefit ratio
Eastern Europe and Central Asia								
Albania	3.7	10	1.2	0.480	6.8	22.8	2.3	0.321
Armenia	13.3	43.5	5.2	0.478	14.5	47	5.5	0.444
Bulgaria	1.8	12.7	0.1	0.702	13.7	33.2	3.3	0.410
Croatia	1.5	10.8	1.3	0.611	12.5	34.4	4.5	0.467
Georgia	14.1	44.0	7.4	0.353	17.1	46.8	8.4	0.332
Kyrgyz Republic	4.0	12.4	1.4	0.455	4.2	13.1	3.2	0.376
Lithuania	1.2	3.7	0.4	0.539	11.6	32.7	4.1	0.332
Moldova	3.4	16.2	1.8	0.815	19.1	39.3	6.7	0.354
Romania	2.7	12.3	1.5	0.747	23.8	50.2	16.8	0.445
Serbia	2.5	9.6	1.1	0.601	27.1	50.3	9.8	0.408
Ukraine	1.7	7.2	0.8	0.720	16.5	41.7	5.0	0.358
Conditional cash transfers								
Benchmark countries								
Brazil	6.1	14.7	1.2	0.551	9.6	20.1	1.9	0.392
Mexico	16.2	39.5	4.1	0.458	21.9	50.3	5.2	0.373

Source: Atlas of Social Protection—Indicators of Resilience and Equity (ASPIRE) (database), World Bank, Washington, DC, http://datatopics .worldbank.org/aspire/, latest available data.
Note: Table shows percentage increase in poverty headcount, poverty gap, or inequality as a result of withdrawal of all programs or programs one by one. This counterfactual compared to actual poverty rate in the presence of a program shows the poverty reduction achieved. LRIS = last-resort income support.
a. As a percentage of pretransfer index.

Changing Role of Last-Resort Programs in Eastern Europe and Central Asia

LRIS programs have maintained a good record and have shown consistency over time, but some entered the spiral of diminishing coverage and falling budgets. As a result, many countries went into the most recent crisis without LRIS programs capable of responding to suddenly increased demands.

In this section, we first look at the key indicators of performance for LRIS programs in selected countries in Eastern Europe and Central Asia before the 2008 crisis, then review changes in their budgets before and during the crisis, and finally show how they performed during the 2008 crisis.

Evolution of LRIS Performance before the 2008 Crisis

Not all countries have sufficiently disaggregated and comparable data, but we can look at key indicators over time for four countries: Albania, Armenia, Bulgaria, and Romania. Interestingly, these countries fall into different groups: two represent countries with consolidated social assistance systems where LRIS plays a pivotal role (Albania and Armenia), whereas the other two represent a more fragmented model (Bulgaria and Romania). They also differ in terms of generosity and coverage: Albania representing a case of very frugal benefits, Armenia running a relatively more generous regime, and Bulgaria and Romania characterized by average levels of LRIS generosity. Bulgaria and Romania target the benefit very narrowly to the extreme poor, whereas Albania and Armenia have a less focused approach to the selection of the target group.

Looking at changes over time for these four countries with comparable data, figure 2.7 represents changes in coverage, figure 2.8 illustrates targeting outcome, and figure 2.9 represents generosity over the precrisis period.

Figure 2.7 shows side-by-side coverage for the lowest quintile and lowest decile (poorest 10 percent) of population. To represent the leakage, the figure also shows the coverage of the richest quintile and decile. Several observations

Figure 2.7 Coverage of LRIS in Selected Countries over Time, Precrisis

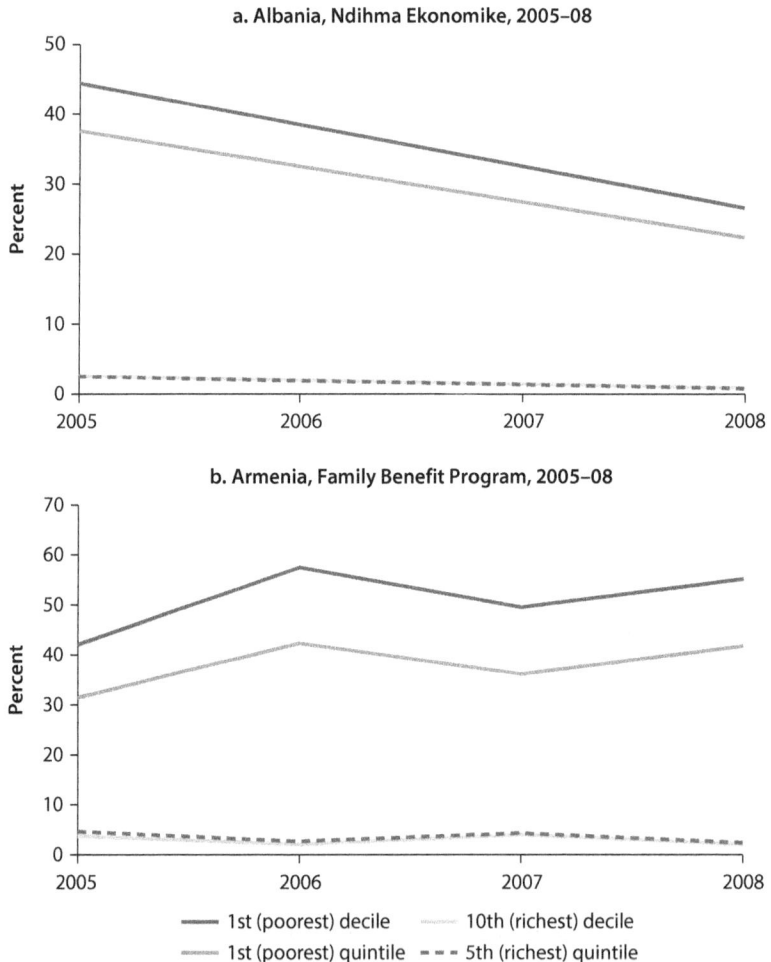

a. Albania, Ndihma Ekonomike, 2005–08

b. Armenia, Family Benefit Program, 2005–08

——— 1st (poorest) decile ——— 10th (richest) decile
——— 1st (poorest) quintile ‑ ‑ ‑ 5th (richest) quintile

figure continues next page

Figure 2.7 Coverage of LRIS in Selected Countries over Time, Precrisis *(continued)*

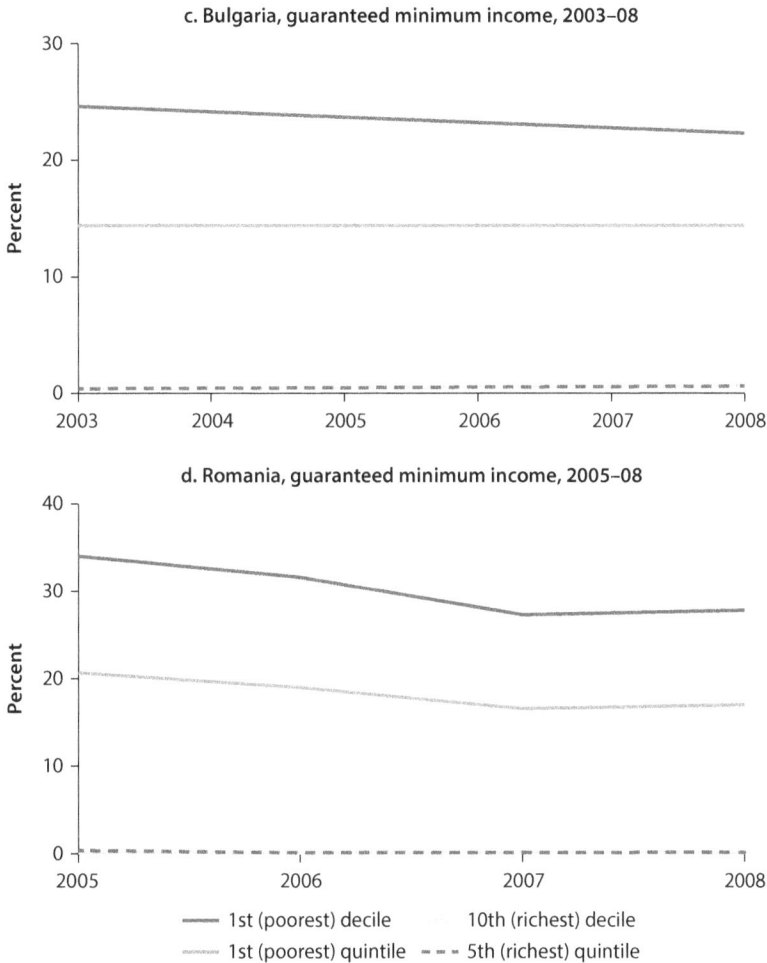

c. Bulgaria, guaranteed minimum income, 2003–08

d. Romania, guaranteed minimum income, 2005–08

—— 1st (poorest) decile   10th (richest) decile
········ 1st (poorest) quintile   — – — 5th (richest) quintile

Sources: Calculations based on Living Standards Measurement Survey (Albania, Armenia), 2005–08; Multi Topic Household Survey (Bulgaria), 2003–08; and Household Budget Survey (Romania), 2005–08.
Note: LRIS = last-resort income support.

can be made. First, targeting outcomes in terms of coverage were impressive everywhere, but especially so in Armenia where over one-half of the poorest decile is covered by LRIS. In Romania and Bulgaria, where the benefits are supposedly targeted to the poorest of the poor, only one-quarter of the bottom decile is covered. Second, the coverage was falling in Albania and Romania, remained more or less stable in Bulgaria, but was expanding in Armenia. Third, in all cases inclusion errors were in check, and only a tiny fraction of the rich could get into the program. This exclusion worked well over time.

Bulgaria and Romania maintained the accuracy of targeting over time, with almost 80 percent of benefits going to the poorest 20 percent of beneficiaries (figure 2.8). In Albania and Armenia, the share of benefits reaching the poorest

Figure 2.8 Targeting Accuracy: Share of Total LRIS Benefits Accruing to Bottom and Top Quintiles and Deciles of Beneficiaries

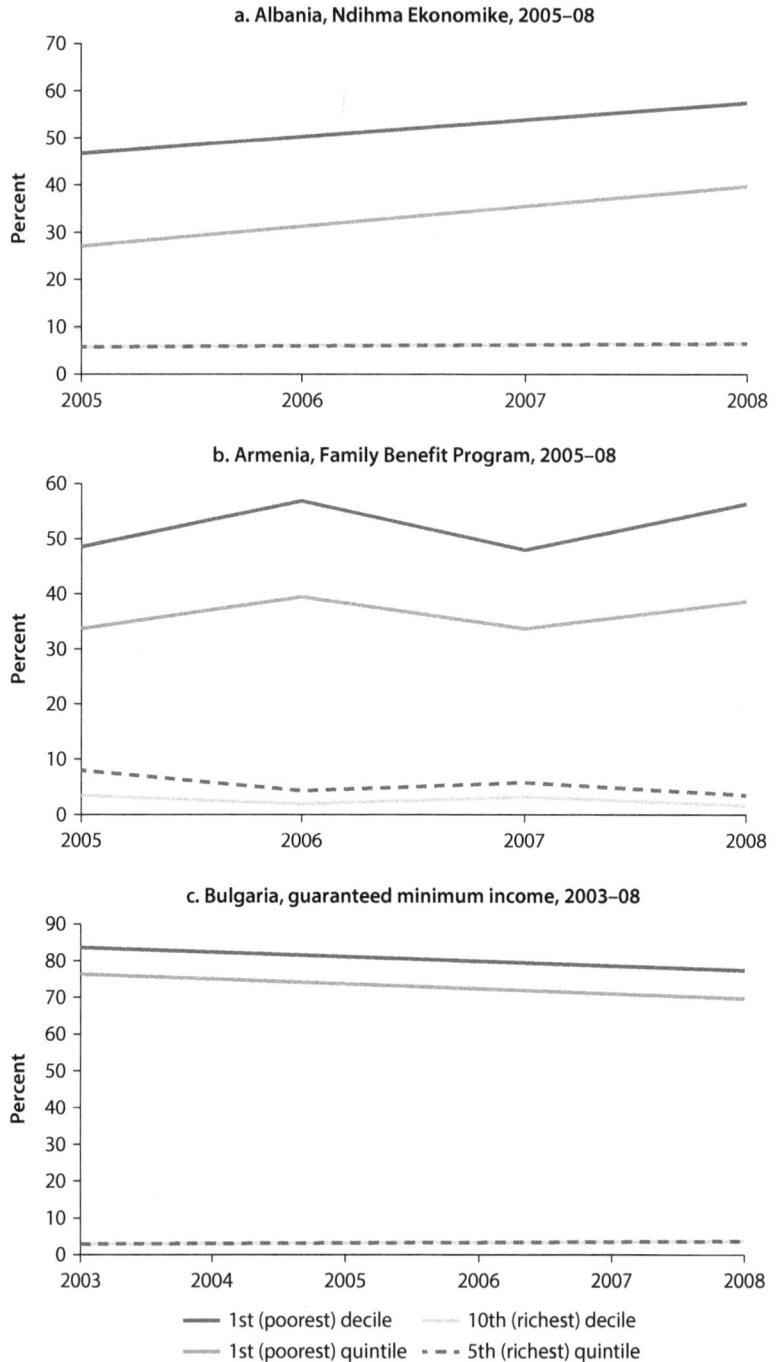

a. Albania, Ndihma Ekonomike, 2005–08

b. Armenia, Family Benefit Program, 2005–08

c. Bulgaria, guaranteed minimum income, 2003–08

——— 1st (poorest) decile   ——— 10th (richest) decile
——— 1st (poorest) quintile   - - - 5th (richest) quintile

figure continues next page

Figure 2.8 Targeting Accuracy: Share of Total LRIS Benefits Accruing to Bottom and Top Quintiles and Deciles of Beneficiaries *(continued)*

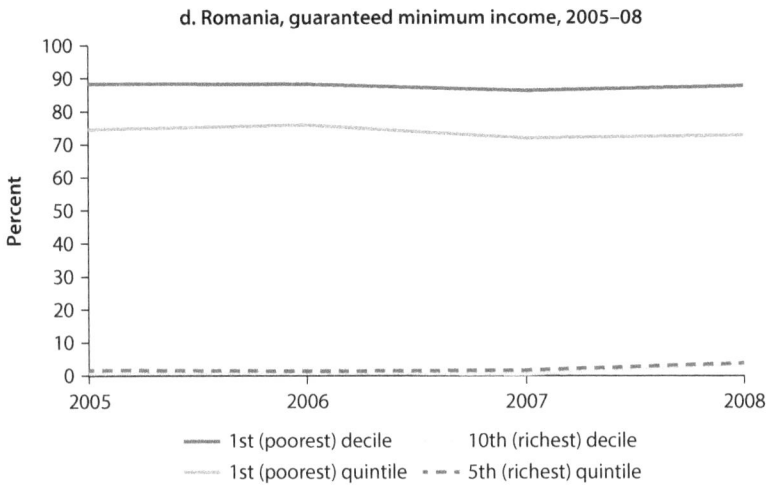

d. Romania, guaranteed minimum income, 2005–08

— 1st (poorest) decile   10th (richest) decile
— 1st (poorest) quintile - - - 5th (richest) quintile

Source: See figure 2.7.
Note: LRIS = last-resort income support.

Figure 2.9 Generosity of LRIS, Ratio of Benefits to Consumption by Beneficiaries

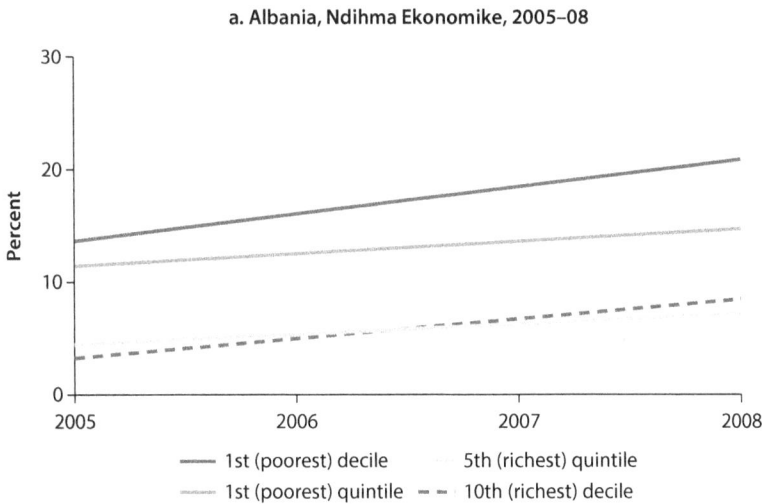

a. Albania, Ndihma Ekonomike, 2005–08

— 1st (poorest) decile   5th (richest) quintile
— 1st (poorest) quintile - - - 10th (richest) decile

figure continues next page

Figure 2.9 Generosity of LRIS, Ratio of Benefits to Consumption by Beneficiaries
(continued)

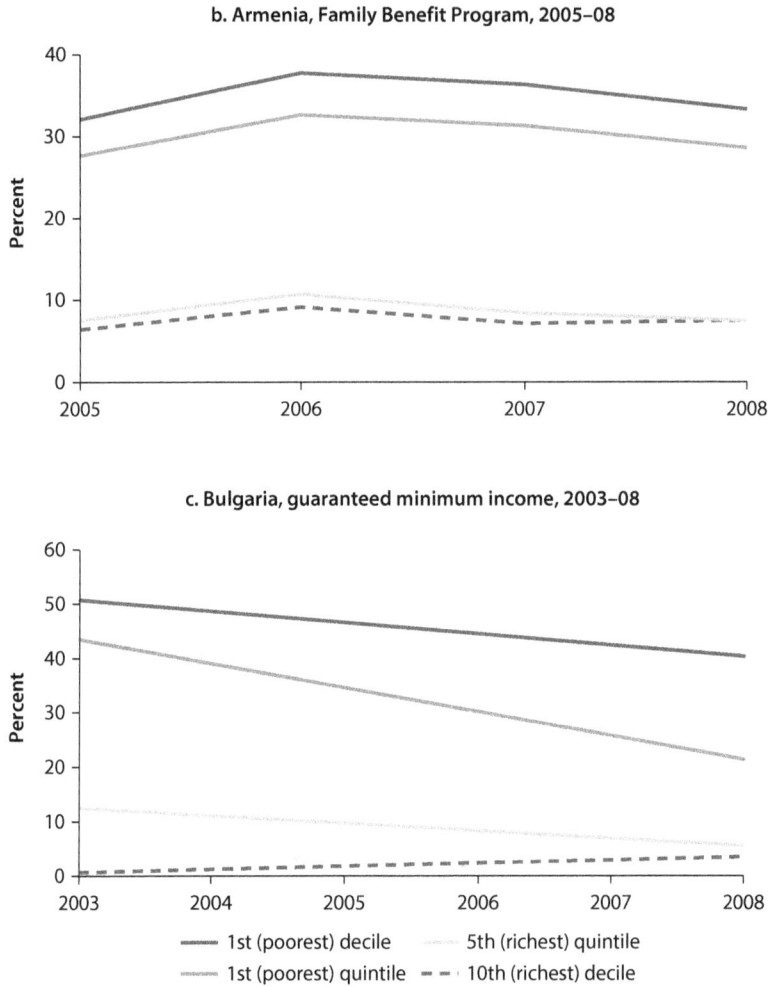

b. Armenia, Family Benefit Program, 2005–08

c. Bulgaria, guaranteed minimum income, 2003–08

— 1st (poorest) decile   5th (richest) quintile
— 1st (poorest) quintile   — — 10th (richest) decile

figure continues next page

Figure 2.9 Generosity of LRIS, Ratio of Benefits to Consumption by Beneficiaries
(continued)

d. Romania, guaranteed minimum income, 2005–08

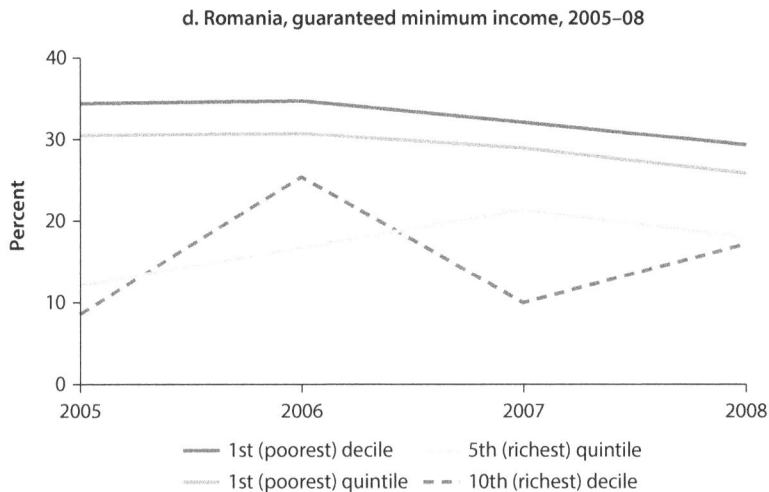

Source: See figure 2.7.
Note: LRIS = last-resort income support.

has improved somewhat over time, though remaining somewhat lower than in Bulgaria and Romania. In the case of Armenia, this improvement was achieved at the same time as expanding the coverage of the poor, a particularly impressive fact. Albania was also able to increase the share of benefits going to the poor, but this change was accompanied by a reduction in the coverage of the poor by almost one-half. Leakage rates of 3–5 percent of transfers going to the richest quintile were constant and are in line with the best examples around the world; they are inevitable in any real-life social benefit system.

Over time, because benefits were not increased with inflation and growth in household incomes and expenditures, the adequacy of transfers declined markedly (figure 2.9). Generosity in Bulgaria and Romania fell over time to reach very modest levels below 30 percent of consumption even for the poorest population covered by the programs. A similar order of magnitude was observed in Armenia, which remained rather stable over time, first with a slight increase and then a larger decrease. Overall, Albania has the least generous benefit system, even though over time it has increased somewhat.

By 2008, at the onset of the crisis, LRIS benefits were modest in all countries—just enough to bridge the poverty gap of the average poor but not enough to get the extremely poor out of poverty. The upside of modest benefit sizes is that disincentives to employment are few. The downside is a smaller dent in poverty.

Evolution of LRIS Budgeting before the 2008 Crisis

The evolution of GDP spent on LRIS in the context of overall social assistance is illustrated in figure 2.10. In most countries in figure 2.10, the size of LRIS

Figure 2.10 Social Assistance Spending by Category of Program as a Share of GDP: Evolution Pre- and Postcrisis

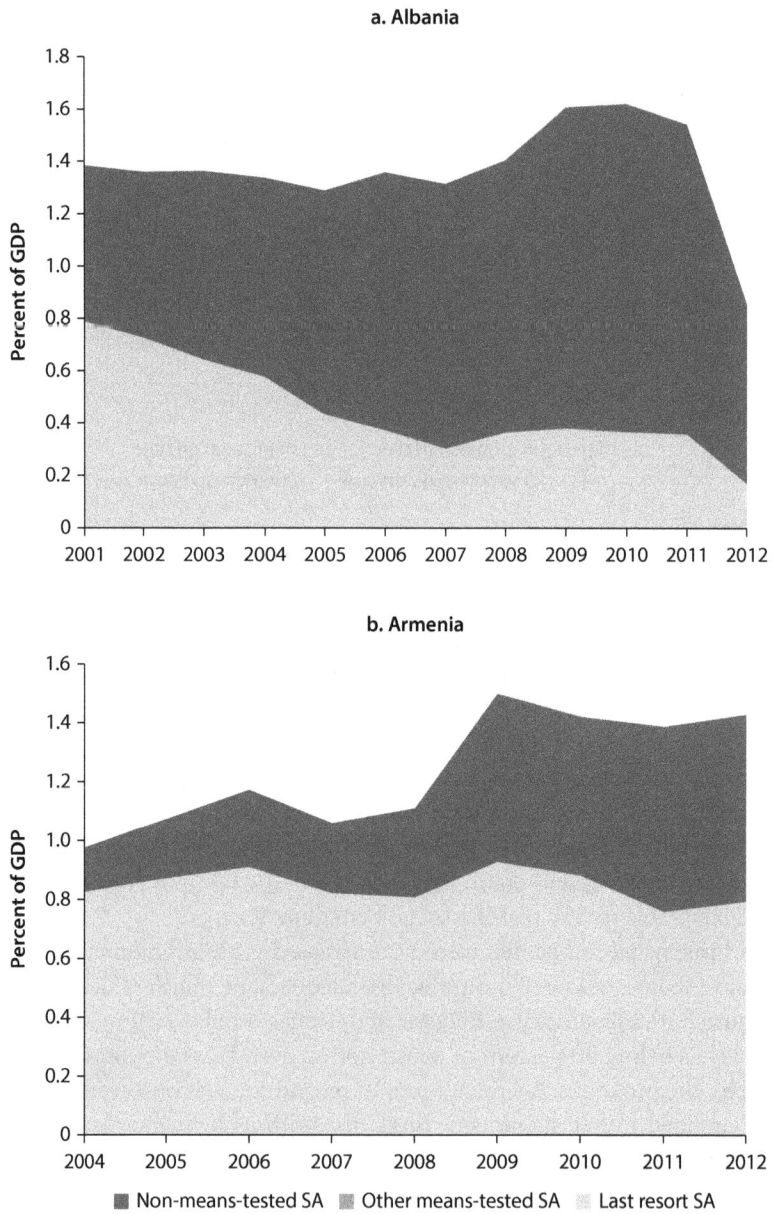

a. Albania

b. Armenia

■ Non-means-tested SA   ▨ Other means-tested SA   ▨ Last resort SA

figure continues next page

Figure 2.10 Social Assistance Spending by Category of Program as a Share of GDP: Evolution Pre- and Postcrisis *(continued)*

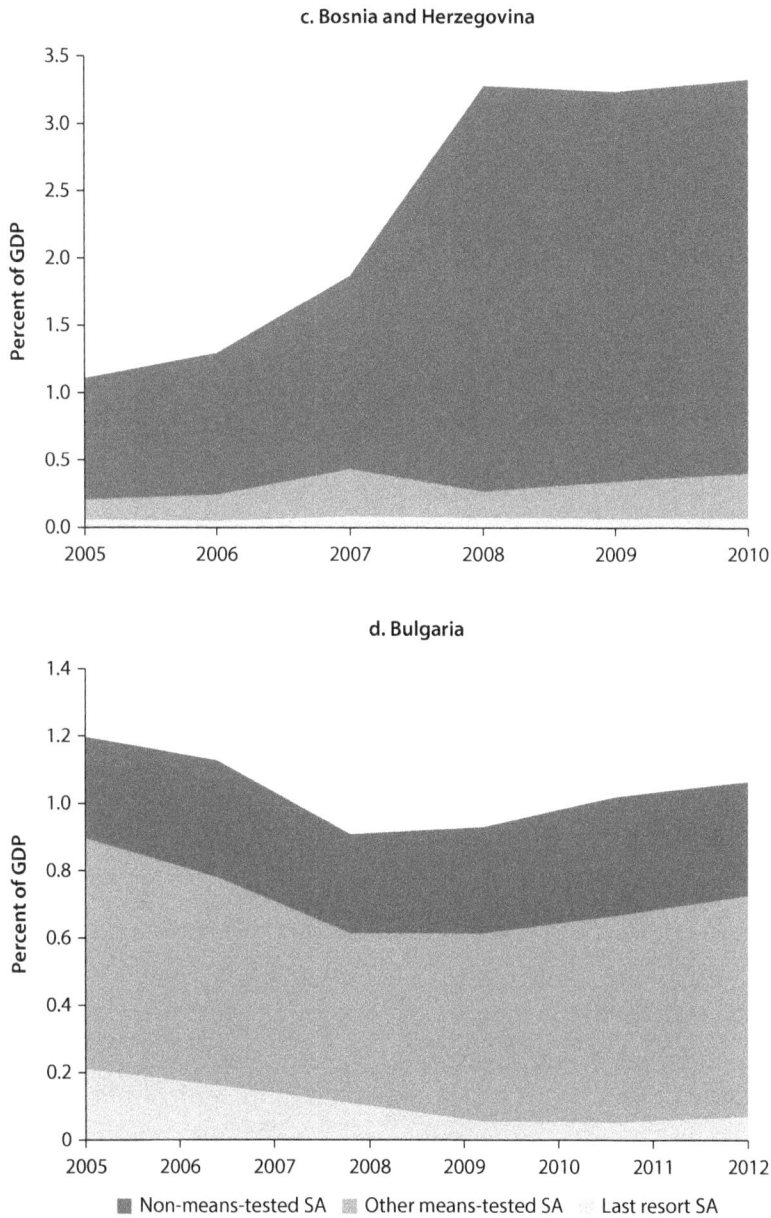

c. Bosnia and Herzegovina

d. Bulgaria

■ Non-means-tested SA   ▨ Other means-tested SA   Last resort SA

figure continues next page

Figure 2.10 Social Assistance Spending by Category of Program as a Share of GDP: Evolution Pre- and Postcrisis *(continued)*

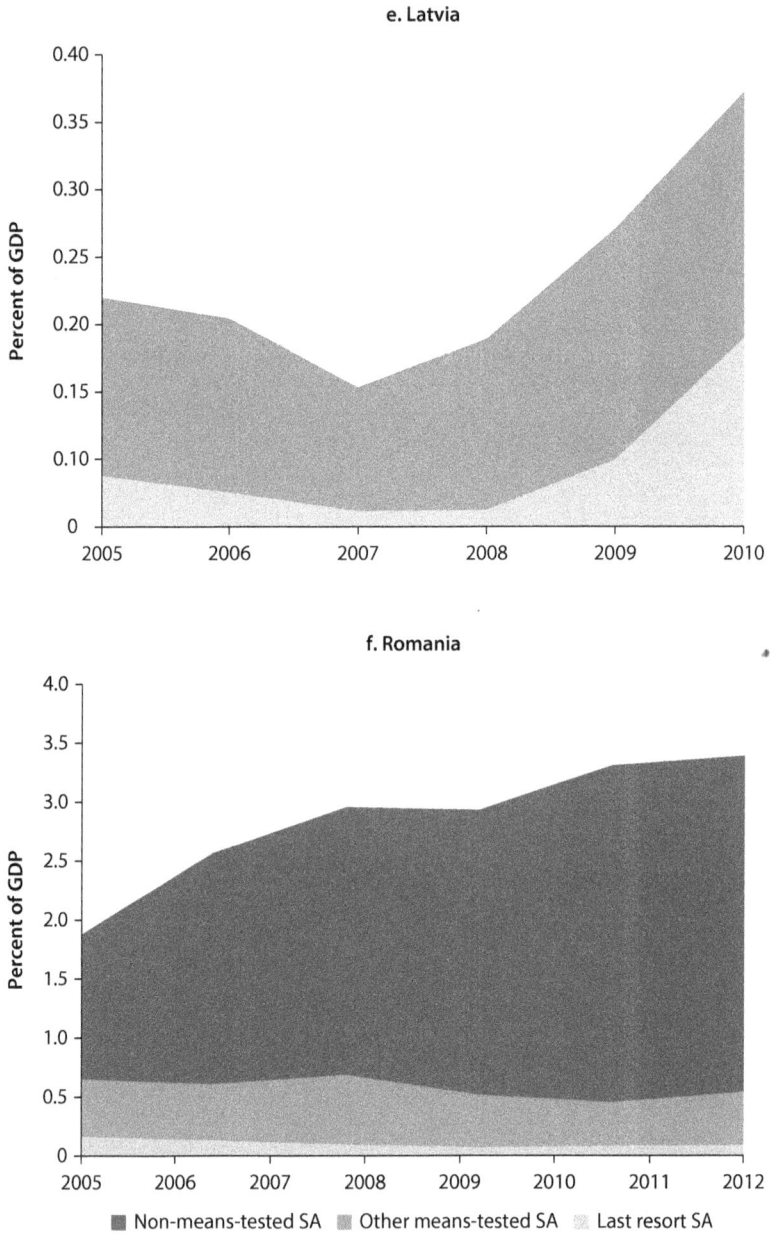

e. Latvia

f. Romania

■ Non-means-tested SA   ▦ Other means-tested SA   ▨ Last resort SA

figure continues next page

Figure 2.10 Social Assistance Spending by Category of Program as a Share of GDP: Evolution Pre- and Postcrisis *(continued)*

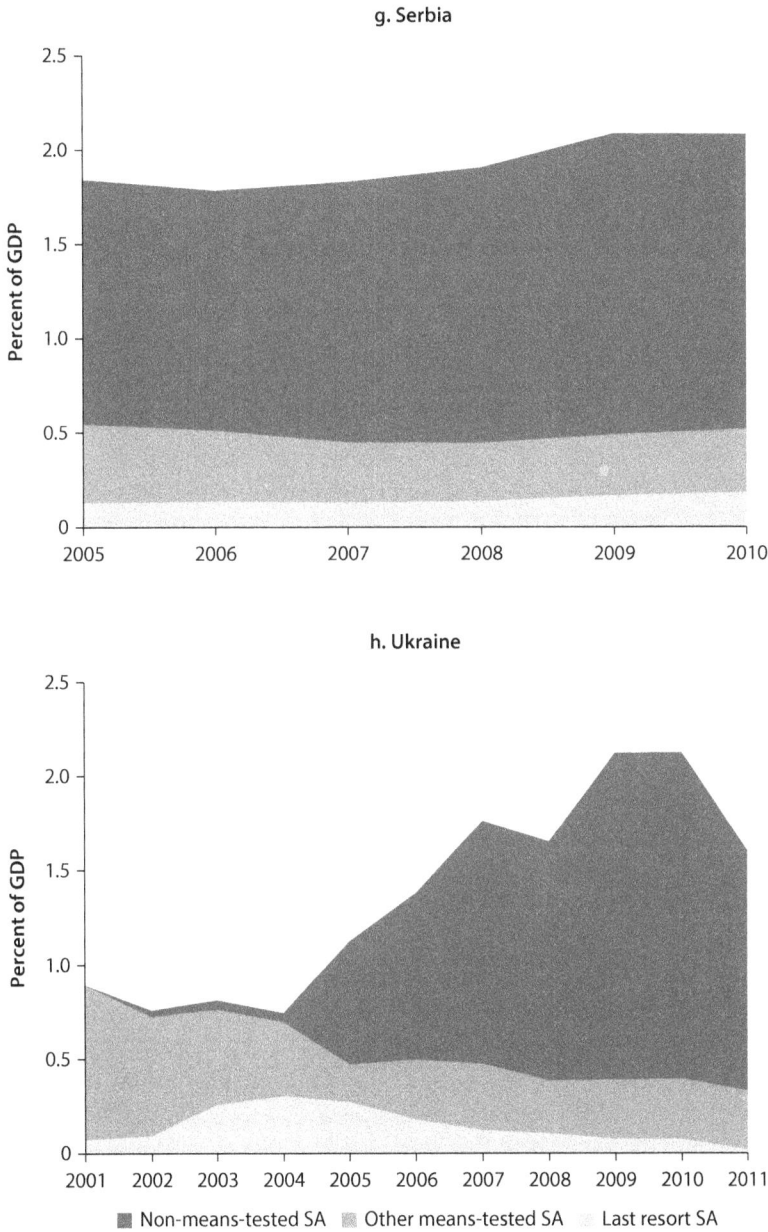

g. Serbia

h. Ukraine

■ Non-means-tested SA ▨ Other means-tested SA ▫ Last resort SA

Source: Europe and Central Asia Social Protection Expenditure and Evaluation Database (SPeeD), latest year, World Bank, Washington, DC (see figure 2.1).
Note: GDP = gross domestic product; SA = social assistance.

programs relative to GDP or social assistance spending fell between 2003 and 2008. The largest contraction occurred in Albania and Armenia, followed by Bulgaria, and Ukraine. Serbia is the only exception where the expenditure on the last-resort material support for low-income households program went up from a very low level of 0.02 percent of GDP in 2000 to 0.16 percent in 2009.

Political economy factors seem to have played a role in the gradual erosion of LRIS. As LRIS programs became smaller and smaller, they served a group that was increasingly marginal and indigent, hence possibly less politically vocal. Country evidence indicates that a large proportion of the LRIS program caseload consisted of hard-to-serve adults, disconnected from the labor market and subject to multiple barriers to employment.[13] Often, governments were reluctant to expand or even maintain benefit or spending levels for nonworking adults, assuming that social assistance had cornered them into a poverty and inactivity trap.[14]

Over the same period, categorically targeted programs grew in terms of budget and coverage. More than 10 years of sustained and significant growth have shifted the preferences of many governments and line ministries in the region away from targeted expenditures to the poor and toward programs that benefit broader categories of people, many of whom are not especially poor.

A number of groups received an increasing share of social assistance spending during this period, including families with children, war veterans, and persons with disabilities. Dwindling fertility in Central and Eastern Europe, Russia, and Ukraine induced many countries to put in place cash transfer programs for newborns (birth grants, maternity and paternity earning replacement programs, and more generous child allowances for infants and young children). Spending on disability programs also rose, but in most countries this started from a very low base; people with disabilities were insufficiently protected in the early days of transition. Although this was a positive development reflecting rebalancing of social assistance, it happened often at the cost of cutting poverty-targeted programs.

In many countries, the LRIS programs contracted from moderate size to small to insignificant. For example, in Bulgaria GMI coverage fell from 5 percent of the population in 2003 to about 1 percent in 2008 (see figure 2.11). The factors behind the decrease in the Bulgarian GMI are complex and include a lack of indexation of the GMI threshold during this period, the pull effect of a public works program aimed toward the long-term inactive adult population, and the push effect of a policy of maximum two-year time limits for benefit eligibility.[15] During this entire period, the value of the GMI threshold was kept at 55 leva (Lev) per capita per month. However, in real terms (constant purchasing power), the value of the GMI dropped to Lev 37 in 2008, a loss of one-third of its purchasing power.

LRIS during the Crisis
For many countries in the western part of the Eastern Europe and Central Asia region, the response to the crisis involved scaling up a mix of social protection

Figure 2.11 Coverage of the Bulgarian GMI Program, 2003–09

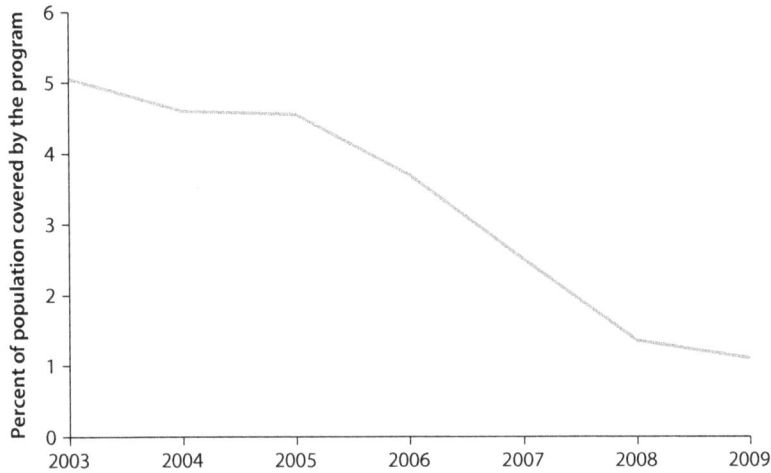

Source: World Bank 2012a.
Note: GMI = guaranteed minimum income.

programs. Because the placement of LRIS programs varied across different types of social protection systems, the role they played in the crisis might have been expected to differ as well. In countries where LRIS programs were a key pillar of social assistance, they would be expected to provide the main shock absorber in the economic crisis. In countries where LRIS was increasingly marginalized, its failure to provide sufficient response would be anticipated. Unemployment benefits or more universal programs (such as child allowances) would then represent the first line of response. In reality, however, many countries fall between these two extremes, using all available programs, and some even attempted reforms in their benefit systems during the crisis.

In Georgia, Latvia, and Lithuania, the number of people served by the LRIS programs increased in response to the crisis (figure 2.12). In Latvia and Lithuania, the number of LRIS beneficiaries arcs upward somewhat behind and lower than the trajectory of the number of registered unemployed, as would be expected, because not all people who lost employment would fall immediately into poverty deep enough to be eligible for the LRIS program. In Romania and Serbia, the number served by the LRIS programs remained more or less stable, but amounts received have increased, as they did in Latvia (World Bank 2012b); in Bulgaria, the LRIS recipients were so marginalized before the crisis that any changes to the number of beneficiaries were invisible compared to the need and changes in other programs. In Armenia and Ukraine, the number of beneficiaries fell during the crisis—contrary to the changing need—with corresponding increases in poverty rates. In Armenia, one of the responses to the crisis and fiscal tightening was to redouble efforts to eliminate targeting errors so the reduced coverage could do a better job of serving the poor (Isik-Dikmelik 2012).

Figure 2.12 Coverage of the LRIS and Other Social Assistance Programs during and after the 2008 Crisis, Selected Countries in Eastern Europe and Central Asia

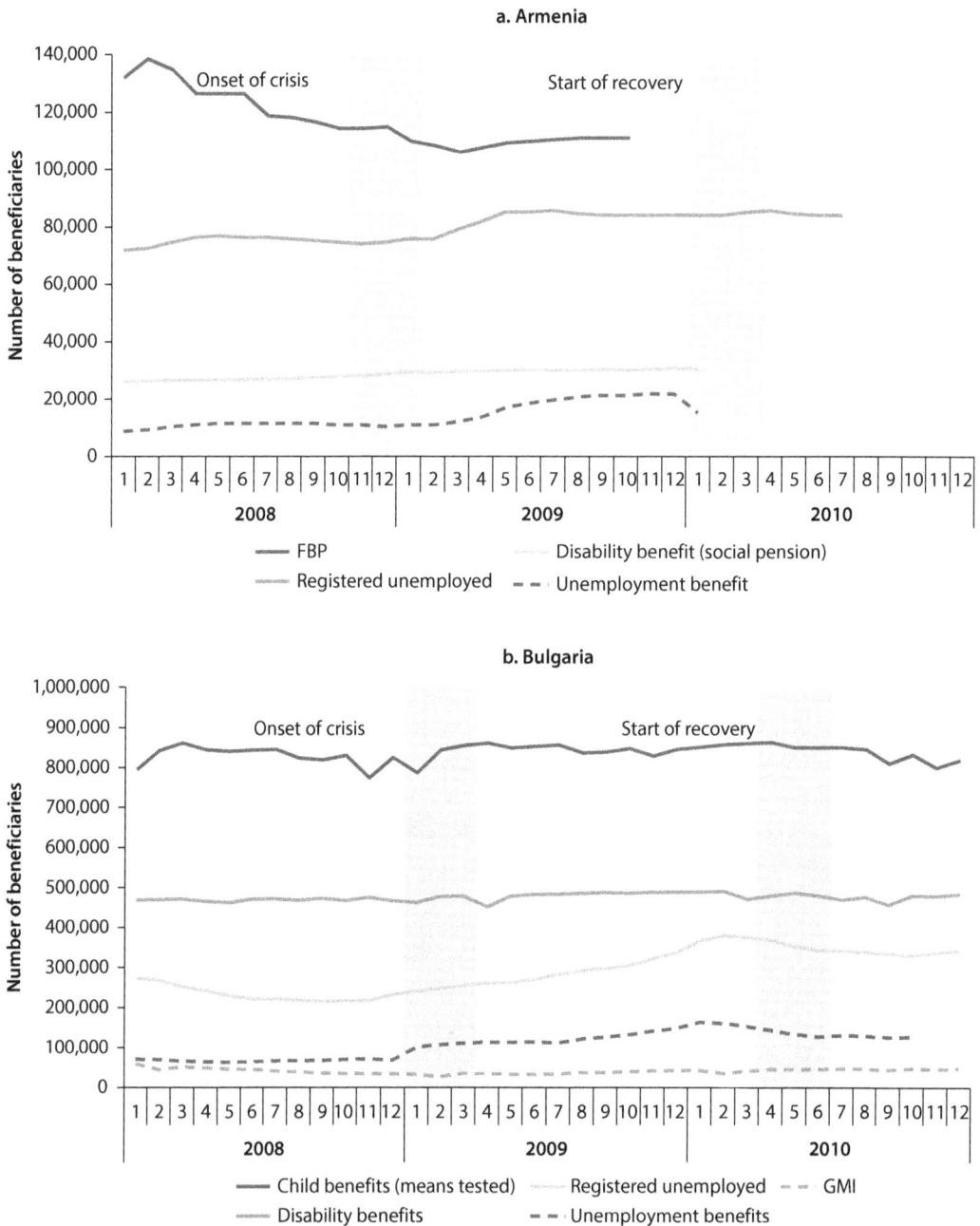

a. Armenia

b. Bulgaria

figure continues next page

Figure 2.12 Coverage of the LRIS and Other Social Assistance Programs during and after the 2008 Crisis, Selected Countries in Eastern Europe and Central Asia *(continued)*

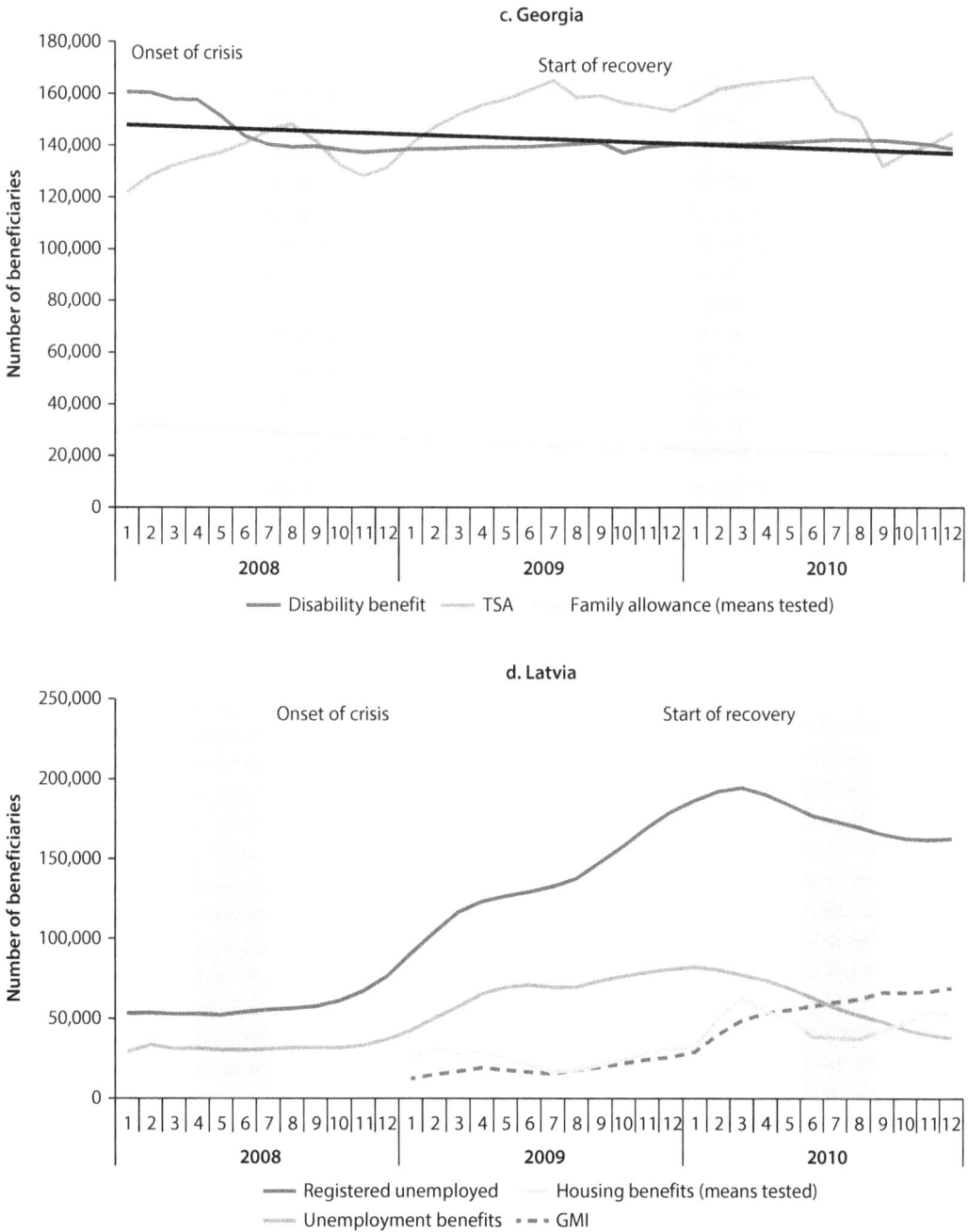

c. Georgia

Disability benefit — TSA — Family allowance (means tested)

d. Latvia

Registered unemployed — Housing benefits (means tested) — Unemployment benefits — GMI

figure continues next page

Figure 2.12 Coverage of the LRIS and Other Social Assistance Programs during and after the 2008 Crisis, Selected Countries in Eastern Europe and Central Asia *(continued)*

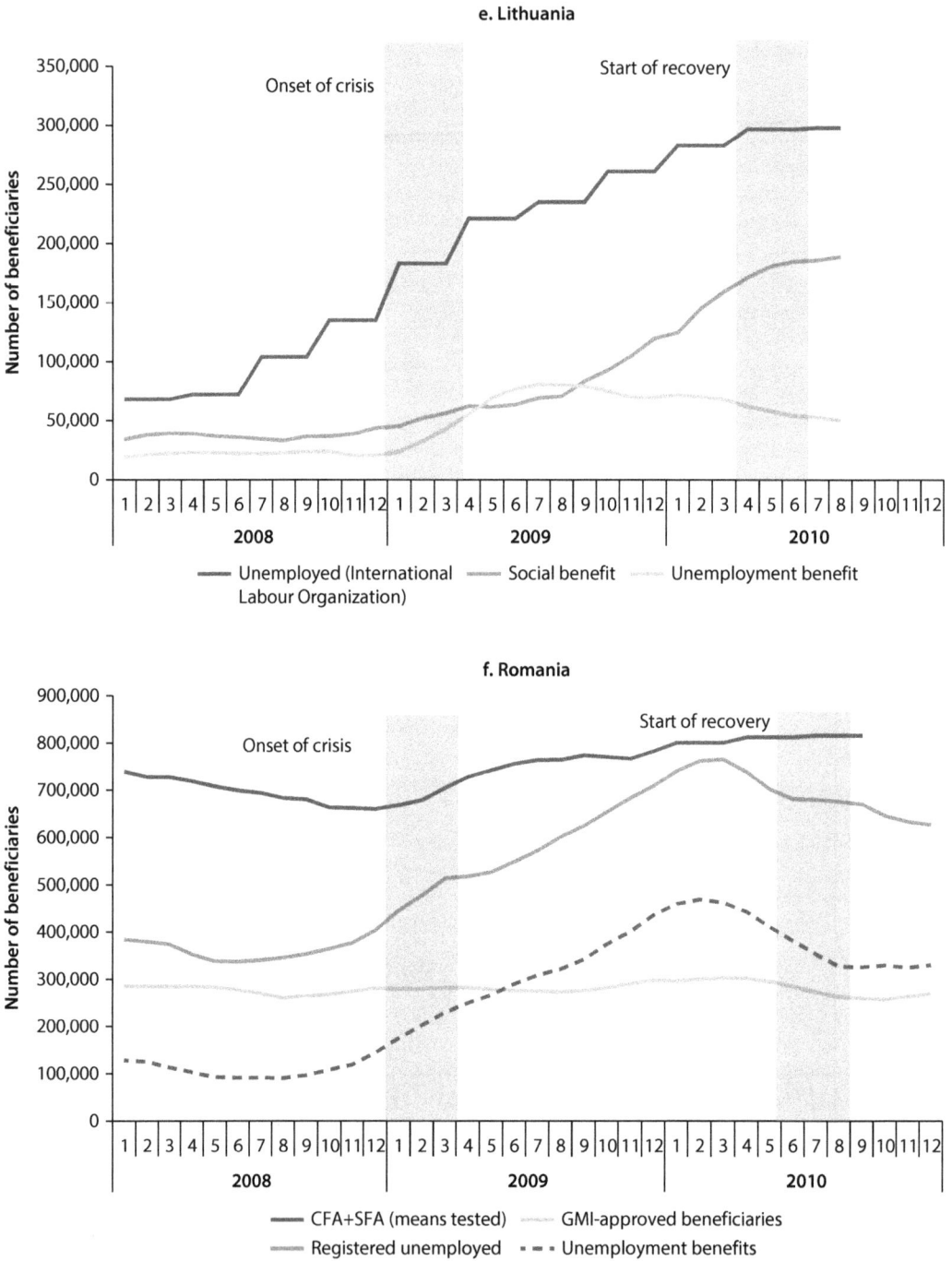

e. Lithuania

f. Romania

figure continues next page

Figure 2.12 Coverage of the LRIS and Other Social Assistance Programs during and after the 2008 Crisis, Selected Countries in Eastern Europe and Central Asia *(continued)*

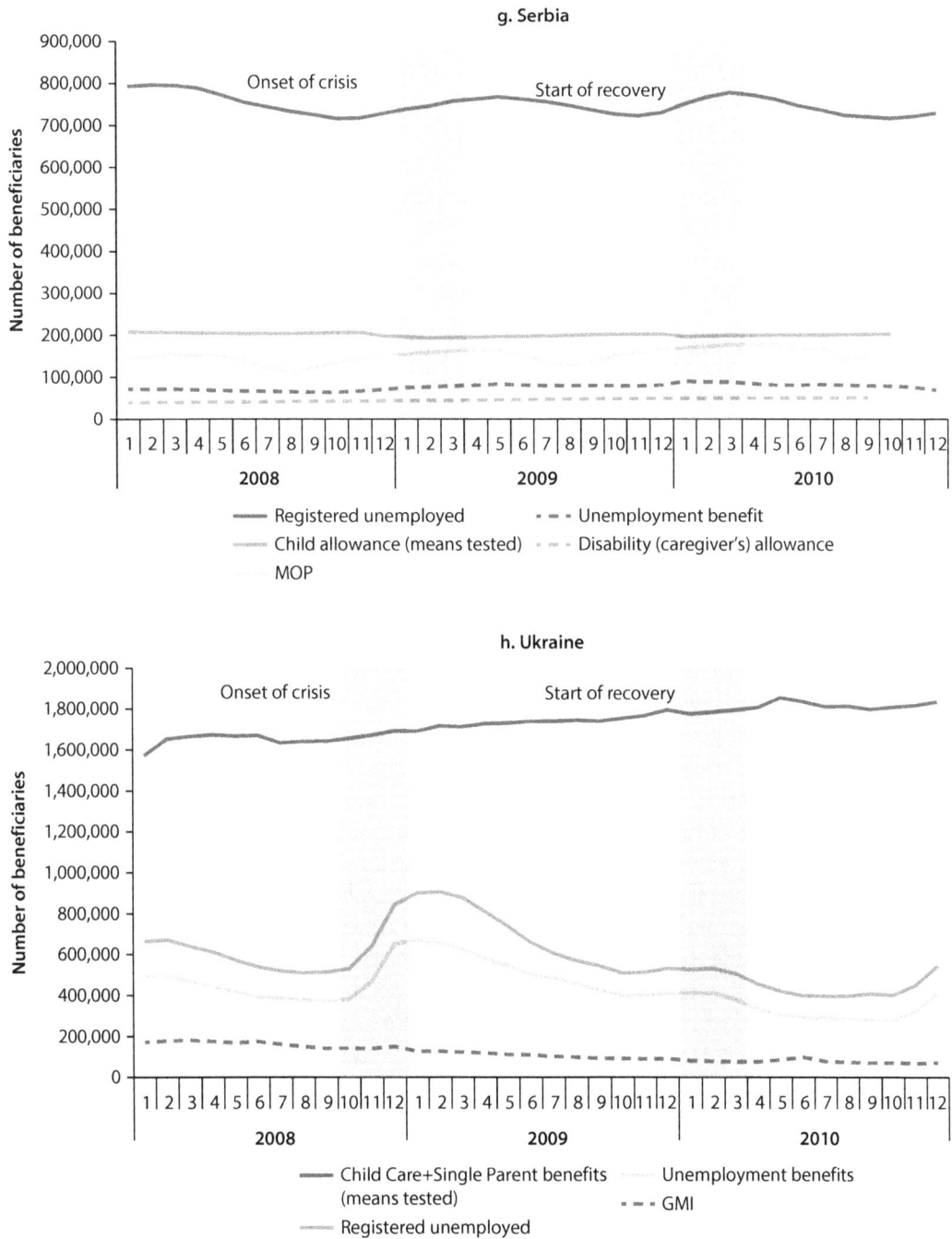

g. Serbia

h. Ukraine

Source: Isik-Dikmelik 2012.

Note: In the x-axis, numbers 1–12 denote months of the year. CFA = Romania Complementary Family Allowance; FBP = Family Benefit Program; GMI = guaranteed minimum income; MOP = material support for low-income households; MT = means tested; SFA = Single Parent Family allowance; TSA = targeted social assistance.

Overall, the use of LRIS to cushion the social effects of the crisis was below expectations. As a result, the bulk of the response to the shock of the crisis (complementing the naturally large role played by unemployment insurance where it existed) was through raising the value (and less often coverage) of categorical benefits, such as child allowances and disability benefits. From a fiscal and poverty-reduction perspective, this type of response was suboptimal because categorical benefits are typically less focused on the poor and have no exit or graduation strategy, leading to creation of open entitlements that allow the increased costs to continue over time (Isik-Dikmelik 2012).

The decrease in the LRIS caseload observed in Bulgaria and Ukraine during the crisis shows lack of crisis responsiveness. Some countries continued to follow the declining trajectory for LRIS coverage (and consequently budgeting) that had preceded the crisis, and some even drastically reduced the scope of LRIS (Kyrgyz Republic and Ukraine) (Isik-Dikmelik 2012). An important lesson can be learned from these experiences about how the LRIS implementation rules made crisis responses more difficult and how this result could be changed without compromising the targeting outcomes.

Conclusions from the Program Overview

The messages from this chapter can be summarized in a few points. First, we see that last-resort programs in Eastern Europe and Central Asia have managed to focus on the poor or extreme poor, and did it consistently over time. Most of these programs use means testing, operate in an environment with a sizable informal sector (unlike that of the OECD), and still generate robust targeting outcomes. They operate against a background of many other social protection programs, using a fraction of the total social assistance resources to focus on those who fall between the cracks of other programs.

In several cases, overly tight eligibility rules in the context of robust economic growth put these programs on a downward spiral of falling coverage, decreasing budgets, and reduced capacity that made them incapable of responding to the severe recession of 2008. Increasing the coverage of a well-targeted program (such as LRIS) during a crisis is not a simple task. Not only is it likely to take some time and a concerted administrative effort, but also some design parameters need to allow crisis response measures within the LRIS program.

These conclusions motivate the rest of the analysis presented in this book. The next chapters drill down into selected country case studies to highlight the key design and implementation arrangements associated with good targeting performance of LRIS programs in Eastern Europe and Central Asia and offer guidance for the design of targeted programs that are more responsive to crisis.

Notes

1. The two exceptions are Turkey and Turkmenistan. Turkey has a conditional cash transfer program that serves as income support to the poor.

2. The Western Balkans are Albania, Bosnia, Kosovo, the former Yugoslav Republic of Macedonia, Montenegro, and Serbia. Baltic countries are Estonia, Latvia, and Lithuania. Central European countries are the Czech Republic, Hungary, Poland, the Slovak Republic, and Slovenia

3. The EU10+ are Bulgaria, Croatia, the Czech Republic, Estonia, Hungary, Latvia, Lithuania, Poland, Romania, the Slovak Republic, and Slovenia. Middle-income CIS are Belarus, Kazakhstan, the Russian Federation, and Ukraine. Low-income CIS are Armenia, Azerbaijan, Georgia, the Kyrgyz Republic, Moldova, Tajikistan, and Uzbekistan.

4. The informal economy has no unique definition or measure. It typically refers to economic activities and transactions that are sufficiently hidden so they are unmeasured or untaxed, and one presumes that economic agents are at least passively aware that bringing these activities to the attention of authorities would imply tax or other legal consequences. Policy makers and researchers who approach the informal economy from a social protection perspective tend to focus on employment, where legal or contractual requirements are not complied with (for example, mandatory contributions to social security and pension schemes). By contrast, if the potential for fraud associated with informality of declared incomes is of concern, a definition of informality that focuses on the types of individuals most likely to be engaged in hard-to-verify activities (and profile of these activities) may be more useful. This approach would be very different from one focused on measuring nonobserved economy share of GDP.

5. Weigand and Grosh (2008) have developed a database compiled from individual World Bank country reports on overall level of spending (and by social assistance or social insurance and by labor market programs), covering 87 countries with information from about 2005.

6. To compare poverty reduction effects of transfers, one needs a measure of individual or household welfare. As in all other studies in Eastern Europe and Central Asia, we use current consumption. Standardized consumption aggregates (Alam et al. 2005) are constructed using the same basket of goods and services. To assess the welfare level of the population and incidence of transfers, we subtract their values from consumption to give pretransfer consumption per capita, which is used to construct all deciles, quintiles, and pretransfer poverty indexes.

7. For instance, the Albania Living Standards Measurement Study does not include a question on disability assistance benefits. As a result, performance measures for the last-resort program in Albania, the Ndihma Ekonomike, cannot be compared with the disability benefits program.

8. Latvia reaches this rate for both the 2007 Household Budget Survey (HBS) and the 2008 HBS, which suggests that a well-designed and well-administered survey instrument can capture social transfers almost completely. Unfortunately, this is not the case for most countries, and we should interpret what follows with caution.

9. See World Bank, Atlas of Social Protection: Indicators of Resilience and Equity (ASPIRE) database, http://www.worldbank.org/aspire.

10. One can argue that social assistance itself should be put into the context of social insurance, which covers almost one-half the poor in Eastern Europe and Central Asia. But not all the poor are eligible for social insurance, and in many instances the support provided by social insurance is not sufficient to overcome poverty. Hence, social assistance plays a crucial role.

11. Note that narrow targeting is not a general feature of all social assistance in Eastern Europe and Central Asia. A smaller percentage of benefits goes to the poorest for all consolidated social assistance transfers, less than 50 percent in most cases.

12. The ASPIRE (Atlas of Social Protection: Indicators of Resilience and Equity) database is a collection of recent household survey data with social protection information from nearly 100 developing countries, available at http://datatopics.worldbank.org /aspire/, or http://www.worldbank.org/aspire/.

13. See Kotseva and Tsvetkov 2010, using the example of policy reform in Bulgaria that limited GMI assistance to 18 months for able-bodied, long-term unemployed individuals. The majority of the beneficiaries subject to the time limits were rural women with many children, a low level of education, and belonging to the Roma ethnicity— hence with little if any political voice.

14. See World Bank (2011), where Levin and Ersado use a regression discontinuity design approach to estimate whether participation in the Poverty Family Benefit Program in Armenia triggers work disincentives. The study did not indicate evidence of work disincentives, but it shows how widespread such concerns were among policy makers.

15. The policy was first reduced to 12 months and then abolished after the financial crisis of 2008.

References

Alam, A., M. Murthi, R. Yemtsov, E. Murrugarra, N. Dudwick, E. Hamilton, and E. Tiongson. 2005. *Growth, Poverty, and Inequality: Eastern Europe and the Former Soviet Union*. Washington, DC: World Bank.

Bidani, B., and V. Sulla. 2011. "The Distributional Impact of the Global Economic Crisis in Europe and Central Asia: Has Poverty Increased? An Update on Income Poverty and Inequality." PowerPoint presented at the conference "Poverty in ECA," sponsored by the World Bank, Almaty, Kazakhstan, September 20.

Coady, D., M. Grosh, and J. Hoddinott. 2004. *Targeting of Transfers in Developing Countries: Review of Lessons and Experience*. Regional and Sectoral Studies, Washington, DC: World Bank.

Grosh, M., C. del Ninno, E. Tesliuc, and A. Ouerghi. 2008. *For Protection and Promotion: The Design and Implementation of Effective Safety Nets*. Washington, DC: World Bank.

Immervoll, H. 2009. "Minimum-Income Benefits in OECD Countries: Policy Design, Effectiveness and Challenges." IZA Discussion Paper 4627, Institute for the Study of Labor, Bonn.

Isik-Dikmelik, A. 2012. "Do Social Benefits Respond to Crises? Evidence from Europe and Central Asia during the Global Crisis." Social Protection and Labor Discussion Paper 1219, World Bank, Washington, DC.

Kotseva, M., and A. Tsvetkov. 2010. "Main Results of the Evaluation of the Net Effect from Intermediary Employment Services." Ministry of Labor and Social Policy, Sofia.

Kozek, W., M. Zieleńska, and J. Kubisa. 2013. "National Report: Poland—Combating Poverty in Europe: Re-organising Active Inclusion through Participatory and Integrated Modes of Multilevel Governance." Institute of Sociology, University of Warsaw, Warsaw.

Ravallion, M., and S. Chen. 2011. "Weakly Relative Poverty." *Review of Economics and Statistics* 93 (4): 1251–61.

Roskomstat. 2011. *The Social Situation and the Standards of Living of the Russian Population* [In Russian: Sotsial'noe polozhenie i uroven' zhizni naselenia Rossii.] Moscow: Rosijski komitet po statistike (Roskomstat).

Schneider, F., A. Buehn, and C. E. Montenegro. 2010. "Shadow Economies All over the World: New Estimates for 162 Countries from 1999 to 2007." Policy Research Working Paper 5356, World Bank, Washington, DC.

Sundaram, R., V. Strokova, and B. Gotcheva. 2012. *Protecting the Poor and Promoting Employability: An Assessment of the Social Assistance System in the Slovak Republic.* Report, World Bank, Washington, DC.

Weigand, C., and M. Grosh. 2008. "Levels and Patterns of Safety Net Spending in Developing and Transition Countries." Social Protection Discussion Paper 0817, World Bank, Washington, DC.

World Bank. 2010. *Social Safety Nets in the Western Balkans: Design, Implementation, and Performance.* Report 54396-ECA, Europe and Central Asia Region, World Bank, Washington, DC.

———. 2011. *Armenia: Social Assistance Programs and Work Disincentives.* Report 63112-AM, Europe and Central Asia Region, World Bank, Washington, DC.

———. 2012a. *Bulgaria: Household Welfare during the 2010 Recession and Recovery.* Report 63457-BG, Europe and Central Asia Region, World Bank, Washington, DC.

———. 2012b. *Implementation Completion and Results Report on a Series of Two Loans in the Amount of Euro 200 Million (US$285.98 Million Equivalent) to the Republic of Latvia for a Safety Net and Social Sector Reform Program.* Report ICR2306, World Bank, Washington, DC.

———. 2012c. "Belarus: Improving Targeting Accuracy of Social Programs." Social Assistance Policy Note 68791, World Bank, Washington, DC.

———. 2013. *Western Balkans Activation and Smart Safety Nets AAA: Synthesis Note.* Unpublished report, World Bank, Washington, DC.

CHAPTER 3

Overview of Key Arrangements: Institutional Actors, Regulations, and Program Financing

Institutional arrangements, rules and regulations, and financial resources are key ingredients for implementing any policy or program. The way those elements were shaped in the last-resort income support (LRIS) programs in Eastern Europe and Central Asia provides useful lessons and insights not only for the forward-looking regional agenda, but also for new programs and similar interventions in other regions. This chapter outlines the institutional and financing arrangements of the LRIS programs in the six country cases under review and distills lessons from the programs' various approaches to administrative and financial decentralization.

The way programs are implemented depends on the institutional actors involved, the allocation of various functions and responsibilities, and the administrative capacity of the program. Implementation also depends on the links between the various actors, including accountability mechanisms and incentives, which, in turn, are shaped by the specific institutional, political, and cultural context of the country. The implementation arrangements of LRIS programs in Eastern Europe and Central Asia were shaped, to different degrees, by two factors: (a) the legacy of the social protection systems of the former socialist regimes and (b) the decentralization reforms affecting all transition countries during the 1990s. Some of the countries included in this review, such as Lithuania, have built on existing social protection institutional mechanisms, which they eventually reformed and to which they added new functions. Other countries, such as Albania, created completely new structures for program administration and delivery.[1]

With very few exceptions, all the former socialist countries in the region have in common several characteristics or initial conditions that can be attributed to their legacy and that distinguish them from developing countries in other regions. The first characteristic is the existence of preexisting social protection systems, including both contributory (social insurance) and noncontributory (social assistance) components. As a general rule, before the 1990s, the social protection benefits and services were provided to wage employees, and the delivery of benefits (mostly child allowances) was simple, being done in most cases through state enterprises and wage bills. Second, a relatively well-institutionalized administrative infrastructure existed from top (central level) to bottom (regional and sometimes local level) because of the preexistence of a government bureaucratic apparatus. Until the early 1990s, this apparatus functioned in a highly centralized and hierarchical decision-making environment. Third, these countries had a culture of written regulations, formal communication, and vertical accountability in public organizations. Finally, all countries have had in common since the early 1990s the existence of a line ministry that is in charge of social protection and, in most cases, has deconcentrated branches at the subnational level.

The institutional arrangements of the programs vary from country to country and reflect not only the legacies and institutional mechanisms of the social protection systems, but also the challenges of the decentralization patterns in the respective countries,[2] including a country's history and its actual decision-making processes. Decentralization plays an important role in the administration of social assistance benefits, especially in the case of poverty-targeted programs. Unlike the universal or categorical programs, poverty-targeted programs require a high degree of "local knowledge" of the clients' living conditions (for entitlement and eligibility testing), especially in cases in which eligibility criteria are not easy to verify (for example, because of a high degree of informality of incomes and employment or because of livelihoods based on subsistence agriculture). Poverty-targeted programs also require more frequent contact with beneficiaries (for recertification purposes). Even when entitlement is based on easy-to-verify criteria, the points of service (front line) should be located as close as possible to the beneficiaries to reduce the cost of the application and recertification processes. Most of the programs examined in this chapter follow that rule.

Institutional Arrangements

Most countries in the Eastern Europe and Central Asia region have several tiers of administration involved in the management and implementation of LRIS programs. In general, the institutional map of the programs is a rather complex one. Roles and responsibilities are allocated across different levels of government or agencies. Some functions (for example, service delivery) are primarily integrated and concentrated in one place, while others (for example, program management, including planning and monitoring and evaluation) recur throughout the institutional map, being distributed across different administrative tiers.

In most of the cases reviewed in detail, the institutional map of the program overlaps with the administrative-territorial organization of the country (table 3.1).

Table 3.1 Administrative-Territorial Organization and Overlap with the Program Institutional Map[a]

	Administrative-territorial organization of the country			Subnational tiers involved in program administration	
Country	Number of subnational administrative-territorial tiers, and total population in the country	Number and average size (population) of regions (level-1 subnational units)	Number and average size (population) of lower-level units	Regional level	Local level
Albania	2 tiers, 3.6 million	11 regions plus capital city; 300,000, excluding capital city	374 local governments 65 urban units; 27,000, excluding capital city 309 rural units, 6,000	12 Regional State Social Service Administrations	385 Ndihma Ekonomike offices; 374 local government councils
Armenia	2 tiers, 3.2 million	11 *marzer* plus capital city; 250,000, excluding capital city	929 municipalities; 2,700, excluding capital city 59 urban units 870 rural units	11 Health and Social Assistance Departments	55 (sub) Regional Social Service Agency Centers
Bulgaria	2 tiers, 7.2 million	28 districts, 250,000	264 municipalities, 27,000	28 Regional Social Assistance Directorates	272 Local Social Assistance Directorates
Kyrgyz Republic	3 tiers, 5.2 million	7 *oblasts* plus the capital city; 585,000, excluding capital city	40 *rayons* 22 towns and cities 477 rural *aiyl okmotu*, 7,000	7 *oblast* Departments of Social Protection	40 *rayon* Departments of Social Protection; 477 rural local governments
Lithuania	2 tiers, 3.5 million	10 counties, 370,000	60 municipalities, 66,000 550 wards	No role	60 Departments (Centers) of Social Assistance; 550 wards
Romania	2 tiers, 21.5 million	41 counties plus capital city; 470,000, excluding capital city	3,176 local governments 320 urban units, 37,000 2,856 rural units, 3,400	42 Directorates of Social Assistance	3,176 local governments; Social Assistance Services and Departments in urban areas
Uzbekistan	3 tiers, 25 million	12 provinces, 1.7 million	162 districts, 150,000 120 cities, 40,000 12,000 citizen assemblies (mahallas), 400	12 *oblast* Departments of Labor and Social Protection	382 *rayon* and City Departments of Labor and Social Protection; 12,000 mahalla committees

Source: Based on country case studies.

a. The information corresponds to the period 2004–06 and remains valid through 2010–11 with the exception of some population figures or number of local governments, which have slightly changed.

However, this is not necessarily the rule. For example, in Albania and Romania each territorial-administrative tier is involved in program administration, performing various functions, while in Lithuania the regional tier has no role. In Armenia, the Regional Social Service Agencies, which implement the program, cover more than one municipality at a time. In Lithuania and Uzbekistan, where the size of the lowest administrative tier is large, some functions are delegated to territorial subunits of the local governments (wards or *elderates* in Lithuania,[3] and *mahallas* in Uzbekistan[4]). These arrangements were influenced to a large degree by factors such as the size of territorial units (economies of scale), the institutional map of the social protection ministry and agencies, the decentralization model in the country and the administrative capacity at various levels of government, and the objective of locating service points as close as possible to beneficiaries.

At the central level in all seven cases, a line ministry is in charge of social protection, which coordinates horizontally with the ministries of finance and of public administration and with other national agencies. The central government, in particular the line ministry, is in charge of policy design, elaboration of the regulatory framework, program budget planning, and overall program monitoring.

At the regional level (administrative regions, counties, and *oblasts*), the deconcentrated branches of the line ministry or a range of specialized departments under the authority of regional governments have roles in monitoring, controlling, delivering guidance and training to implementation units, and, in some cases, planning and funds allocation.

The service delivery, including eligibility determination, benefit award (entitlement), enrollment, registration of beneficiaries in the databases, recertification, and payrolls, is in most cases the responsibility of the lowest administrative levels (*rayons*, municipalities, cities, towns, communes, and wards). At this level, the programs are implemented in most cases by elected local governments with specialized departments (in large urban localities) or with full- or part-time staff assigned to social assistance functions (in rural localities). Thus, in most cases service delivery is delegated to local governments, and only in rare cases is deconcentrated to regional or local departments and services of the line ministries (box 3.1).

In Albania (figure 3.1), Lithuania, Romania, and Uzbekistan, program implementation is delegated to the lowest tier of the territorial administrative organization (local governments). In the Kyrgyz Republic, a mix of deconcentration and delegation is used. In rural areas, implementation is delegated to local governments (*aiyl okmotu*), and in urban areas, the responsibility lies with the deconcentrated branches of the line ministry. In Armenia, because of the high fragmentation and low capacity of rural local governments, the program is implemented by subregional agencies under the coordination of the regional governments (*marzer*).[5] In Bulgaria a pure deconcentrated model is used, and the program is implemented by the departments of the line ministry at the municipality level (figure 3.2).

Box 3.1 Forms of Decentralization in Service Delivery

Different functions can be performed by different tiers of government and at different levels—central, regional, and local (that is, different competencies can be attributed to different government levels).

Forms of decentralization:

- Deconcentration: Central ministries and agencies transfer activities and responsibilities to their subnational branches and offices.
- Delegation: Subnational governments (and not local or regional branches of ministries) are given responsibilities for delivering public services, but are subject to supervision by the central government. Policy making remains with the central government, while (selected) administrative functions are decentralized to local governments.
- Devolution: Central government transfers the authority for decision (policy) making, finance, and management to autonomous units of local government.
  - In addition, some activities can be outsourced, such as benefits delivery or maintenance of databases.

In general, the institutional arrangements and the relationship among the various actors are more complex in a decentralized context than a centralized one. Delegating program implementation to local governments has multiple advantages. However, this approach also has challenges, such as the large variation in the administrative capacity across local governments and the hierarchical and horizontal accountability aspects, including the principal-agent problem (that is, ensuring and enforcing the service quality standards). The main dilemmas that central governments face in a decentralized context are how to hold the elected local governments accountable for errors (or intended miscompliance with rules) and what types of incentives to provide to improve performance in service delivery. This topic will be discussed in more detail later, but in brief, Eastern Europe and Central Asia accountability in service delivery is based primarily on rules rather than performance.

Setting the Program Rules

The LRIS programs reviewed in this book are nationwide programs, aiming to provide equal treatment to citizens belonging to their target groups. The definition of target groups and eligibility criteria is in all cases the responsibility of the central governments. In most of the countries under review, the implementing agents (that is, local or regional governments) are bound by the nationwide legislation; they have little or no space for adjusting the rules (for example, target groups, eligibility criteria, incomes to be imputed and assets to be taken into account, or conditions). This is the case in Armenia, Bulgaria, the Kyrgyz Republic (box 3.2), and Lithuania.

Figure 3.1 Delegation of Implementation to Local Governments, Albania

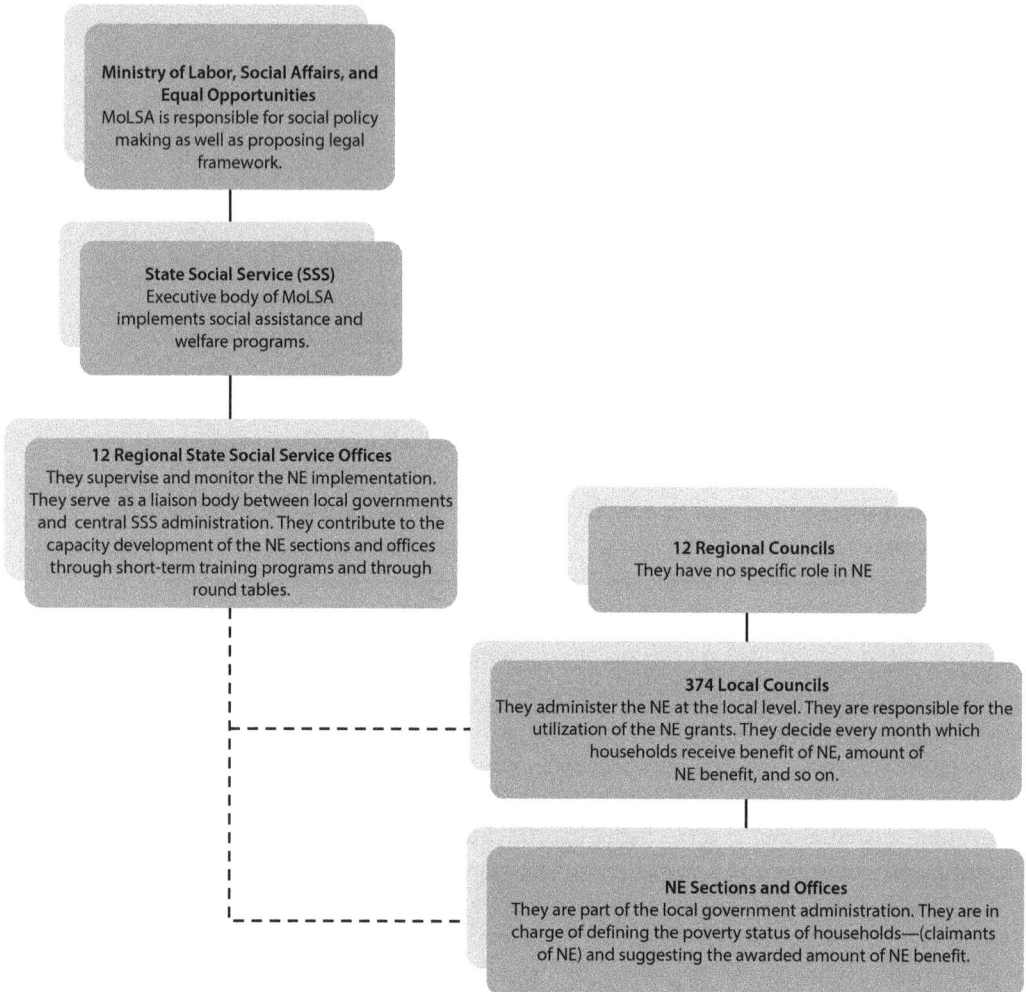

Ministry of Labor, Social Affairs, and Equal Opportunities
MoLSA is responsible for social policy making as well as proposing legal framework.

State Social Service (SSS)
Executive body of MoLSA implements social assistance and welfare programs.

12 Regional State Social Service Offices
They supervise and monitor the NE implementation. They serve as a liaison body between local governments and central SSS administration. They contribute to the capacity development of the NE sections and offices through short-term training programs and through round tables.

12 Regional Councils
They have no specific role in NE

374 Local Councils
They administer the NE at the local level. They are responsible for the utilization of the NE grants. They decide every month which households receive benefit of NE, amount of NE benefit, and so on.

NE Sections and Offices
They are part of the local government administration. They are in charge of defining the poverty status of households—(claimants of NE) and suggesting the awarded amount of NE benefit.

Sources: Based on Kolpeja 2005; Ayala Consulting 2010.
Note: NE = Ndihma Ekonomike.

In some countries, however, specific elements have been left to the discretion of other actors, such as local or regional governments. In Albania, Romania, and Uzbekistan, local governments have been given the freedom to adjust or create the rules, within given limits, in particular with respect to eligibility criteria, assessment of means, and conditions of entitlement. In Albania and Romania, the local councils are allowed to use additional local eligibility and exclusion criteria (regulated through formal, local council decisions), but these criteria cannot contradict the general national rules. In Uzbekistan, the national regulations regarding eligibility criteria have a guidance role, and the mahalla committees have a high degree of discretion regarding entitlements.

Figure 3.2 Deconcentration of Implementation, Bulgaria

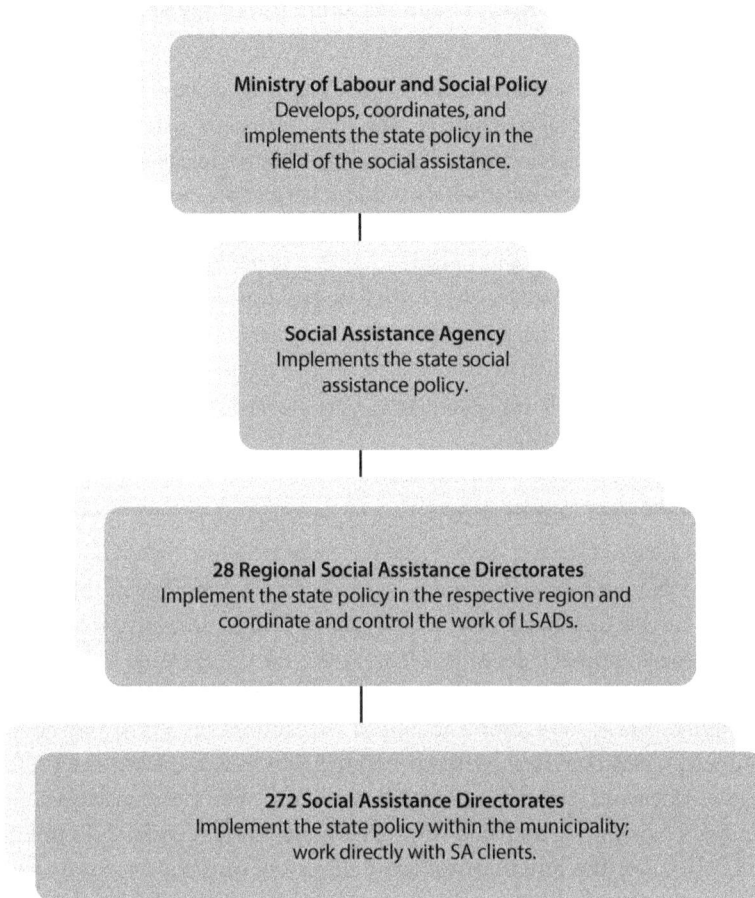

Ministry of Labour and Social Policy
Develops, coordinates, and
implements the state policy in the
field of the social assistance.

Social Assistance Agency
Implements the state social
assistance policy.

28 Regional Social Assistance Directorates
Implement the state policy in the respective region and
coordinate and control the work of LSADs.

272 Social Assistance Directorates
Implement the state policy within the municipality;
work directly with SA clients.

Sources: Based on Shopov 2006, 2012.
Note: LSAD = Local Social Assistance Directorate; SA = social assistance.

Several good reasons exist for the central government to allow local governments or implementation agencies some degree of discretion to adjust or intervene in the program design. For example, when the program costs are shared (that is, local governments are cofinancing a share of the cost), local governments could and do claim some degree of discretion over the rules. Another reason is the weak capacity or knowledge of the central government to operationalize and adapt some broad poverty criteria to regional and local circumstances, especially in environments characterized by high informality of livelihoods. At the same time, granting discretion to local governments over specific elements of program design requires not only enhanced supervision and monitoring, but also an institutionalized procedure to appeal local government regulations that are not consistent with the principles stated in the primary legislation. In Albania and Romania, the institution responsible for checking the consistency between local

---

Box 3.2 Regulations in the Kyrgyz Republic: Unified Monthly Benefit—An Example of Nationwide Regulations

In the Kyrgyz Republic, the Unified Monthly Benefit (UMB) is regulated at the national level and no discretion is given to local governments. The social protection system is regulated by an umbrella law that states the principles and the main institutions responsible for social protection provisions. The UMB and other social assistance benefits are regulated by the law titled "On the State Benefits in the Kyrgyz Republic" and by a number of decrees, resolutions, and instructions. These instructions are constantly updated according to the feedback received from the implementation units. Specific instructions exist with respect to household income assessment, completion of the application forms for UMB, and documents necessary for granting the benefit. In addition to this guidance, an operational manual was developed. The manual is revised regularly to incorporate new aspects or issues revealed during implementation.

Source: Kyrgyzstan Center for Social and Economic Research 2006.

---

decisions and the national law is the prefecture (the representative of the central government at the regional level), which can appeal in administrative court the legality of a local council's decision. Usually, the deconcentrated branches of the line ministries (RSSS [Regional State Social Services] in Albania and DJMPS [County Directorates of Labor and Social Protection] in Romania) check the local councils' decisions during their monitoring visits and inform the prefecture if the local decisions are not consistent with the national legislation. Similar arrangements exist in Uzbekistan. In practice, these arrangements do not always work well. Because the line ministry has neither the direct authority to sanction nor the capacity to follow up the appeal, the (inconsistent) local rules may remain in force in some cases.

Allowing the local governments to adjust certain program parameters (for example, eligibility criteria or conditions) has advantages and disadvantages (table 3.2). On the one hand, this practice may increase the legitimacy of the program by allowing the community to adapt the program to local "preferences" and may improve the targeting performance by making use of local knowledge. Discretion in creating or adjusting the rules may lead to local innovations that are adopted quickly when they prove to be effective. In Romania, for example, tying the benefit to participation in community work was first introduced as a local regulation by a few local governments. This practice diffused, being adopted by more and more local councils, and was later incorporated in the national legislation. On the other hand, discretion can also lead to a high degree of heterogeneity in implementation and to distortions in the program's intended outcomes. In Albania, some local governments used discretion to entitle certain types of "deserving poor," such as single elderly or single mothers, to receive the maximum level of benefit despite their actual incomes. In Romania and Uzbekistan, discretion was used to exclude from the program adults who could work during

Table 3.2 Pros and Cons for Local Governments' Discretion to Adjust Program Parameters (Target Groups, Eligibility Criteria, and Benefit Levels)

Pros	Cons
Parameters can be adapted to local conditions and local preferences. Communities have direct influence. Increased legitimacy of the program.	Heterogeneity in implementation may occur. Too much discretion may result in horizontal inequity. Overall targeting outcomes may be affected.
Local innovations may arise, becoming natural pilots for future rule modifications.	
Local governments can prioritize when funds are scarce.	Exclusion errors may occur. Underfinancing of the program may be hidden (by issuing local regulations that limit demand and allow local governments to reject applications that would be otherwise legitimate from a strict poverty perspective). Program outcomes may be affected.
Local governments can participate in policy making. Local governments are accountable to their constituencies for program outcomes.	Local decisions conflict with national regulations. Risk exists for fuzzy accountability.

the agricultural season, irrespective of their ability or inability to find work. A high degree of discretion left to local governments can also lead to horizontal inequities, that is, two households with similar poverty status but located in different localities or regions could have different probabilities of entitlement.

An important issue in almost all countries reviewed in this book is the lack of clear procedures for program administration. Because most countries in Eastern Europe and Central Asia lack an operations manual for the program, the procedures regarding file management, case management, and information management are only loosely regulated and are rather uneven across localities, especially in cases where implementation is delegated to local governments. Excluding the Kyrgyz Republic and to some extent Armenia, the programs rely mostly on primary and secondary legislation—laws, decrees, ordinances, ministerial orders, internal guidelines, and central or local government decisions. Usually the program regulatory framework consists of a national law and complementary implementation guidelines, which may be issued as a law, as in Romania, or as a ministerial decree, as in Armenia. These documents are, in most cases, not sufficient or clear enough to provide guidance for implementation. In Romania, for example, about 55 percent of the local governments' staff surveyed[6] said that the legislation and the methodological norms provided clear guidance for the application of the law and for program implementation only to a minimal extent or not at all. Updates and clarifications on procedures are issued through internal orders or ministerial decisions or communicated only during workshops or by phone or fax. However, such updates are never consolidated in a single, consistent document (except in Armenia and the Kyrgyz Republic).[7] Albania, Lithuania (box 3.3), and Romania piloted the introduction of procedure manuals that set standards demanding more qualified staff, better information technology systems, and more resources and enforcement than was available, and thus, the manuals were never fully implemented.

Income Support for the Poorest • http://dx.doi.org/10.1596/978-1-4648-0237-9

Box 3.3 Piloting Uniform Administration Procedures in Lithuania

In 2001–02, Lithuania implemented a project (Programme for Social Protection Reform and Social Acquis Implementation, within the framework of European Union Phare Consensus III) to establish uniform administration procedures for the cash social assistance programs across municipalities. In four pilot municipalities, the project analyzed the entire process of organization and provision of cash social assistance: application forms, completion of the forms, computation of benefits, check for errors, documentation flows, creation of a combined information base with other related authorities, office equipment, databases, number and structure of human resources, functions, and so on. Within the framework of the project, material was developed and distributed: a procedural manual for "Awarding Social Benefits"; a methodological manual for "Risk Management, Active File Handling, and Information Management"; and an "Income Identification Methodology" for professionals at municipal social assistance units.

These tools were recommended to municipalities but were not made mandatory. The municipalities could choose what manuals to use and what was applicable to their conditions. A 2004 evaluation showed that municipalities were using the manuals to a relatively minimal extent: 39 percent of the municipalities used "Income Identification Methodology"; 35 percent used "Awarding Social Benefits"; and 7 percent used "Risk Management, Active File Handling, and Information Management." Explanations for low usage were that the procedures required additional material, human, and information technology resources; increased the workload of the social workers; and required better-qualified staff.

The conclusion reached from the exercise is that in the absence of prerequisites, such as training, adequate information technology, and enforcement, national-level issuance of uniform procedures for administration of cash social assistance at the municipal level is not reasonable.

Source: Zalimiene 2006.

Program Financing

The total cost of cash transfer programs can be split into two broad categories— the administrative cost of the program (staff, premises, equipment and systems, fees for contracted-out services such as payments, and so on) and the cost of benefits. In theory, depending on the approach to decentralization, each of these costs can be the responsibility of the central government or the local governments, or it can be shared.

In general, the approaches to program financing of the six countries studied follow to a large degree the implementation arrangements. In Bulgaria, where the line ministry and its deconcentrated branches implement the program, financing the program (including administrative costs and benefits) falls naturally under the responsibility of the central government. In the Kyrgyz Republic, the government keeps the program financing responsibility at the central level, except for the administrative costs of rural local governments (aiyl okmotu), which are supported from local budgets. In Armenia, the central government finances the benefits and the administrative costs at the central level, while the administrative costs of the regional social service agencies are covered by the regional governments (marzer). In Albania, Lithuania, and Romania, where the program implementation is delegated to local governments, most of the administrative costs incurred at the local level are supported from the local budgets. The benefits are also paid from local budgets,[8] but the central governments are involved in financing the benefits by using different models of provision and allocation of funds, which are further discussed below.

Thus, as a rule across the country case studies, when implementation is delegated to local governments, the administrative costs incurred at the local level are usually supported by the local budgets, whereas the line ministries finance only the administrative costs related to their own staff and activities and the fees corresponding to payment services. A notable exception to this rule is in Lithuania where, to ensure a homogenous level of quality in implementation across municipalities, the local governments are allowed to use 4 percent of the program funds to cofinance administrative costs.[9]

In other regions, the central governments use administrative costs in innovative ways to improve program administration. A good example is Brazil's Bolsa Família conditional cash transfer, in which joint management agreements are signed between the Ministry of Social Development and municipalities. The agreements formalize roles and responsibilities and establish minimum standards for program operation. The ministry monitors the quality of implementation by using an index of management capacity based on a four-point scale, which covers key indicators of registration quality and verification of compliance with conditionality. Based on the scores, the ministry pays a pro-rated administrative cost to municipalities. Poor-performing municipalities that do not receive the financial incentive are offered technical assistance to improve performance. Such incentives can help balance relationships among stakeholders at different government levels and minimize errors, while supporting positive program outcomes such as targeting or service delivery (Bassett et al. 2012). A similar example is the Supplemental Nutrition Assistance program in the United States, where states receive an administrative cost subsidy based on the level of program compliance they achieve.

In all six countries whose LRIS programs were reviewed, the financing of benefits rests ultimately with the central government, except for some attempts to decentralize, which are discussed next.

Financing the Benefits in a Decentralized Context—A Series of Experiments

Generally, redistribution is a function of the central government, which is in the best position to address regional inequalities and promote equitable access to program benefits. From a risk management perspective, social assistance is most efficiently financed from the largest possible risk pool (that is, at the national level). Devolving the responsibility for financing benefits can fragment the risk pool (World Bank 2010a). However, when beneficiaries' selection is delegated to local governments, the central government is responsible for finding balancing mechanisms to ensure adequate program coverage and, at the same time, limiting excess demand for funds and increasing the implementation units' accountability. Central governments have several options to provide funds in decentralized contexts (see box 3.4), and the various approaches used in Eastern Europe and Central Asia cover almost all of them. Albania is using conditional nonmatching grants, while Lithuania is using conditional block grants. Until 2010, Romania implemented a mixed approach of conditional block grants and cost sharing, and now is using conditional nonmatching grants.

In an attempt to address the increasing demand for funds and better align local governments' accountability and incentives, some countries in Eastern Europe and Central Asia (for example, Bulgaria and Romania) experimented over the years with several approaches to decentralize financing of social assistance benefits, including devolution and cost-sharing programs.[10]

In 1996, Romania shifted from centralized to fully decentralized (devolved) program funding (100 percent from local government's own revenues). The results proved to be fatal for the program. Local governments, and especially those of poor localities, did not have the capacity to secure the necessary funds and began to limit demand by not approving new applications and not recertifying existing beneficiaries. Decentralization of program financing led to a dramatic decrease in the number of beneficiaries—from 10 percent of the population in 1995 to about 1 percent in 2001—and to the collapse of the program (which as a consequence was reformed in 2002).

Bulgaria experimented with matching grants (cost sharing) until 2003, using various shares of local government contribution—50 percent between 1999 and

---

Box 3.4 Financing Social Assistance in a Decentralized Context

How Central Governments Can Provide Funds for Social Assistance Programs in a Decentralized Context

- Conditional nonmatching grants (funds are earmarked to a specific program).
  - The size of the grant can be based on demand or forecast, on a formula, or a combination.
- Matching grants (or cost sharing) require that funds be spent for specific purposes and that the recipient (that is, local government) match the funds to some degree.
  - Such transfers can be open ended (no limit on funds as long as they are matching) or closed ended.
- Conditional block grants include several social assistance cash transfers; the local governments have discretion on how to allocate between various social schemes.
- In theory, central governments could use other types of grants such as unconditional (block) grants, but this approach risks crowding out the safety nets in favor of other types of spending (for example, investments).

2001 and 25 percent in 2002—while keeping the program implementation functions (including benefit award) with the deconcentrated branches of the line ministry. A cost-sharing approach was also used by Romania between 2002 and 2010. In theory, introducing the obligation of cofinancing provides incentives for the local governments to use the funds in an accountable manner and to not abuse the program, especially when the capacity of the central government to monitor and supervise is weak. However, this approach also poses challenges—especially for the poor (and most needy) localities that have limited revenues and financial capacity and cannot afford the cost.

The cost-sharing approach had rather negative outcomes in both Bulgaria and Romania, though for different reasons. In Bulgaria, this approach led to significant arrears in payments (three to five months) mainly because of the unusual arrangement of centralized implementation and decentralized financing (that is, the local governments had no incentives to provide their share of funds because they had no influence in the beneficiary selection process). In Romania, the cost-sharing approach also led to payment arrears and to significant numbers of unpaid beneficiaries. However, in Romania's case, the reason was rather a combination of political economy factors, weak financial capacity of local governments, and unclear rules of cost sharing. The lack of clear regulations raised significant challenges for program implementation, in general, and for transparency and accountability mechanisms, in particular. In practice, the gaps in regulations were filled through ad-hoc informal rules (see box 3.5).

The Romanian experience with devolution of program financing is consistent with the findings in other countries in Eastern Europe and Central Asia[11] and speaks in favor of maintaining funding from central governments for at least a minimum package of social assistance cash benefits. Latvia is another example providing evidence in this respect. There, the local governments

---

Box 3.5 Romania: Gaps in Cost-Sharing Regulations

In Romania, during eight years of program implementation (2002–09) the Guaranteed Minimum Income Law stated that the program is cofinanced by local governments. However, no regulation specifying the cost share between the central and local government was in place. This is the case of a rather "intentional gap" in the legislation, which allowed the Ministry of Finance to avoid firmly committing to a specific share of program financing from the state budget. Instead, a verbal instruction was issued specifying a share of 80 percent from the state budget. Many local governments took this figure for granted and planned a program budget accordingly. However, because the share of cofinancing was not formally regulated, neither the Ministry of Finance nor the local governments could be held accountable for nonpayments or partial payments of the benefits. During that period, the benefit received by a beneficiary household was estimated to be on average between 72 and 78 percent of the entitlement.

Source: Florescu, Pop, and Tesliuc 2006.

---

both finance and implement the guaranteed minimum income (GMI) program, and as a result, more than 40 percent of total social assistance transfers were going to people living in the capital city, even though they were, on average, considerably better off than those residing in other parts of the country (Grosh et al. 2008). Moreover, because local governments were required to carry a balanced budget, they were not able to expand the program during the economic and financial crisis, when it was most needed. Recognizing this constraint, the central government temporarily revised the GMI financing arrangements by putting in place a central government financing guarantee (50 percent cofinancing) to supplement the local spending on GMI until 2012 (Isik-Dikmelik 2012).[12]

While the cost-sharing approach cannot be ruled out on the basis of experiences presented here, it is important to note that several preconditions must be met for the approach to work, including consistent implementation arrangements, clear rules, and assurance that municipalities (especially the poor ones) have the financial capacity to share the program costs.

Only two of the six countries implemented conditional block grants—Lithuania and Romania (the latter only for a few years, starting in 2002). The principle behind this approach is to allow local governments the discretion to prioritize among several programs within the social assistance category. Although this approach seems to be working in Lithuania, in Romania it led (again) to underfinancing of LRIS programs (the GMI) in favor of other benefit programs such as personal assistants for the disabled and heating benefits (which were also included in the conditional block grant).

Budget Planning and Allocative Processes

Planning LRIS budgets involves several institutional actors especially when implementation is decentralized. In practice for the countries included in this book, three major factors influence the overall projected budget: (a) historical caseload and spending (that is, the spending in previous years), (b) indexation of benefits and eligibility thresholds, and (c) ceilings or budget constraints imposed by the ministries of finance.

As a general rule in Eastern Europe and Central Asia, budget planning is not linked to outcomes, such as poverty reduction targets, and in many cases, the indexation (adjustment for inflation) of benefits is not regulated, being done in an ad hoc manner.[13] Among the countries included in this book, the Kyrgyz Republic is the only one where, according to the law, the budget projection should be based on an annual poverty reduction target of 5 percent. However, the existing evidence on budget trends indicates a lack of compliance with this law.

When implementation is delegated to local governments and the programs are financed from local budgets (even if supported through grants from the national level), the LRIS budget planning usually works in a bottom-up process through which the local implementation units assess the need for funds based on historical caseload and spending and send a budget proposal to the next administrative level. In most cases, the historical spending refers to the number of applications and expenditures from the previous year, (except in Lithuania, where, by law, the average spending from the past three years should be taken into account) together with other indicators such as unemployment. The projected budgets may be reviewed or revised at the regional level. The regional levels send the aggregated budget requests to the central level, usually to the line ministry. The line ministries integrate the LRIS budgets in their total budget and submit it to the ministries of finance, where adjustments are made (for example, in Albania and Bulgaria, ceilings or quotas are applied). The Kyrgyz Republic is an exception; the planning is based on a figure set by the Ministry of Finance and communicated to the line ministry.

The mechanisms of funds allocation among regions and localities vary across countries with respect to both transparency and complexity. In countries with centralized financing and deconcentrated implementation, there is no binding preallocation by regions and localities, and the transfer of funds is done monthly or once every few months according to requests from local implementation units. In decentralized contexts, the budgets for the programs are allocated to regions or localities, and the requests for funds are also done regularly, either every month or every few months. However, as the number of actors and levels involved in the funds allocation mechanisms and the complexity of the arrangements increases, the process may become less transparent, and political factors may start playing a significant role. In Lithuania, the allocation process is simple and transparent: the funds are allocated directly by the Ministry of Finance to the local governments according to a clear formula, and transfers are done quarterly. In Albania, the regional branches of the line ministry are involved in deciding the size of the grants to localities, but the central government allocates grants on the basis of fund requests and a list of indicators. However, there are concerns regarding the reliability of these indicators (box 3.6).

Until recently in Romania, the regional governments had the final decision on the allocation of funds among localities. The Ministry of Finance would transfer the grants to regional (county) governments, which would redistribute them to local governments. Qualitative research from 2004 indicated that this process left room for political interference, especially because no clear allocation criteria were being used.

A similar approach is used in Uzbekistan, where the funds are distributed by the central government (ministry) to oblasts and rayons, which, in turn, distribute the funds to mahallas with no clear allocation criteria or indicators. The lack of a transparent fund allocation mechanism consistent with the program's objectives affects the targeting performance of the program (by increasing the inclusion and exclusion errors) and the local governments' ability to plan, and ultimately leads to horizontal inequities (that is, two households with similar poverty status that are located in different regions will not have the same probability of entitlement). In 2003 in Uzbekistan, only 6 percent of the poor were located in Tashkent (the capital city), but about 27 percent of the low-income benefit funds were allocated to that region (table 3.3).

Box 3.6 Financing Arrangements in Albania

Ndihma Ekonomike: Institutional Actors and Mechanisms Involved in Financing the Benefits

By law, the Ndihma Ekonomike (NE) may be financed from several sources—the central budget, local budgets, and grants from nongovernmental organizations. In practice, the central budget is the unique source of funds for the NE program. The funds are distributed to local governments through conditional grants (that is, they are earmarked) to eliminate the risk of the grants being used for other purposes.

The Ministry of Finance is in charge of funding the program, based on the request for funds provided by the State Social Service (SSS) Administration, which is an agency subordinated to the Ministry of Labor, Social Affairs, and Equal Opportunities (MoLSA). The request for funding is done on a yearly basis. When preparing the request, the Budget Directorate of the SSS takes into account a number of criteria, which may vary from year to year. For example, until 2005 the following factors were taken into account: (a) forecasts for the next year based on local governments' requests for funds and on expected impacts of policy changes, if any; (b) employment policies and their impact on NE beneficiaries; (c) number of current NE beneficiaries, disaggregated by type of benefit and household size; (d) results of inspection and reports from inspectors; and (e) indexation factors. The SSS at the central level (the Budget Directorate) was deciding on the grant amounts for each municipality or commune every two months, based on several indicators considered to be accurate poverty correlates. Indicators include the number of unemployed, the number of pensioners and invalids, the number of persons with disability allowance or an invalid-related pension, the number of rural households without agricultural land, and so on. SSS specialists assigned each indicator a specific weight, based on its assumed influence on the local economic and social situation.

The allocation of funds suffered from two shortcomings. First, the process was not very transparent, because the indicators used, as well as the weights, were at the discretion of the SSS. Second, local governments could manipulate the reported values of the indicators to get higher allocations. In 2010, MoLSA started to plan the block grant allocations using more transparent poverty indicators.

Sources: Kolpeja 2005; Ayala Consulting 2010; World Bank 2010b, 2011.

Lessons from Implementation Arrangements

The most important lessons from LRIS programs in Eastern Europe and Central Asia come from the region's experience with decentralization. The first is a prominent warning against decentralized funding. Although many aspects of the LRIS programs could be organized in either a centralized or a decentralized fashion, experience shows that financing should remain the responsibility of the central government. Decentralized financing runs the risk of creating inequities and leaving the poorest unprotected.

Moreover, decentralization of program financing may lead to serious resource constraints for the program not only for the poorest localities, but also for those

Table 3.3 Regional Allocation of Benefits versus Poverty Distribution, Uzbekistan, 2003

Region	Food poverty line Share of the poor (%)	Program threshold Share of the poor (%)	Share of poverty gap (%)	Distribution of funds for the low-income benefit program (%)
Ferghana	33	31	22	13
Central	18	19	22	18
Southern	16	19	21	31
Northern	12	14	18	8
Mirzachul	9	10	12	3
Tashkent	12	6	4	27
Total	100	100	100	100

Source: World Bank 2007.

that are not so poor. In the face of resource constraints, eligibility criteria for most benefits can be ad hoc, because local welfare offices use discretion when rationing available resources. These sorts of regional inequalities in social assistance can be particularly troubling when they are linked, as they so often are, to ethnic or other social divisions. In addition, a dynamic argument against decentralized and block-grant financing of LRIS programs can be based on experience that shows that locally cofinanced LRIS programs do not respond to economic crises even in more developed countries.

Central governments have many options for financing cash social assistance programs implemented by local governments. Conditional nonmatching grants or conditional block grants seem to work well, though the latter may have some downsides. Matching grants, in contrast, should be carefully designed, first, by ensuring that local governments do not bear more than 10–20 percent of the cost and, second, by ensuring that mechanisms are available through which poor localities are able to cofinance the transfers.

Even when the central government assumes the responsibility to finance targeted transfers, allocation of funds may remain an issue. Among the countries reviewed in this book, only a few have clear and transparent formulas or mechanisms for fund allocation. The need to set up such mechanisms to prevent horizontal inequities and political interference is another lesson from the case studies.

The rules and regulations governing program implementation should be defined in a manner consistent with both program goals and administrative resources. The development of program procedure manuals for program administrators is an essential element for effective implementation, especially in the context of decentralized or complex implementation arrangements. This element was missing in many countries in Eastern Europe and Central Asia. Although providing program administrators some degree of discretion over program rules may be justified when implementation is decentralized, when discretion is granted, its limits should be clearly defined, and supervision and accountability relationships should be functional.

Finally, an important lesson refers to embedding incentives for better implementation and service delivery by local governments. In addition to proper monitoring mechanisms, which can address typical principal-agent dilemmas that are characteristic of national programs implemented by local governments (a very common feature in Eastern Europe and Central Asia), policy makers should consider introducing performance incentives in LRIS programs.

Notes

1. The Albania Ndihma Ekonomike was a pilot program in Albania's decentralization reform.
2. Decentralization started in most countries in Eastern Europe and Central Asia in the mid-1990s and was characterized by trial-and-error processes. Some countries rolled out decentralization of some functions and competencies fast, but they later recentralized to some degree.
3. Because municipalities are relatively large (over 60,000 inhabitants, on average), some municipalities have set up wards as structural territorial units of the municipal administration, covering a certain part of the municipal territory. The number of wards in a municipality, their boundaries, and the functions delegated to the wards are established through decisions of the municipal councils. The activities of the wards are funded by the municipal budget.
4. The mahalla committees are "neighbourhood committees," or "organs of self-administration of citizens" (Coudouel, Marnie, and Micklewright 1998, 4). Their members are in principle elected by citizens, although there are claims that they are being appointed by the elders of the mahalla and that in some cases the appointment is influenced by local authorities. In any case, the chairperson and the secretary of a mahalla committee are paid a salary by the local authorities for performing some delegated functions, including receiving applications for social benefits, checking eligibility, and registering beneficiaries.
5. The marzer are coordinated by a governor appointed by the central government.
6. GMI evaluation survey, 2003 (U.K. Department for International Development, Government of Romania, and World Bank). The local government survey included 115 localities (large and small, urban and rural).
7. Another issue typical for Eastern Europe and Central Asia, which may affect the consolidation of procedures (and practices), is the frequent change of central legislation regarding the LRIS program or regarding other related programs that may affect the implementation of eligibility rules for LRIS.
8. In Romania, the financing of benefits was centralized in 2011. However, during the reference period covered by the country case studies, the benefits were paid from local budgets.
9. On average, the 4 percent covers about half of the total administrative cost at the local level.
10. Other examples of countries with devolved (fully decentralized) program financing are Bosnia and Herzegovina, Poland, and the Russian Federation. However, in the case of Poland, financing is decentralized only for those benefits for which the rules are left to the discretion of the local governments, or in those cases when local governments decide to top up a national benefit (World Bank 2010a). This approach is also used in Albania and Lithuania.

11. See World Bank (2010a) for a discussion on decentralizing the financial responsibility of social assistance programs, with references to Eastern Europe and Central Asia.

12. The U.S. Temporary Assistance for Needy Families program is another example showing that fiscal pressure at the subnational level during economic crises can constrain the ability of locally cofinanced social benefit programs to respond effectively to a crisis even in more developed countries (Zedlewski, Loprest, and Huber 2011).

13. Indexation will be further discussed in relation to eligibility thresholds.

References

Ayala Consulting. 2010. *Functional Review of the Ndihma Ekonomike Program.* Unpublished report, World Bank, Washington, DC.

Bassett, L., S. Gianozzi, L. Pop, and D. Ringold. 2012. "Rules, Roles, and Controls: Governance in Social Protection with an Application to Social Assistance." Background paper to the Social Protection and Labor Strategy, Social Protection and Labor Discussion Paper 1206, World Bank, Washington, DC.

Coudouel, A., S. Marnie, and J. Micklewright. 1998. *Targeting Social Assistance in a Transition Economy: The Mahallas in Uzbekistan.* Innocenti Occasional Papers, Economic and Social Policy Series 63. Florence, Italy: UNICEF International Child Development Centre.

Florescu, R., L. Pop, and E. Tesliuc. 2006. *Program Implementation Matters for Targeting Performance—Evidence and Lessons from Eastern and Central Europe: Country Study—Romania.* Unpublished report, World Bank, Washington, DC.

Grosh, M., C. del Ninno, E. Tesliuc, and A. Ouerghi. 2008. *For Protection and Promotion: The Design and Implementation of Effective Safety Nets.* Washington, DC: World Bank.

Isik-Dikmelik, A. 2012. "Do Social Benefits Respond to Crises? Evidence from Europe and Central Asia During the Global Crisis." Social Protection and Labor Discussion Paper 1219, World Bank, Washington, DC.

Kolpeja, V. 2005. "Ndihma Ekonomike (NE) Program Implementation Matters for Targeting the Performance: Evidence and Lessons from Albania." Paper prepared for the seminar "Program Implementation Matters for Targeting Performance: Evidence and Lessons from Eastern and Central Europe," Bucharest, June 6–7.

Kyrgyzstan Center for Social and Economic Research. 2006. *Program Implementation Matters for Targeting Performance—Evidence and Lessons from Eastern and Central Europe: Country Study—The Kyrgyz Republic.* Unpublished report, World Bank, Washington, DC.

Shopov, G. 2006. *Program Implementation Matters for Targeting Performance—Evidence and Lessons from Eastern and Central Europe: Country Study—Bulgaria.* Unpublished report, World Bank, Washington, DC.

———. 2012. *Implementing Activation and Graduation Measures for Social Assistance Beneficiaries—Bulgaria: A Review of Experiences.* Unpublished report, World Bank, Washington, DC.

World Bank. 2007. *Republic of Uzbekistan Living Standards Assessment Update.* Report 40723-UZ, Washington, DC.

———. 2010a. *Latvia: From Exuberance to Prudence. A Public Expenditure Review of Government Administration and the Social Sectors. Volume 2: Analytical Report.* Report 56747-LV. Washington, DC: World Bank.

———. 2010b. *The Social Safety Net in Albania.* Unpublished report, Washington, DC.

———. 2011. *Social Safety Nets in the Western Balkans: Design, Implementation, and Performance.* Report 54396-ECA, Washington, DC.

Zalimiene, L. 2006. *Program Implementation Matters for Targeting Performance—Evidence and Lessons from Eastern and Central Europe: Country Study—Lithuania.* Unpublished report, World Bank, Washington, DC.

Zedlewski, S., P. Loprest, and E. Huber. 2011. "What Role Is Welfare Playing in This Period of High Unemployment?" Fact Sheet 3, Unemployment and Recovery Project, Urban Institute, Washington, DC. http://www.urban.org/UploadedPDF/412378-Role-of -Welfare-in-this-Period-of-High-Unemployment.pdf.

CHAPTER 4

Eligibility

Most last-resort income support (LRIS) programs in the Eastern Europe and Central Asia region use a form of a means test (MT) to select some of the poorest families as beneficiaries. As shown in chapter 2, these programs perform well in selecting mostly poor beneficiaries (good targeting accuracy), but some suffer from low coverage of the poor. The ability to accurately identify the poorest beneficiaries amid higher informality than in developed countries remains a puzzle. For example, many analysts link the absence of a MT for LRIS programs in most southern European Union countries to the high informality in these countries (OECD 1998a, 1998b; de Neubourg, Castonguay, and Roelen 2007). With an even higher share of informal economy than southern Europe, most Eastern Europe and Central Asia countries have managed to operate LRIS programs with very good targeting accuracy. This chapter dissects the targeting methods and eligibility procedures that are most common in Eastern Europe and Central Asia countries and explains the key factors behind the good targeting accuracy.

At the core of the eligibility determination process is a test of household income and wealth or assets. In a stylized form, this test can be summarized as follows:[1] households with incomes and wealth below the program thresholds are eligible. The income test uses an administrative definition of income, which departs from the comprehensive, economic definition, either by disregarding or by imputing the hard-to-verify, informal incomes. The typical example of presumptive income is the agricultural income, which is estimated on the basis of ownership of agricultural assets (land, livestock, and agricultural machinery) and their expected yield. For good targeting accuracy, the difference between the administrative and economic income should be minimized by limited use of disregards and well-calibrated presumptive incomes. Most countries complement the income test with a wealth or asset test. Unlike Organisation for Economic Co-operation and Development (OECD) countries, few countries in Eastern Europe and Central Asia use a composite measure of household wealth and a corresponding threshold (for example, Lithuania). Most countries use a list of assets and specific thresholds to exclude asset-rich households from the program. The use of an administrative income that is smaller than the economic income translates into a relatively small income-eligibility threshold. Consequently, this approach provides access to the program for two types of beneficiaries: those without earnings or those with informal earnings and low assets. Often, the use of asset filters that have not been tested empirically leads to a high level of exclusion among income-poor beneficiaries. In the end, most programs select only a subset of the very poor.

Although the principal selection mechanism is the MT, it is often combined with other targeting methods, such as categorical, geographic, and self-selection. Program beneficiaries are selected on the basis of some form of a MT, which may or may not be combined with categorical selection criteria such as demographic, health, or socioeconomic characteristics of the household or its members. Pure geographic targeting is not used in Eastern Europe and Central Asia—the programs are available in all localities and areas. However, elements of geographic targeting are implicitly present through the algorithm of funds allocation across municipalities (for example, Albania and Lithuania) or by assignment of different coefficients, poverty weights, or scores to households as a function of their location (for example, Armenia and the Kyrgyz Republic). In addition to the income and asset tests, many programs include built-in conditions or requirements, which, if not fulfilled, alter the eligibility status of the household or individual. These conditions relate mostly to the availability to take up work and participation in active labor market programs of those beneficiaries who are able to work. Noncompliance with these requirements leads to self-selection of beneficiaries.

Eligibility Determination: Key Design Elements

Means Test: Determining the Welfare Status in the Presence of Informal Incomes

The MT involves an assessment of means through income and asset tests and the choice of a threshold to distinguish between those who are eligible and those who are not. Usually, the metric used for the MT is a monetary one.[2] Armenia is the only country included in our case studies using a vulnerability score instead of a monetary metric, which brings it closer to a proxy-means test (PMT). However, the main elements used in a regular MT (that is, the income and asset tests) play a major role in the case of Armenia, too.

Income Test

Almost all LRIS programs in Eastern Europe and Central Asia use an income test to determine the welfare status of potential beneficiaries. As a general rule, the list of incomes taken into account for eligibility determination is a comprehensive one, following closely the economic definition of total income (table 4.1).

The calculation of total income would include all sources of revenue for all members of the assistance unit (family or household), as well as the incomes that are not attributable to specific members (for example, incomes from agriculture and social protection family benefits). Indeed, in the majority of Eastern Europe and Central Asia countries, the applicants are required to declare all incomes:

Table 4.1 Types of Incomes Included in the Comprehensive, Economic Definition of Income

Type of income	Definition
Income from wage employment	Wage income in cash or in kind, including from seasonal and occasional work
	Bonuses
Nonfarm self-employment income	Earnings in cash or in kind from sale of output[a]
Farm and agricultural income	Earnings from the sale of crops[a]
	Earnings from the sale of processed crop products[a]
	Earnings from the sale of animal products[a]
	Consumption of self-produced food[a]
Income from transfers	Social insurance pensions
	Unemployment benefits
	Social assistance and noncontributory benefits in cash or in kind (child allowances, disability benefits, and so on)
	Scholarships
	Private interhousehold transfers in cash and in kind, remittances
	Charity
Income from capital and assets	Income from renting out dwellings, land, equipment, and consumer durable goods
	Interest on savings, dividends
	Revenue from sale of land, livestock, buildings, and durable goods
Other income	Income from lottery and gambling
	Other

Source: Adapted from McKay 2000.
a. Sales revenue net of cost.

from employment, including nonfarm self-employment; from agriculture; from social protection transfers, including contributory and noncontributory benefits, and scholarships; from private transfers; and from capital and assets, including rent, dividends, interest, and sales.

Easy-To-Verify Income versus Hard-To-Verify Income. Measuring and verifying income as an indicator of welfare raises challenges, especially in countries with significant informality of incomes (for example, cash and in-kind incomes from agriculture, incomes from employment in the informal sector, remittances, incomes from informal agreements of renting or leasing land or houses, and so on). Several factors correlate with the difficulty in verifying and measuring incomes, such as the relative size of the informal (hard-to-verify) incomes, their distribution across welfare groups, and the administrative capacity to verify and cross-check information.

The first two factors can be illustrated with survey data for three typical situations by plotting the shares and (absolute) size of verifiable (formal wages and social protection transfers) and nonverifiable incomes in total income across the income distribution (the population being ranked from the poorest to the richest in terms of total income per capita). When the share of hard-to-verify incomes is relatively small and grows monotonically with income, the ranking of households based on a verifiable income provides a good approximation of the distribution of the full, per capita income and the risk of inclusion errors is relatively low[3] (for example, in Bulgaria; see figure 4.1). When the share of hard-to-verify incomes is high and not positively correlated with income, the risk of inclusion errors (or of rank reversal) is higher (for example, in the rural Kyrgyz Republic, figure 4.1).

Figure 4.1 Composition of Household Income over the Welfare Distribution

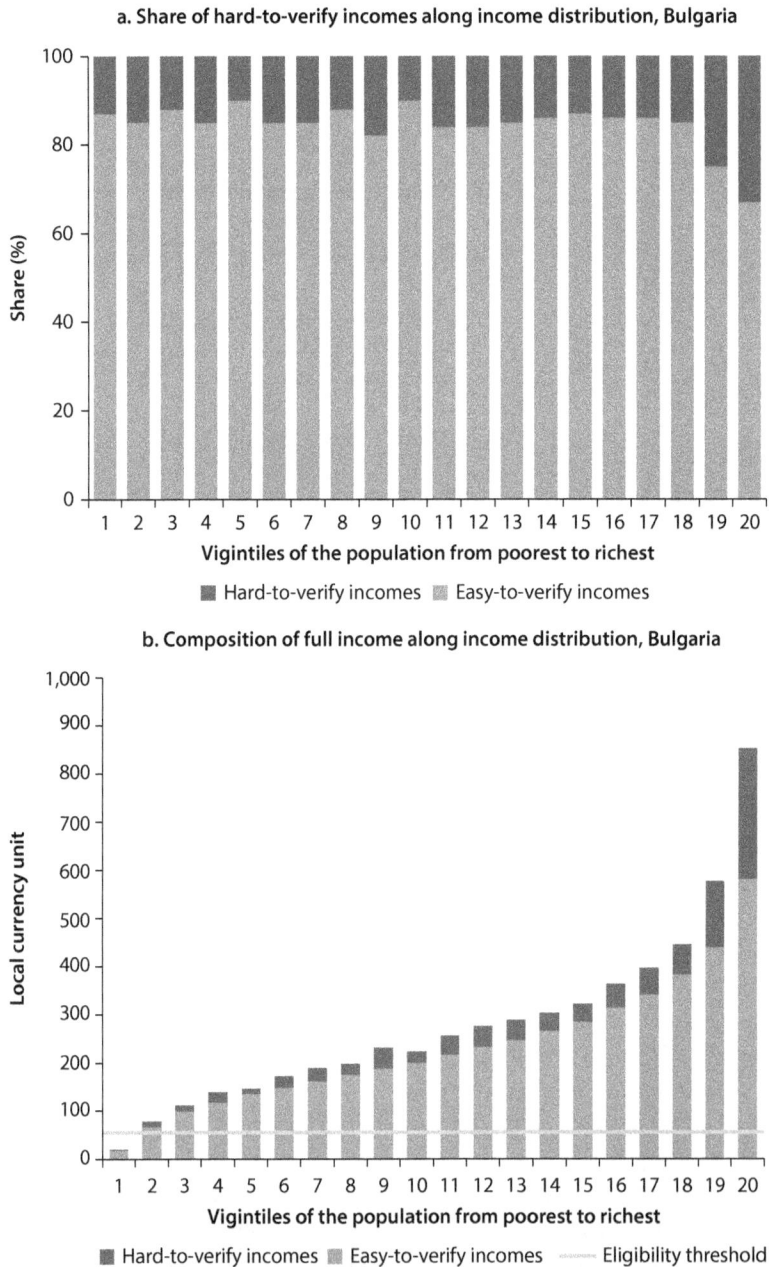

a. Share of hard-to-verify incomes along income distribution, Bulgaria

Vigintiles of the population from poorest to richest

■ Hard-to-verify incomes ▨ Easy-to-verify incomes

b. Composition of full income along income distribution, Bulgaria

Vigintiles of the population from poorest to richest

■ Hard-to-verify incomes ▨ Easy-to-verify incomes ⎯ Eligibility threshold

figure continues next page

Figure 4.1 Composition of Household Income over the Welfare Distribution *(continued)*

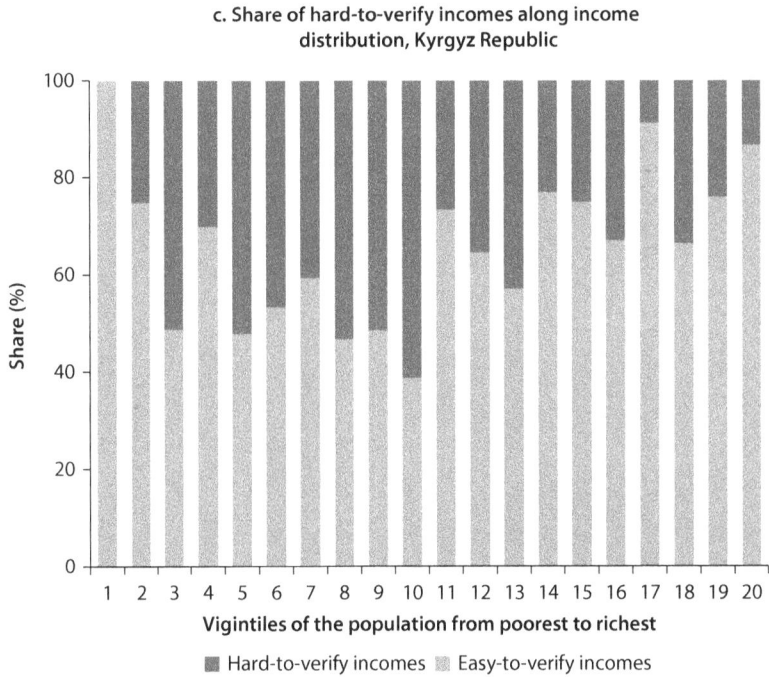

c. Share of hard-to-verify incomes along income distribution, Kyrgyz Republic

Vigintiles of the population from poorest to richest

■ Hard-to-verify incomes   ▨ Easy-to-verify incomes

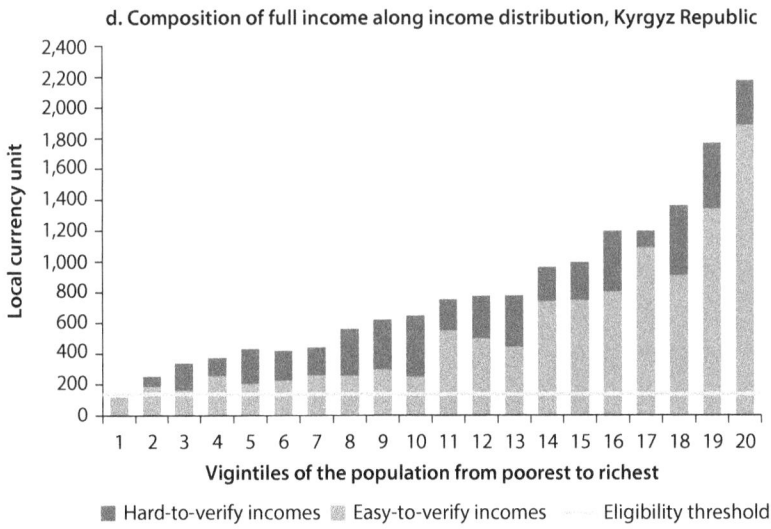

d. Composition of full income along income distribution, Kyrgyz Republic

Vigintiles of the population from poorest to richest

■ Hard-to-verify incomes   ▨ Easy-to-verify incomes   — Eligibility threshold

figure continues next page

Figure 4.1 Composition of Household Income over the Welfare Distribution *(continued)*

e. Share of hard-to-verify incomes along income distribution, rural areas, Bulgaria

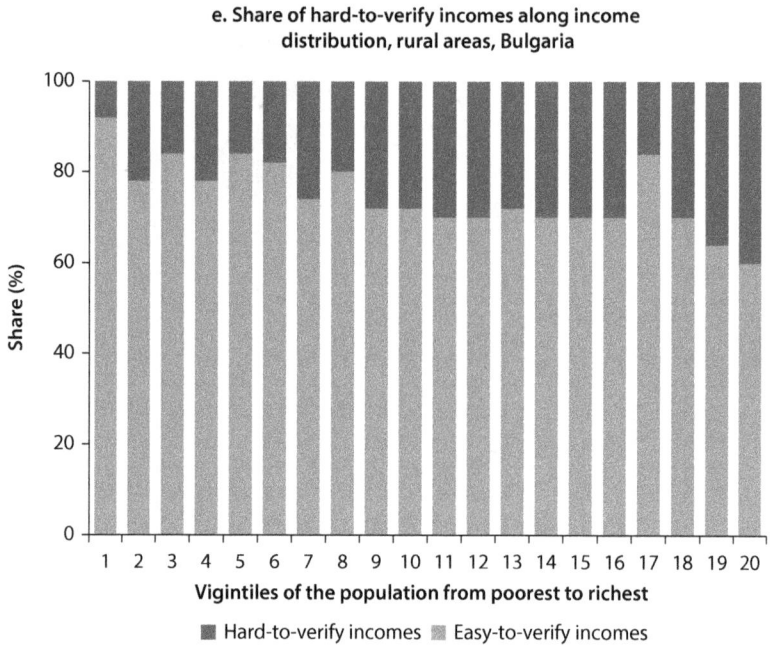

Vigintiles of the population from poorest to richest

■ Hard-to-verify incomes ▨ Easy-to-verify incomes

f. Composition of full income along income distribution, rural areas, Bulgaria

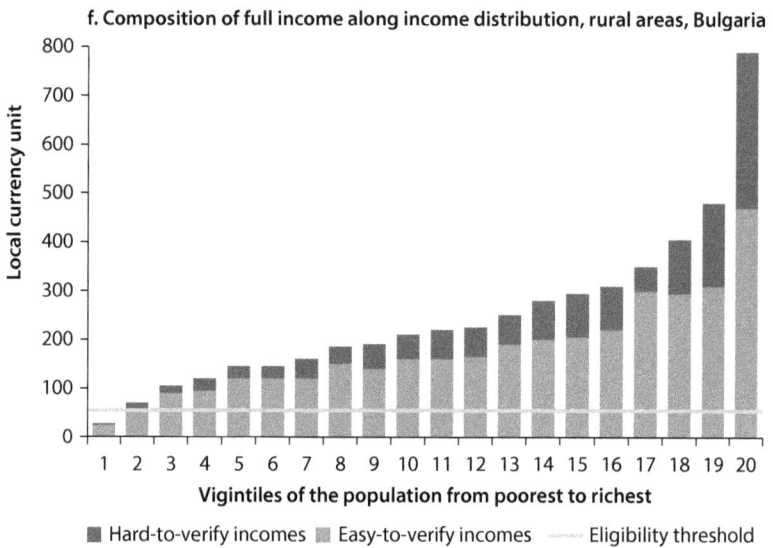

Vigintiles of the population from poorest to richest

■ Hard-to-verify incomes ▨ Easy-to-verify incomes —— Eligibility threshold

figure continues next page

Figure 4.1 Composition of Household Income over the Welfare Distribution *(continued)*

g. Share of hard-to-verify incomes along income distribution, rural areas, Kyrgyz Republic

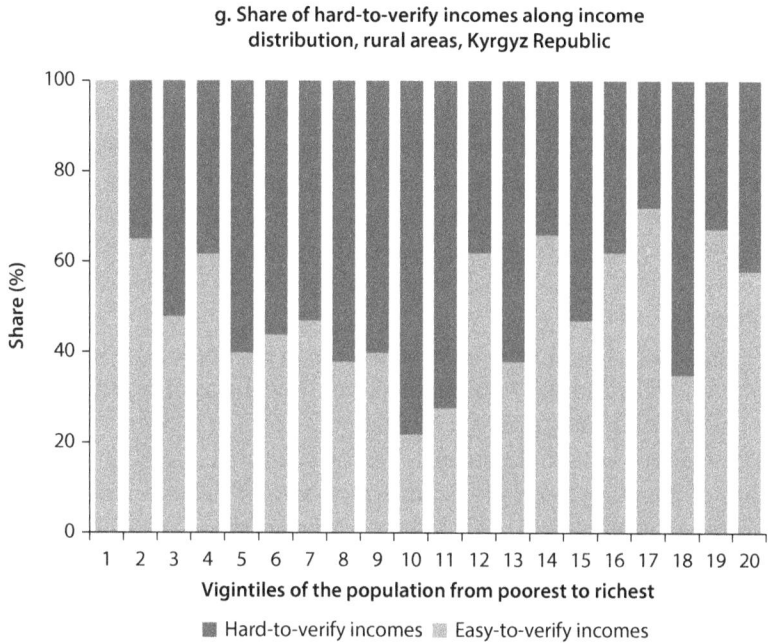

Vigintiles of the population from poorest to richest

■ Hard-to-verify incomes ▩ Easy-to-verify incomes

h. Composition of full income along income distribution, rural areas, Kyrgyz Republic

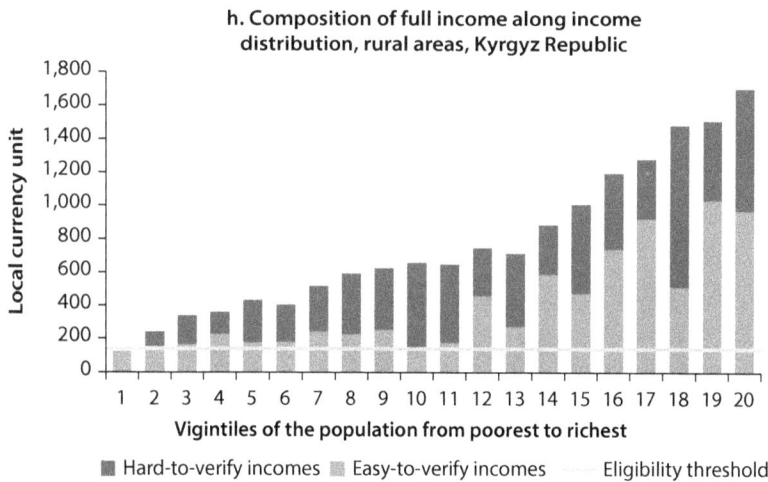

Vigintiles of the population from poorest to richest

■ Hard-to-verify incomes ▩ Easy-to-verify incomes ---- Eligibility threshold

Sources: Calculations based on survey data: Bulgaria, 2007 Living Standards Measurement Study; Kyrgyz Republic, 2007 Household Budget Survey.

Interviews with the frontline staff members and beneficiaries in the case study programs suggest that hard-to-verify incomes are seldom reported or checked. Hard evidence on this, especially from the Eastern Europe and Central Asia region, is still scarce but growing. Two studies, one on a Russian means-tested program around 2006 and another on the Romanian guaranteed minimum income (GMI) program in 2013, have found large discrepancies between the income reported by beneficiaries when they apply for benefits (administrative records) and the income they declare in household surveys.

Income Underreporting in Means-Tested Programs in Tomsk Region, the Russian Federation, 2006. In Russia, a World Bank team partnered with two local research institutes to examine why income-tested programs operating under similar rules as in the OECD have comparatively poor targeting accuracy. The study (Institute for Urban Economics, Independent Institute for Social Policy, and World Bank 2007), combining quantitative and qualitative methods, covered five regions of the country, including the Tomsk region, which benefited from more in-depth data collection.

First, the study found that income was severely underreported even in a detailed and well-managed household survey. The Tomsk Poverty Monitoring Survey (June 2006) was the first in Russia since 1997 to collect comprehensive information about household income and consumption. Based on this detailed information, the study found that underreporting of income was widespread: households reported their income to be, on average, about two-thirds of house-hold consumption (figure 4.2). Given that the Tomsk region was registering robust growth during 2006, one would have expected incomes to exceed consumption with the difference being savings. The underreporting was present in almost all administrative subdivisions of Tomsk *oblast* (an adminis-trative division), except the city of Seversk, where employment was

Figure 4.2 Severely Underreported Incomes Even in Household Survey, Tomsk Oblast, Russian Federation

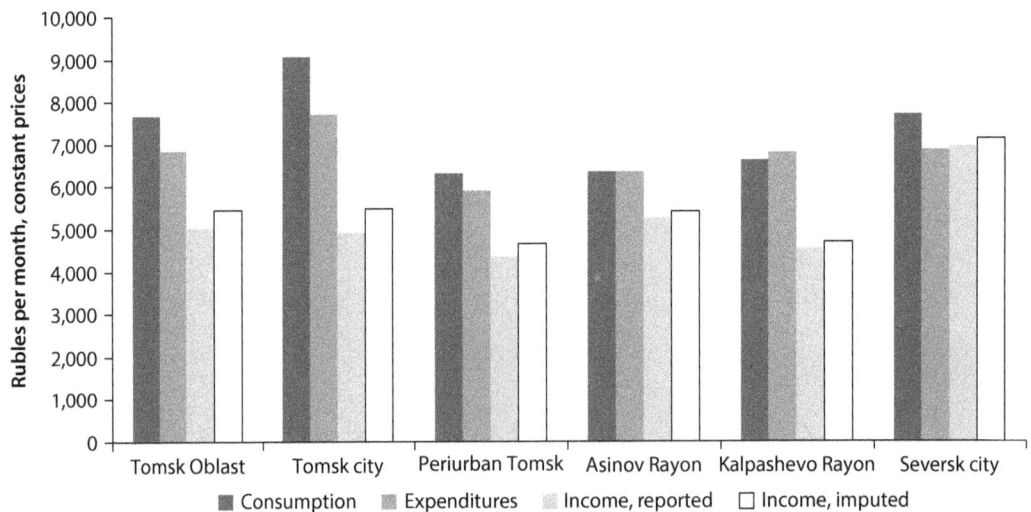

Source: Institute for Urban Economics, Independent Institute for Social Policy, and World Bank 2007; estimates based on Tomsk Poverty Monitoring Survey, 2006.
Note: Income was significantly underreported in the survey. The consumption aggregate includes monetary expenditures as well as consumption out of own production.

predominantly formal and consisted of more military personnel. This conforms with expectations from the household survey literature—that households whose sole or main income is from a single, explicit, and regular paycheck will find it easier to report income than those whose incomes are from varied sources, especially those incomes that may be irregular in timing and amounts or be the net result of many transactions for which profit and loss bookkeeping does not take place. Indeed, this is the reason why many studies use consumption-based measures of welfare in researching welfare in developing countries (see Grosh and Glewwe 2000). The more accurate reporting in the city of Seversk could also be due to the dominant type of household in the city: military families more accustomed to a very orderly, disciplined life.

Second, the study found that the incomes declared by applicants to the social assistance (SA) offices suffered from additional underreporting. For this test, the study compared the share of beneficiaries reporting a certain type of income in the survey with the similar share derived from applications for the respective programs.[4] Both the sample of beneficiaries in the survey and the sample of applications from the administrative files were randomly selected and were representative of the whole population of beneficiaries. Both samples covered the same time period (2006). The random selection of beneficiary files was called "quality control review." The results of these comparisons are summarized in figure 4.3. Significant underreporting was present in both programs (illustrated by the orange bars, which show the difference between the average income of a certain type reported in the survey minus the income reported to the SA offices), but it was somehow higher in the child allowance programs (whose absent recertification and verification procedures triggered larger differences between the type of incomes declared at application time and the current level of income captured in the survey).

Third, the study found that informal, hard-to-verify income was seldom reported and that some formal incomes were underreported in applications for benefits. Some underreporting had plagued formal incomes, such as wages (especially from the private sector involving specific wage elements such as bonuses), as well as other SA benefits. Informal, hard-to-verify incomes from farming, hunting, self-employment, or remittances were rarely reported at all. These findings were triangulated with the results of a qualitative assessment. Frontline staff members processing eligibility were aware of that underreporting, were able to identify the type of incomes with more severe underreporting, and complained about their inability to check the accuracy of the income reported in applications. However, absent hard data, they tend to think that the phenomenon is marginal, as confirmed in this interview with a head of an SA center from the Institute for Urban Economics, Independent Institute for Social Policy, and World Bank (2007) study:

> We cannot check the accuracy of the information given to us. We do not have legal powers as well as staff who could do it. They (n.a. beneficiaries) drive impressive cars, build impressive houses, but they do not have any remorse to request a benefit

Figure 4.3 Share of Beneficiaries Reporting a Certain Type of Income in Their Application for a Social Assistance Program versus in a Household Survey

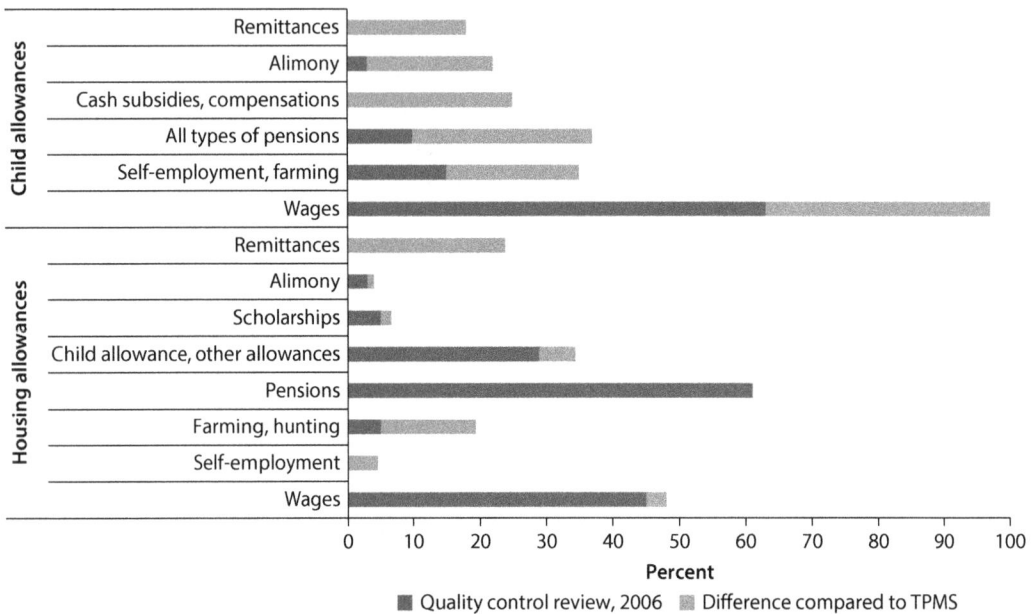

Sources: Institute for Urban Economics, Independent Institute for Social Policy, and World Bank 2007; Tomsk Poverty Monitoring Survey, 2006.
Note: Comparison of two contemporaneous representative samples of beneficiaries—one from the Tomsk Poverty Monitoring Survey, another one from a random sample of beneficiary files (quality control review) in Tomsk, Russian Federation, 2006. TPMS = Tomsk Poverty Monitoring Survey.

of 91 rubles. But there are not many of them. They do not influence the program significantly…. Our main problem is entrepreneurs. It seems impossible to verify their income. They give us references from the Tax Office, where they write in print this large that they cannot guarantee the accuracy of this information. If an applicant is employed by an entrepreneur, the entrepreneur declares any amount, and we have no right to check what the actual wage was. We do not have such powers. We do not have people and means to check it all. (p. 69)

Income Underreporting in the GMI Program, Romania, 2012. The evidence from Romania's GMI program in 2012 supports and even strengthens the findings from Russia. Urban GMI beneficiaries tend not to report informal, hard-to-measure, and hard-to-verify incomes. In the case of Romania, a representative sample of GMI beneficiaries from the Household Budget Survey (August to October 2012) was compared with the administrative records of all beneficiaries of that program during the same period. The comparison includes the share of beneficiaries reporting a particular income source in the survey and in administrative data (statistics similar to those in Russia in 2006), as well as the average reported income. The comparison is restricted to urban beneficiaries as a way to filter out rural households whose eligibility is not based on agricultural income, but on an asset test (rural beneficiaries are not required to report their

Figure 4.4 Income Not Reported by Urban GMI Beneficiaries, Romania, August–October 2012

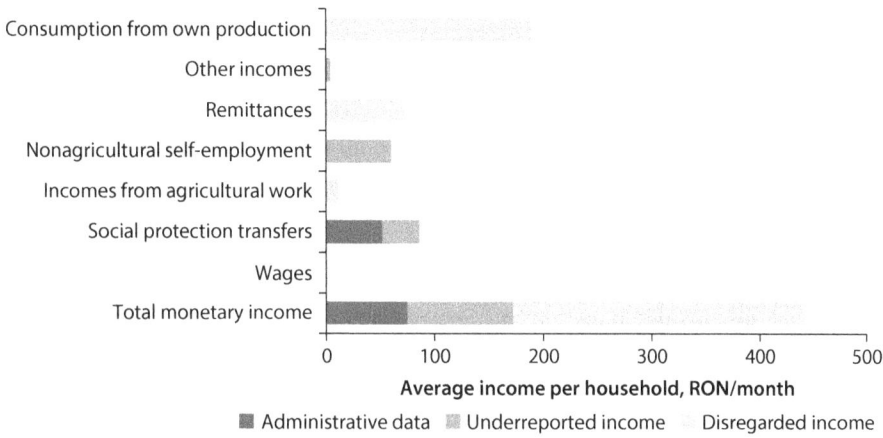

Source: Tesliuc et al., forthcoming.
Note: Comparison of the average monthly income per household reported by guaranteed minimum income beneficiaries in the Household Budget Survey (representative sample of beneficiaries) and in administrative data (program management information system). GMI = guaranteed minimum income.

Figure 4.5 Type of Income Sources Not Reported by Urban GMI Beneficiaries, Romania, August–October 2012

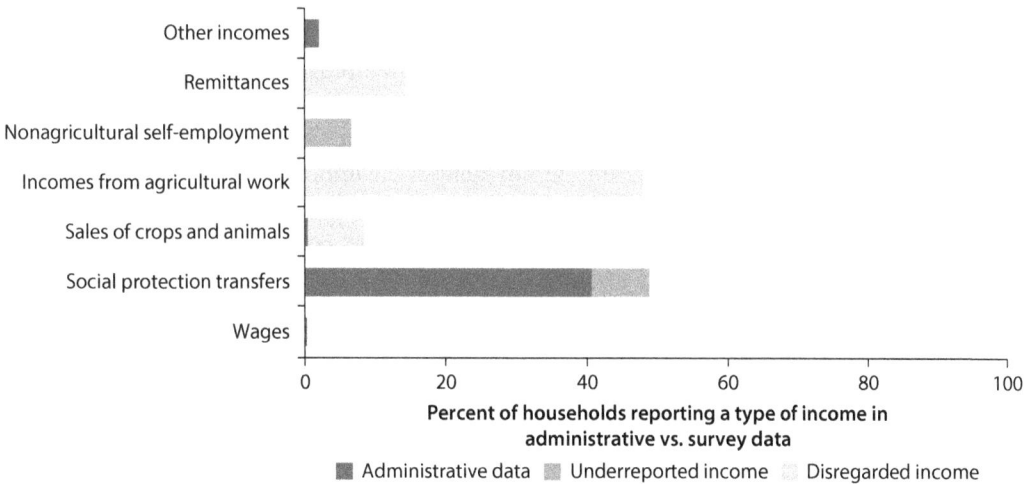

Source: Tesliuc et al., forthcoming.
Note: Figure shows comparison of the percentage of households reporting a particular income source in the Household Budget Survey (representative sample of GMI beneficiaries) and in administrative data (program management information system). GMI = guaranteed minimum income.

agricultural income). The results are summarized in figures 4.4. and 4.5. In figure 4.4, the blue bars indicate the average income reported by (all) beneficiaries in their applications for the GMI program, and the orange and green bars indicate the difference between the income reported in the survey and the income reported when applying for the program (underreporting in orange, and disregarded incomes in green). As in Russia, informal, nonagricultural employ-ment is not reported, as well as some social protection incomes. Several types of income (consumption from own production, incomes from agricultural works, and remittances) are not included in the administrative definition of income used to determine GMI eligibility and, hence, are not reported.

Findings Consistent with Expectations. One would expect the underreporting of income to be greater in applications for SA programs than in household surveys, for at least two reasons: (a) in the survey, substantially more effort and time is spent collecting information about income and consumption compared to the summary assessment typically done in the social protection offices; and (b) households do not have any pecuniary incentive to conceal some hard-to-verify income sources in order to receive benefits.

The Income Test in Practice: From Economic to Administrative Incomes. The success of the means-tested programs depends on the capacity to measure and verify the means of the applicants. As shown above, although the list of incomes to be counted includes by design a wide range of revenues, not all of them are easy to test. In practice, four categories of incomes are observed: (a) easy-to-verify and counted, (b) hard-to-verify and imputed, (c) hard-to-verify and probably missed (not declared or underestimated by applicants), and (d) disregarded (both easy- and hard-to-verify). The easy-to-verify incomes may vary from country to country, depending on the capacity to cross-check information,[5] but at the mini-mum they consist of incomes from formal employment and social protection benefits. The hard-to-verify and imputed incomes (presumptive incomes) are usually those from agriculture or occasional labor. Other incomes, such as those from remittances, from self-employment in the informal sector, or from informal lease or rent of assets, are to be declared by the applicant but are difficult to verify, measure, or impute. Depending on the country, certain incomes are disregarded—usually some specific SA transfers like one-time or temporary SA benefits, disability benefits, child benefits, or charity (see table 4.2). Incomes may be disregarded to avoid the exclusion of some groups benefiting from par-ticular types of SA benefits,[6] or even as an approach to encourage activation (reintegration in, or participation in, the labor market).

Presumptive Incomes. Most countries address the challenge of hard-to-verify-incomes by supplementing the test of formal incomes with an assessment of presumptive (informal) incomes. The imputation of presumptive incomes in addition to measuring the easy-to-verify incomes makes this method a hybrid means test (HMT), which can be considered an intermediate targeting method between the MT and the PMT. Under the HMT model, the welfare status of the applicant is assessed using an income indicator that is the sum of verifi-able income (from wages and social protection transfers) and the estimated unverifiable income. Figure 4.6 illustrates the impact of accounting for some part of the hard-to-verify income (the presumptive income) on the number of

Table 4.2 Treatment of Different Income Sources in Means-Tested Programs in Eastern Europe and Central Asia

Administrative income		Required to declare	Verifiable and measurable	Imputed (presumptive incomes)	Disregarded
From wage employment	Formal wages	✓	Easy (though seasonal wages may be a problem)	No	No[a]
	Informal wages	✓	Difficult	In selected countries[b]	No
From nonfarm self-employment	Formal	✓	Rather difficult	According to tax legislation	No
	Informal	✓	Difficult	No	No
From farming and agriculture	Crops Processed products	✓	Difficult	Yes[c]	No[d]
From public transfers (social protection)	Social insurance and social assistance benefits, cash, or in-kind benefits[e]	✓	Easy	No	Selected noncontributory benefits, cash, or in-kind benefits
From private transfers	Remittances Charity	✓[f]	Difficult	No[g]	No
From rent or lease of assets (land, dwellings)	Formal	✓(e)	Easy	No	No
	Informal	✓(e)	Difficult	No	No
From capital	Dividends, interest	✓(e)	Rather difficult	No	No
Other		✓	Difficult	No	No

Source: Based on case studies and program legislation.
a. In Romania, 15 percent of wage income is disregarded, as an incentive to work.
b. This applies to occasional work in Albania and Romania.
c. Bulgaria does not include imputed income.
d. In some countries, part of the farming income is disregarded: Bulgaria does not count the income from land conceded by the state in the first year after concession; the Kyrgyz Republic does not count income from livestock; and Romania does not impute income for land and livestock below certain limits.
e. These include pensions, unemployment benefits, social assistance (noncontributory) allowances (child, family, disability, and so on), scholarships, humanitarian aid, and so on.
f. Armenia does not include imputed income.
g. Imputed income is not included in Albania, where any household having a member abroad is assumed to receive remittances.

accepted applications. Not taking into account the hard-to-verify income increases the number of accepted applications from OA to OB (figure 4.6, panel a). Taking into account the presumptive income will reduce the number of accepted applications to OC, thus, eliminating some of the leakage of benefits (the population segment CB; figure 4.6, panel b).

The typical case of hard-to-verify and imputed incomes in Eastern Europe and Central Asia is represented by the incomes from agriculture,[7] which, in addition to being difficult to verify, are also difficult to measure. This difficulty happens for several reasons. First, farm income is computed over a longer time period (the agricultural season) than in other economic branches where such estimates could

Figure 4.6 Hard-to-Verify Incomes and the Impact of Imputing Presumptive Incomes on the Number of Beneficiaries

a. Income test under means-test approach

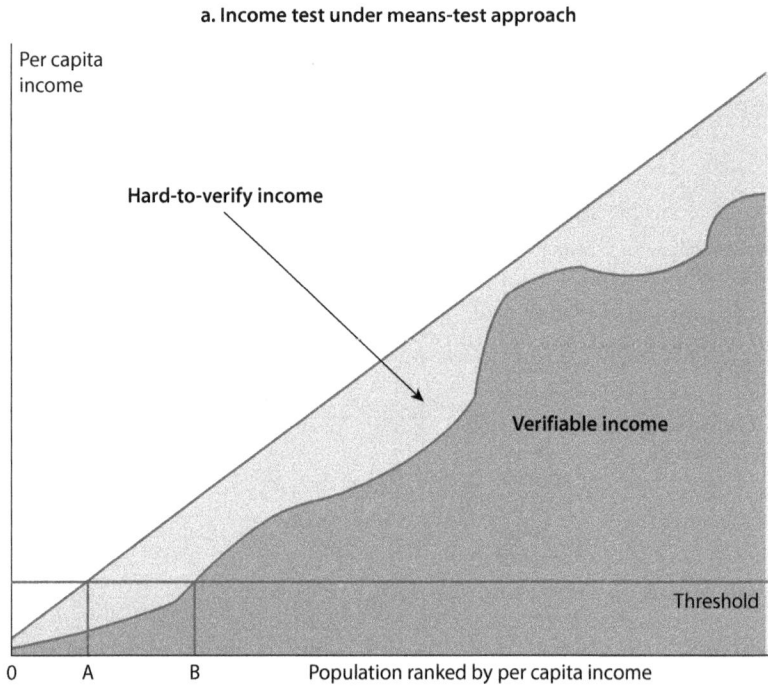

b. Income test under hybrid means test approach

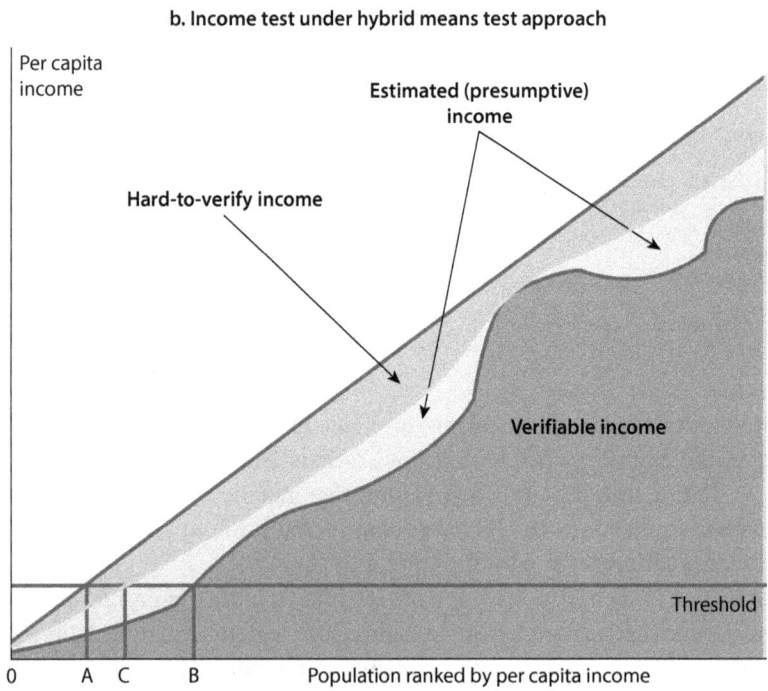

Source: Tesliuc, Leite, and Petrina 2009.

be generated monthly. In the Eastern Europe and Central Asia region, the agricultural season for vegetal production is typically a year and for livestock production is several months, depending on the type of livestock. Over the agricultural season, expenses are incurred during planting or breeding time, whereas, revenues are collected solely after harvest. Only then can farmers find the net revenues from costs and find their profit. In contrast, day laborers or formal employees would know their income (wage) at the end of the day or end of the month, respectively. Second, the estimation of the farm income is as complex as for other sole entrepreneurships, further compounded by the length of the agricultural season. Third, not all revenues or the expenditures on inputs (for example, labor, equipment, and fertilizers) are monetized, because a part of the production is consumed by the household, and some inputs are produced or supplied by the household (for example, fodder and some labor). Small farmers, often at risk for poverty and targeted by LRIS programs, often consume a larger share of their production in kind, bypassing markets, which makes the valuation of their outputs and inputs a complex task. This portion of farm income appears in the "consumption out of own production" estimate in household surveys.

Most of the countries reviewed impute presumptive agricultural incomes based on the estimated return to land and livestock. This is the case in Albania, Armenia, the Kyrgyz Republic, Lithuania, and Romania (up to 2009[8]). In addition to the presumptive income from land and livestock, for beneficiaries capable of working, governments in Albania, Romania, and Uzbekistan[9] also imputed presumed earnings from seasonal occasional work—at local market wage rates—for a given number of days per month during the agricultural season. In Romania, where local governments were allowed to modify eligibility rules within given limits, survey data indicated that almost half of the local governments imputed incomes for occasional work by default, and in rural areas this amounts to 60 percent. About two-thirds of the local governments that imputed informal incomes did so for the entire year, whereas the others applied this rule only during the agricultural season. However, such a practice can lead to significant exclusion errors, because it assumes no shortage of demand for occasional work, and equal access to such work, which is not always the case.[10]

In the case of farm income, the (imputed) return is estimated by type of land or livestock and is usually regulated at the local, regional, or national level, by (or in consultation with) the line agencies or ministries with responsibilities in the agriculture field. In Lithuania and Romania, the presumptive income is imputed only for agricultural assets (land size or number of livestock heads) above certain thresholds (which vary by type of land or livestock) and is regulated at the national level.[11] This approach means that income is not imputed for a minimum quantity of livestock or land considered to be essential for subsistence. In the Kyrgyz Republic, the imputation of incomes from land is done on the basis of income standards by type of land and administrative region and is regulated by national legislation. In Armenia, Croatia, and Ukraine, the imputation of incomes from land is done on the basis of land value and tax information. In Albania, the imputation for both land and livestock is done on the basis of national revenue coefficients by type of land and geographic characteristics. In Uzbekistan, the imputation is done according to local rules.[12]

Both the nationwide and locally regulated imputation methods have advantages and disadvantages. In large countries with significant shares of rural or agricultural populations, the identification of an appropriate mechanism that can take into account the regional prices and cost-of-living factors needed to set up the asset valuation or income imputation procedures may be a difficult task, and central governments are often inclined to leave the task at the discretion of local governments, which supposedly have better information. However, when a high degree of discretion is left with the local governments, horizontal inequities[13] are likely to emerge. In the first three years of LRIS program implementation (2002–04) in Romania, the local governments imputed incomes based on unit prices established through decisions of local councils (box 4.1). The absence of national regulations regarding the evaluation of an applicant's assets (that is, imputation of incomes) induced regional variation in program implementation. The result was extreme variation in values for most assets within similar types of localities (and even between neighboring communities), which in turn led to

---

Box 4.1 Romania: Were Applicants Who Owned Similar Assets Likely to Receive the Same Assessment in All Localities?

A survey carried out in 115 local governments in the context of guaranteed minimum income evaluation (2003) indicated considerable variation in the values attached to the imputed income from and valuation of assets. In almost all cases, these values were determined by the local councils (rarely after a consultation with the county council); the values decided upon were simply reported to the county council. Although this was consistent with the methodological norms in place at that time—values should be determined by the local councils, and local information could be taken into account—this procedure not only used a great many resources with the same job being undertaken by each local council, but also contained the potential for unequal treatment. The survey of 115 local councils undertaken for the program evaluation confirmed the impression of considerable variations in the valuation. The results include two interesting points:

• First, within each type of locality, there was considerable variation in values for most assets. The smallest ratio was 1.8 for domestic birds in large cities while the largest was 1,819.2 for buildings in rural areas. Most assets had a ratio of 5 or more, indicating that a particular asset was likely to be treated very differently within similar types of localities.
• Second, in general, the values were higher for rural areas. It is very difficult to believe that this reflects market conditions, especially in the case of buildings where one would expect values to be higher in large cities. This valuation is more likely to reflect the attempt by poor rural areas to avoid the liability for cofinancing the program than the true market values of assets.

Sources: Ministry of Labor, Social Solidarity and Family, Romania, and Birks Sinclair and Associates Ltd. 2004.

---

horizontal inequities. Later on, in 2004, the program was reformed: clear rules of imputation were put in place, and limits for unit prices had to be provided by county-level agencies using information from deconcentrated branches of the Ministry of Agriculture. A second reform introduced national standards that set minimum and maximum limits at the national level. After 2009, the program renounced this method altogether and instituted a system of asset filters to separate asset-poor farmers from asset-rich farmers (Tesliuc et al., forthcoming).

Though introducing national rules may require more administrative effort, capacity, and collaboration across several agencies in the design stage, this approach appears to overcome some of the disadvantages of the locally regulated approach to assets evaluation. Albania and Armenia use such nationwide approaches, including conversion formulas between different types of livestock (box 4.2). When the price of assets is known to have significant regional variation, the involvement of regional agencies (for example, the 2004 reform in Romania) appears to more expedient.

Box 4.2 Imputation of Farm Income in Armenia and Albania

Armenia

For rural households, the income from agricultural activities is calculated on the basis of cadastral gross income of the land lots considered to be the household's private property minus the amount of compulsory payments and taxes defined by legislation.[a]

The income received from animal husbandry is calculated by first converting the stock of animals owned by each household into standard livestock units, using a set of conversion factors defined by a governmental decree of Armenia, and then multiplying this by the expected gross income calculated by the Ministry of Agriculture for one standard livestock unit.

Albania

Revenues from land are calculated according to the coefficients shown in table B4.2.1 for the different categories of land use, such as field crops, viniculture, horticulture, and fruit trees, with the exception of land under desalination.

Revenues from livestock differentiated according to zones are calculated on the basis of the coefficients shown in table B4.2.2.

Table B4.2.1 Land Categories and Revenue Coefficients, Albania

Item	Land categories								
	I	II	III	IV	V	VI	VII	VIII	IX–X
Revenue coefficient lek/m^2 per year	9	8	7	7	5	5	4	4	3

Source: Council of Ministers, Albania 2005.
Note: m^2 = square meter.

box continues next page

Box 4.2 **Imputation of Farm Income in Armenia and Albania** (continued)

Table B4.2.2 Livestock Unit Conversions and Revenue Categories

Zone	Coefficient
Lowlands	Revenues from 1 cow = 15 sheep or goats = 3 swine = 5 piglets = 20 beehives = lek 22,500/year
Hills	Revenues from 1 cow = 12 sheep or goats = 3 swine = 5 piglets = 20 beehives = lek 18,000/year
Mountains	Revenues from 1 cow = 10 sheep or goats = 3 swine = 5 piglets = 20 beehives = lek 13,000/year

Sources: Ministry of Labor and Social Issues 2004; Council of Ministers 2005.
a. A 2009 study by the National Institute of Labor and Social Research with the support of the U.S. Agency for International Development–Armenia Social Protection Systems Strengthening Program identified possible sources of fraud and error through underreporting of the actual size of the land by the beneficiary families or through underestimation of the cadastre cost of the land (and the subsequent underestimation of land tax derived from that cost) (NILSR 2009).

Reference Period and Assistance Unit. The reference period for which the incomes are assessed may vary from one month (Romania) to three months (the Kyrgyz Republic and Lithuania) to six months (Ukraine) in the case of regular incomes, whereas for incomes from agricultural or nonagricultural self-employment, which consist of irregular or seasonal earnings, the reference period can be up to 12 months.

The assistance unit can be the extended family (Armenia), the household (Albania and the Kyrgyz Republic), or the nuclear family (Bulgaria and Romania). The household is usually defined as a unit living in the same dwelling and sharing the food (cooking together) and other common housing utilities (for example, heating). In many cases, the household overlaps with the extended family. The operational approach to identify a household is based on utility bills (where they exist). The nuclear family is defined as parents and minor children, or students up to 24 years old. In many Eastern Europe and Central Asia countries, especially in rural areas, households with multiple nuclear families (that is, extended families and multigenerational households, but also nonrelated families in some cases), which share some common resources, are not unusual. In such situations, if the assistance unit is the nuclear family, the social worker is supposed to estimate the share of household incomes (for example, from agriculture) that is to be attributed to each family. Targeting nuclear families as opposed to households responds to the concern of weakened support (including the intergenerational support) within extended families, but at the same time this approach may further complicate eligibility assessment, monitoring, and evaluation. For example, most national surveys do not identify nuclear families within households, resulting in difficulty in accurately assessing the program coverage and targeting performance.

Assets Test

The other important eligibility test for means-tested programs, in addition to income, is the level of wealth the household possesses. Estimating a comprehensive measure of household wealth is often more complex than measuring income, especially when wealth is stored in multiple assets, some of them with thin markets. Hence, instead of using a wealth eligibility threshold, most countries in Eastern Europe and Central Asia or the OECD that operate means-tested programs use thresholds for specific assets to screen out high net-worth applicants[14] (asset filters). Assets that are typically included in the test are land, livestock, dwelling, mobile or immobile assets that can be put into productive use and generate income, saving accounts and other financial assets, and durable goods or appliances. Most asset tests consist of simple exclusionary filters (yes or no), with a few examples of sophisticated valuation methods and asset eligibility thresholds (for example, Lithuania and Romania until 2009). When used, the asset thresholds are defined on the basis of a set of minimum standard parameters for assets and living conditions,[15] such as number of rooms, size of living area, land size, and number of allowed durable goods and electronic appliances.

In some cases, asset filters are used to select poor households whose main source of income is disregarded because it proved difficult to assess or verify. This was the case in Romania after 2009, when the SA administration replaced the valuation of agricultural income based on the quantity of assets owned (land, livestock, and agricultural machinery) with exclusionary assets filters.

Most asset tests applied in Eastern European and Central Asian LRIS programs include exclusionary filters (table 4.3) that override the income test and reject applicants even if they are income poor. For example, in Albania, Bulgaria, and Romania, once a household owns any assets beyond the defined thresholds, it is excluded from the program. In other cases (Uzbekistan), assets are taken into account and the decision is left to the discretion of social workers or *mahalla* committees (subunits of local governments) based on overall assessment. In Lithuania, the asset test is applied to the overall value of assets owned by comparing that value to the sum of thresholds for three specific types of assets: (a) land; (b) dwelling; and (c) other assets including vehicles, livestock, durables, savings, and shares (box 4.3).

Asset filters or valuation methods can be regulated at the national or local level. In Albania, Ukraine, and Uzbekistan, the asset test is not regulated in detail at the central level, being done according to local, rather discretionary rules. However, as in the case of income imputation, giving the local level too much discretion in the setting of the list of filters or in the valuation of assets has downsides because it can lead to horizontal inequity or to exclusion errors.

Still, exclusionary asset filters are used on a relatively wide scale. This approach has pros and cons, and the decision is driven by the country context, including capacity, labor informality, and political economy. In some cases, anecdotal (but not verified) stories of beneficiaries coming to claim benefits while wearing luxury clothes or accessories, or even driving expensive cars,[16] are significant factors that drive the introduction of conservative exclusionary filters. Although the use of conservative exclusionary asset filters may prove effective from the perspective of improving the targeting of extreme or chronic poverty by reducing the inclusion errors and at the same time ensuring the legitimacy of the program,[17]

Table 4.3 Asset Test

Country	Land	Livestock	House, dwelling, and built structures	Other productive assets (for example, transportation)	Financial assets and shares	Durable goods or appliances
Albania	Taken into account; no nationwide thresholds or rules; discretion of social worker or local government	Taken into account; no nationwide thresholds or rules; discretion of social worker or local government	Exclusionary filter for additional dwellings other than the current domicile	Taken into account; no nationwide thresholds or rules; discretion of social worker or local government	Exclusionary filter	Taken into account; no nationwide thresholds or rules; discretion of social worker or local government
Armenia	No[a]	No	Exclusion for recent acquisition of real estate; for current housing, score assigned by social worker	No	No	Exclusion for ownership of car; for other durables, discretionary score assigned by social worker based on home visit
Bulgaria	No	No	Exclusionary filter based on standard housing (number of rooms by family size)	No	Exclusionary filter based on a maximum value allowed	No
Kyrgyz Republic	No[a]	No	No	No	No	No
Lithuania	Estimated value at market price included in the overall assets test; norm values set by type of land and area of residence	Estimated value at market price included in the overall assets test, if it exceeds a specific threshold	Estimated value at market price included in the overall assets test; norm values set for standard housing by family size	Estimated value included in the overall assets test	Estimated value included in the overall assets test, if it exceeds a specific threshold	Estimated value included in the overall assets test, if it exceeds a specific threshold

table continues next page

Table 4.3 Asset Test *(continued)*

Country	Land	Livestock	House, dwelling, and built structures	Other productive assets (for example, transportation)	Financial assets and shares	Durable goods or appliances
Romania (until 2009)	Exclusionary filter using land size thresholds by land type (that is, applicant rejected for land above a certain size)	Exclusionary filter using thresholds by livestock type (that is, applicant rejected for livestock above a certain number of heads)	Exclusionary filter for additional dwellings or structures, other than the current domicile	Exclusionary filter based on detailed negative list	Exclusionary filter using a threshold equal to the annual value of the GMI	Exclusionary filter based on detailed negative list of durable goods; positive list of allowed durables also defined
Ukraine	Taken into account; no special methodology; evaluation made at discretion of social inspector	No	Taken into account; no special methodology; evaluation made at discretion of social inspector	Taken into account; no special methodology; evaluation made at discretion of social inspector	No	Taken into account; no special methodology; evaluation made at discretion of social inspector
Uzbekistan	Taken into account; no nationwide thresholds or rules; discretion of mahalla	Taken into account; no nationwide thresholds or rules; discretion of mahalla	Taken into account; no nationwide thresholds or rules; discretion of mahalla	Taken into account; no nationwide thresholds or rules; discretion of mahalla	No	Taken into account; no nationwide thresholds or rules; discretion of mahalla

Source: Based on case studies.

a. Land is not taken into account except for imputing presumptive income. The asset test is different from the imputation of presumptive income, it being an eligibility criterion in itself. GMI = Guaranteed minimum income.

Box 4.3 Lithuania Assets Test

The "regulatory property value" allowing a family (individual) to claim the social benefit (SB) is calculated by cities or towns and by municipal centers according to a nationwide methodology. Each city or town and municipal center must set the standard house value (the standard house is defined at the national level as having 60 square meters [m^2], plus 15 m^2 for each family member) and the standard value of a land lot. The standard value of movable property is set at 45 times the state-supported income (SSI) for one family member over 18 years old, 30 times the SSI per each other family member, and 15 times the SSI per child. The size of the SSI is approved by the governmental resolution. When a person applies for the SB, his or her property value is totaled, and if the amount does not exceed the regulatory property value defined for that particular city or town, the person is considered eligible.

Source: Zalimiene 2006.

this approach may be less effective in identifying vulnerability (exposure to transient poverty) and can lead to exclusion errors in some contexts (for example, when households cannot sell or lease out land because of lack of a functional land market).

The theoretical case for using asset filters as a substitute eligibility criterion for hard-to-verify incomes is quite straightforward. From a targeting perspective, a good asset filter would not exclude any member of the target group, but would exclude the remaining population. However, there are no assets that exhibit such a pattern. The most common one is illustrated in figure 4.7 as the dotted line. To move toward the ideal solution, many countries use many filters, often without doing an ex ante evaluation of the exclusion error based on household survey data.

Selecting the right combination of exclusionary asset filters should be done after an empirical analysis. Otherwise, the filters could exclude many of the poor in the target group, thus reducing the effectiveness of the program. Assets that are owned in large proportion only by noneligible households could reduce the inclusion error for a small increase in beneficiaries' and administrative costs, especially if the assets are easy to verify and hard to conceal by the owner (for example, car ownership). However, reliance on many such filters, without proper ex ante simulation of their impact, could lead to a high level of exclusion error. Before deciding to use such filters, program administrators should carry out an analysis of the filters' impact on both inclusion and exclusion error, based on a representative household survey using information on all key eligibility criteria, including the filters. Three recent empirical analyses in Albania (box 4.4.), Croatia, and Romania illustrate the risks of setting up such filters using only common sense or the beliefs of the SA administrators instead of an empirical assessment.

Figure 4.7 Ideal versus Typical Asset Filter

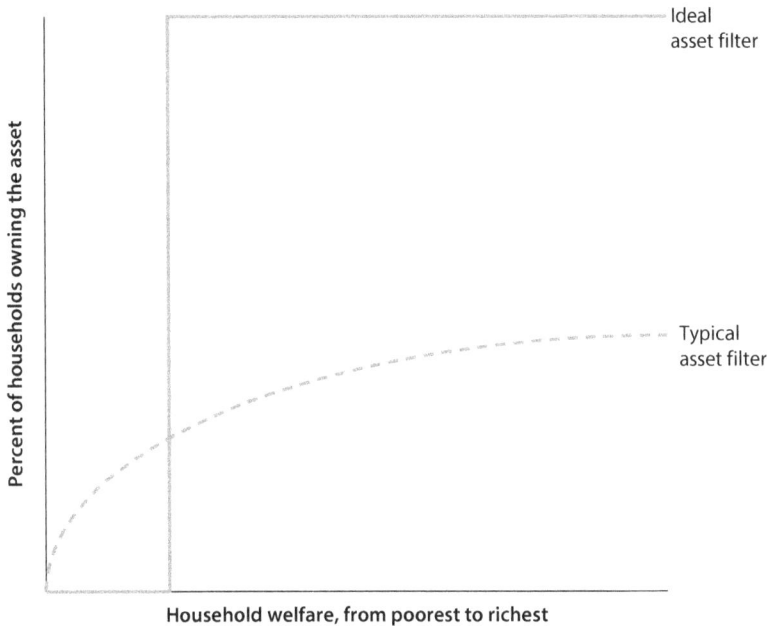

Note: The solid line illustrates the ideal filter; the dotted line is the typical behavior of the asset filters found in practice.

Box 4.4 Too Many Filters Triggered High Exclusion Error among Poor Urban Beneficiaries in the Ndihma Ekonomike Program, Albania, 2008

For urban households, eligibility for Ndihma Ekonomike (NE) is determined on the basis of a means test and a series of filters. Specifically, a household will be denied benefits if it has a member who

- receives a pension (except disability pension);[a]
- owns any form of capital (land, dwelling, or other real estate);
- is economically active (disabled are exempted);
- resides outside of the country;
- is not registered as unemployed and looking for work (farmers and disabled are exempted);
- refuses to work when a job is offered by the employment offices;
- refuses to take land given;
- does not collect the benefit within six working days (except in special cases as defined in the legislation); or
- undertakes fraudulent actions to benefit from NE.

This approach of noncontinuous, multilayered filters distorts eligibility decisions and results in errors of excluding the poor. A simulation of the perfect implementation of these filters for the urban subsample of the poorest decile based on the 2008 Albania

box continues next page

Box 4.4 Too Many Filters Triggered High Exclusion Error among Poor Urban Beneficiaries in the Ndihma Ekonomike Program, Albania, 2008 *(continued)*

Living Standards Measurement Study estimated that 92 percent of those households would be excluded from the program (see figure B4.4.1). The individual filter that generated the highest exclusion error among the urban poorest decile was the employment filter, which excluded a staggering 82 percent of the households.[b] All households in the poorest decile were below the poverty line at the time of the analysis (in 2008 the total poverty headcount was 12.7 percent) and had low incomes and consumption (as measured by the household survey), but were excluded from eligibility for the NE program because of their participation in economic activities (formal or informal employment). Moreover, the employment filter could have triggered potential work disincentives. Excluding families with any member who is economically active raises poor families' incentives to work informally (harder to monitor and verify) or not work at all, in order to qualify for benefits. This assumption is consistent with the findings of the impact evaluation of work disincentives by Dabalen, Kiloic, and Wane (2008).

Figure B4.4.1 The Effect of Filters in Excluding the Urban Poor (Bottom 10 Percent) in Ndihma Ekonomike, Albania
Percent

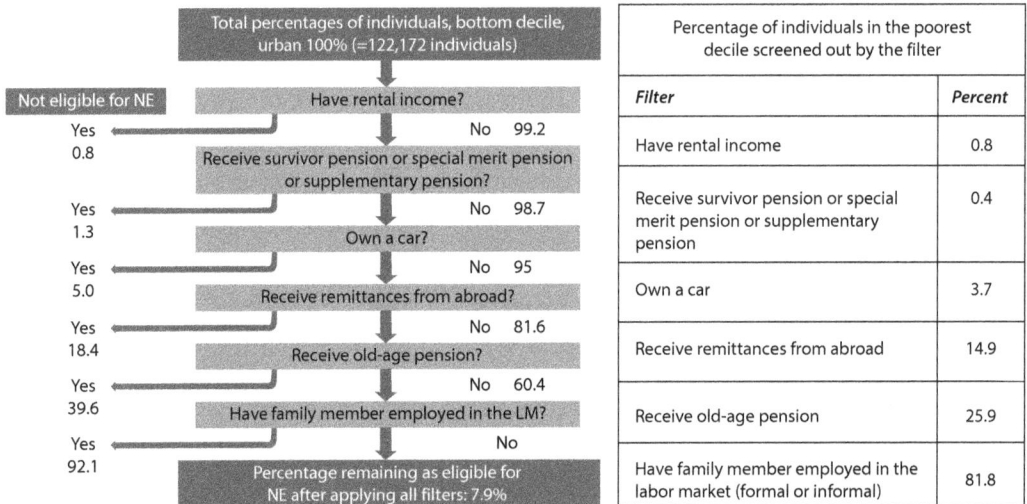

Filter	Percent
Have rental income	0.8
Receive survivor pension or special merit pension or supplementary pension	0.4
Own a car	3.7
Receive remittances from abroad	14.9
Receive old-age pension	25.9
Have family member employed in the labor market (formal or informal)	81.8

Source: Reproduced from World Bank 2010.
Note: The figure indicates the cumulative effect of the one-off filters in excluding individuals in the bottom decile in urban areas. The percentages present the exclusionary impact of each filter individually. LM = labor market; NE = Ndihma Ekonomike.
a. According to the 2008 Albania Living Standards Measurement Survey (LSMS), 20 percent of the NE beneficiary households have a member who receives a disability pension. The 2008 LSMS does not include specific information on noncontributory disability programs. According to the administrative data, about 10 percent of the NE beneficiary families also receive a disability benefit.
b. This simulation assumed that the "have an employed family member" filter was implemented perfectly, assuming full information. In practice, verifying informal employment may be difficult, and as a result the filter may be more precise in excluding those families with a member who has a job in the formal sector. Simulating these differences between formal and informal employment status, if one uses only the formal employment filter, then 41 percent of households in the poorest 10 percent would remain eligible. Based on actual implementation results, 28 percent of the poorest decile receives NE benefits, suggesting that some informal employment is being captured in implementation and used to exclude potential beneficiaries (in addition to formal employment).

Croatia (2010): Impact of Asset Filters on Access to Social Assistance Programs. An important element that determines the inclusion and exclusion error in the LRIS program (the Support Allowance Program) is the asset filters. An empirical evaluation of the potential exclusion error triggered by the asset filters to support allowance beneficiaries was carried out on the basis of the Croatian Household Budget Survey (HBS) data in 2013. The results, shown in table 4.4, led to the following findings:

- First, some of the existing filters based on the quantity of assets owned by applicants are set too low, and they exclude a large share of genuinely poor households. One such example is the "basic housing needs," or allowable living space, which was set at 35 square meters (m²) of usable space for one person plus 10 m² for each additional person. Estimation based on the HBS 2010 (table 4.4) shows that if the filter were perfectly applied, almost 60 percent of the current beneficiaries would lose the right for the support allowance, and that a similar effect would happen for close to 50 percent of beneficiaries from the first quintile. Such a filter is obviously too restrictive for the poor population because the exclusion error would be particularly high. This filter, if applied to other SA programs, would also exclude a large share of genuinely poor beneficiaries.

- Second, not all of these households are excluded in practice from the support allowance. The estimated rate of the exclusion error is higher than the true one; some of the households who should be excluded by the asset test report that they receive the support allowance program. This raises issues of program

Table 4.4 Exclusion from the Program Because of Existing Asset Filters

Percent and HRK

		Existing filters (variants testable by HBS)		
Social assistance program (HBS terms)	Number of observations in HBS (households)	Has secondary real estate	Exceeding basic housing needs (35 + 10 + 10 m²)	Property sale revenue in the past 12 months >€1,000 (HRK 7,500)
		Exclusion in share of total number (bottom quintile) of existing beneficiaries (%)		
Child allowance	342	4 (2)	48 (12)	2 (3)
Compensation for disability and nursing	93	9 (8)	62 (47)	2 (4)
Layette assistance	42	8 (0)	51 (30)	0/(0)
Social assistance in cash	198	7 (5)	57 (48)	2 (3)
Social assistance in kind (food, firewood, clothing, and so on)	26	0/(0)	13 (18)	0/(0)
Estimated fiscal savings (perfect implementation), HRK millions	—	130	1,400	50

Source: World Bank, forthcoming.

Note: HBS = Household Budget Survey; — = not available.

compliance. Such issues could be addressed by stronger mechanisms to combat error and fraud (see chapter 6).

- Third, some of the filters perform well and could be extended to other SA programs, such as "having a second house" or "having large revenues obtained from the sale of property in the previous year." Only a small proportion of current beneficiaries of the support allowance program (up to 7 percent) would lose their benefits if these filters were perfectly enforced.

Romania (2012): Impact of a long list of asset filters on the exclusion error of the population in the poorest decile. The eligibility criteria for the GMI and Family Benefit programs (FBP; an LRIS and a means-tested child allowance) include both an income test and an asset test. The asset test is quite complex. Applicant households should not possess more assets than the quantity specified in a list with 20 items, such as land, livestock, cars or motorcycles, second dwelling, and so on (table 4.5). The extensive list of asset filters has been introduced to make sure that asset-rich farmers are not included in the program. Farm income, mostly informal, was disregarded, and the asset filters were put in its place. The decision on the list of the asset filters was taken without a quantitative analysis of the potential exclusionary effect of the filters. Within two years, the list was

Table 4.5 List of Asset Filters Used for the Romanian GMI, January 2012

Number	Asset filter
1	Any other dwelling(s) besides the one used as residence (owned, leased, or rented out)
2	Consumer cars or motorcycles (less than 10 years old)
3	Trucks and other types of commercial cars
4	Boats, yachts, and the like
5	Tractors, harvesters
6	Oil presses, cereal mills
7	Wood processing equipment
8	Art objects, jewelry and precious metals (over 100 grams), furs, and so on
9	Electronics: video equipment, copying machines
10	Savings over lei 3,000
11	Residential land in excess of 1,000 sq mi in urban areas and 2,000 sq mi in rural areas
12	Agricultural land in excess of 1.5 has for families up to 3 persons; 2 has for families with more than 3 persons
13	2 cows
14	1 horse
15	3 pigs
16	5 sheep or goats
17	5 bee families
18	10 domestic rabbits
19	25 poultry
20	Commercial animal farm

Source: Government of Romania 2012.
Note: GMI = guaranteed minimum income; has = hectares; sq mi = square miles.

put to an empirical test. A special module was added to the running HBS that included all the assets included in the asset tests during one quarter of 2012.

The analysis showed that individually, the asset filters perform relatively well. With the exception of 3 of the 20 filters, they exclude between zero and 3 percent of the 10 percent poorest (figure 4.8; only some of the more frequent filters are shown). Three of the filters, however, had a higher rate of exclusion error (residential land, agricultural land, and ownership of more than 25 heads of poultry). Moreover, there was relatively little correlation or overlap of asset ownership. Thus, combined, the 20 asset filters exclude approximately 32 percent of the first decile and 36 percent of the first quintile (figure 4.8).

This high rate of exclusion error led to a review (in progress at the time of this writing) of the eligibility criteria for means-tested programs. First, the review emphasized that setting asset limits per household, and not per capita or per adult equivalent, leads to horizontal inequities. Larger households, which tend to be poorer, also own a large quantity of these assets and tend to be excluded from the program at a higher rate, even though they have the same per capita consumption or income level as the smaller households. Second, the fact that the

Figure 4.8 Share of Persons from the Poorest Decile Excluded by Asset Filters, Romania, 2012

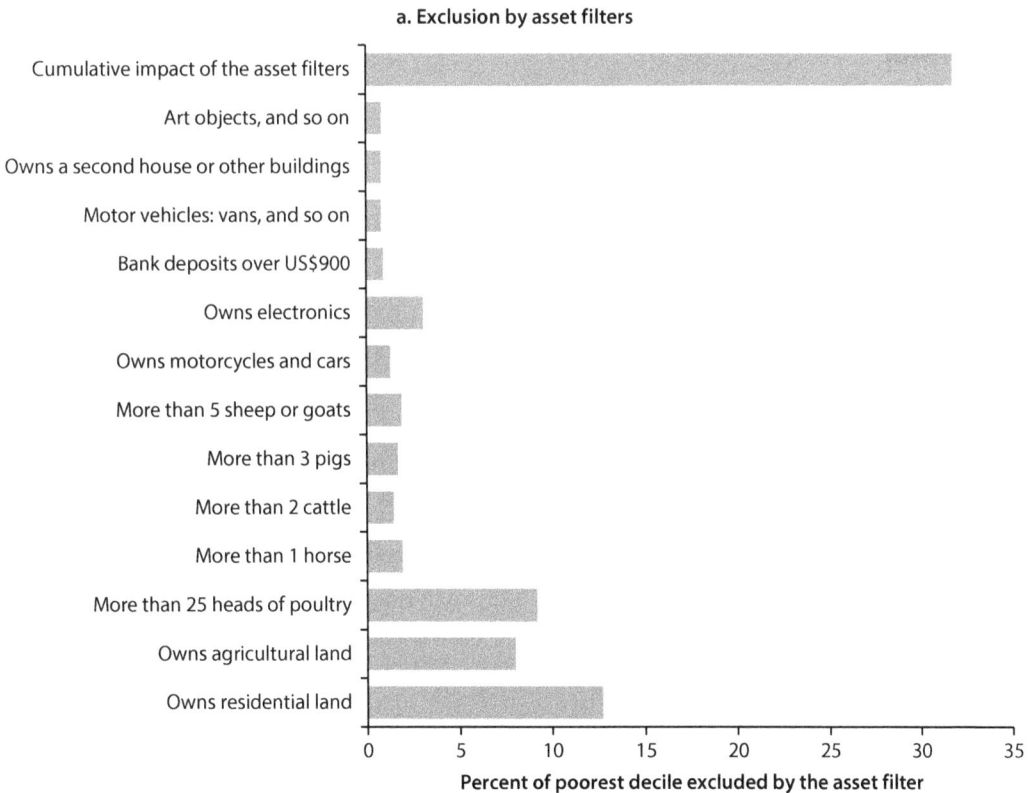

a. Exclusion by asset filters

figure continues next page

Figure 4.8 Share of Persons from the Poorest Decile Excluded by Asset Filters, Romania, 2012 *(continued)*

b. Exclusion error

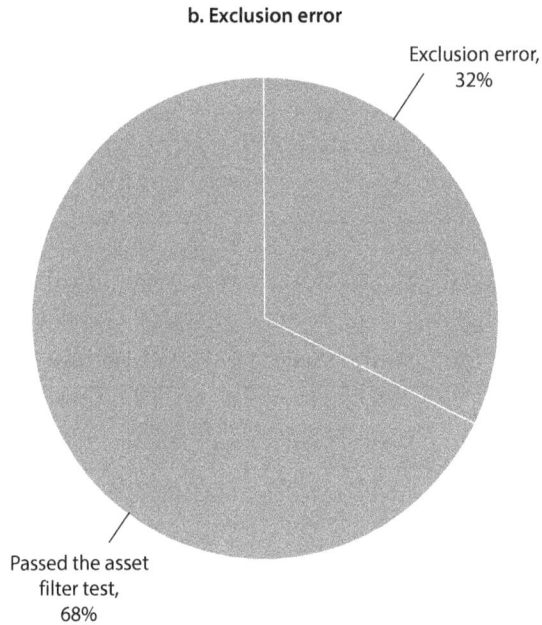

Exclusion error, 32%

Passed the asset filter test, 68%

Sources: Tesliuc et al., forthcoming; Romania, Household Budget Survey, 2012.
Note: Deciles are based on per capita income, net of transfers.

filters are applied individually complicates the estimation of their combined effect on exclusion error.

The recent evidence on the performance of asset filters in means-tested programs suggests that they should be used with caution. Although there are potential benefits of using such filters (for example, excluding rich households through an eligibility criterion that is simple to administer), there are also costs, such as excluding part of the intended target group of the program. For mitigation of this risk, it is important to simulate the likely impact of the filter on excluding both the nonpoor and the poor; to reevaluate the impact often, especially for assets that are built up at a fast rate during a period of growth; and to use as few filters as possible, because their interaction could get out of control. Among the different types of asset filters, those that vary by household size (or the implicit adult equivalent scheme used by the program) would be better at avoiding horizontal inequities (for example, exclusion of small households). Whenever possible, it is more suitable to replace asset filters based on productive assets with presumptive income rules, especially in countries with good tax records on assets and on incomes from specific assets.

Alternative Scoring Approaches

In a few countries in the region—Armenia initially, later Georgia and Turkey, and more recently Albania—rather than using income and asset tests per se, a "scoring" or PMT approach is used. PMTs generate a score for each applicant household based on a few easy-to-verify characteristics, such as the quality of the dwelling, ownership of durable goods, agricultural assets, demographics, education level, and location. The most common method to estimate such a score is based on household survey data using a regression of the welfare status of the households on these characteristics. The regression coefficients then become weights of a relatively simple scoring formula. The total score is the estimate (prediction) of the household welfare status (for example, household consumption per capita) given these observable characteristics. Based on the intended target group of the program, a cutoff score is selected that will produce, in the simulation, the desired number of beneficiaries. Moving from the analytics of the PMT to program implementation, one then uses the scoring formula to select applicants. For each applicant, a score would be computed on the basis of his or her characteristics, and those with scores below the cutoff become beneficiaries. This method was used in Georgia (Lokshin and Posarac 2006) and Turkey, and is planned to be used in Albania.

Although in most cases the PMT formulas are empirically derived on the basis of correlation of a welfare indicator (income–consumption) and some easy-to-observe and measurable proxy indicators, in Armenia the approach was rather normative, or based on expert opinions. The points assigned to each category or group were originally derived from an opinion survey of social workers. The formula has been subsequently updated by an expert panel using judgment, but now informed by substantial household survey analysis that showed that the original weights were reasonable.

In Armenia, the family vulnerability score is computed as a product of 13 indicators. The basic principle behind the score is that some groups are more vulnerable than others. Each family member is thus classified into a group and assigned a number of points, or a vulnerability score, which can vary between 20 and 50 points—higher scores indicate higher vulnerability[18] (see table 4.6). The family gets a score equal to the average vulnerability scores of its members. This score is subsequently weighted using a set of 12 other indicators (see box 4.5). Some of these indicators act, in practice, as filters—being equal to 0 in the presence of some characteristics (for example, having a business or a car or acquiring real estate after 2000), or 1 in its absence. The income indicator weights the score by a factor between 1.2 and 1 if the family income per capita is less than five estimated minimum salaries,[19] and by a factor of less than 1 if the income per capita is higher than five estimated minimum salaries. However, the estimated minimum salary is set at a very conservative value—about 40 percent of the extreme poverty line. There are two interesting features of the Armenian formula: (a) the use of consumption indicators (energy and telephone bills) as proxies to compensate for the lack of accurate information on incomes because of the high informality of earnings; and (b) explicit geographic targeting through the use of location weighting factors.

In theory, the Armenian vulnerability formula does not have absolute bounds; in practice, the upper plausible bound is around 75. The FBP threshold has been

Table 4.6 Scores to Be Used in the Formula for an Average Household Vulnerability Score, Armenia

Social group	Code	Vulnerability point (Pi)
(1) Invalid I group	I11	48
(2) Invalid II group	I22	39
(3) Invalid III group	I33	28
(4) Invalid child	I44	45
(5) Child under age 5 years	A55	35
(6) Child from age 5 to 18 years	A66	33
(7) One-sided orphan child	O23	43
(8) Child without parental care	C56	50
(9) Unmarried woman with child	Un45	26
(10) Divorced person's child	D34	26
(11) Student under age 23	S12	22
(12) Pregnant woman (12 weeks or more)	Pr00	35
(13) Unemployed	U99	22
(13.1) Uncompetitive unemployed	U98	28
(14) Pensioner	Pen88	36
(15) Lonely, nonworking pensioner	Pen87	37
(16) Aged pensioner (75 years old or more)	Pen 86	39
Absent member of the family	n.a.	18
Person having no social group	n.a.	18

Source: Based on information provided by Ministry of Labor and Social Issues, Armenia, adapted from World Bank 2011.
Note: n.a. = not applicable.

Box 4.5 Armenia: Main Elements of the Vulnerability Formula

As of 2011, the following formula has been applied for assessing the eligibility of Armenian families for the Family Benefit Program (FBP):

$$P = P_{initial} \times K_{incapable} \times K_{location} \times K_{housing} \times K_{income} \times K_{car} \times K_{business} \times K_{real\ estate} \times K_{customs} \times K_{electricity} \times K_{phone} \times K_{assessment}$$

where P is the total score, which expresses a household's level of vulnerability. The higher the score, the higher the vulnerability. Families with scores of 30 and above qualify for the monthly FBP payments.

Other elements of the formula are as follows:

- $P_{initial}$ is the average value of the family's social group score. The government has identified and assigned numeric scores to a number of vulnerable social groups, such as disabled persons, children, pensioners, and pregnant women. Each individual can belong to no more than three social groups with the highest score taken at full value, the second-highest score at 30 percent, and the third-highest score at 10 percent. The individual social group scores are then averaged for the household.

box continues next page

Box 4.5 Armenia: Main Elements of the Vulnerability Formula *(continued)*

- $K_{incapable}$ is the coefficient related to the number of family members incapable of working. It is calculated as $K_{incapable} = 1.00 + 0.02\ m$, where m is the number of family members who are children, disabled persons of first or second disability category, or unemployed working-age pensioners.

- $K_{location}$ coefficient measures residence insecurity, based on the geographical area of residence. Its value can be 1 (secure), 1.03 (insecure), or 1.05 (most insecure), and these values are set for each city or village by government decree.

- $K_{housing}$ evaluates family housing conditions, with houses or apartments given the value of 1 and progressively worse housing conditions given higher values (up to 1.2 for tents provided after an earthquake).

- K_{income} is a coefficient for per capita family income. It is calculated on the basis of family members' salaries and wages, pensions, and unemployment benefits, as well as the value of livestock (based on a set value per head) and the value of land (calculated in terms of cadastre value, net of paid land tax). This income is then averaged for the household, and the coefficient is calculated as $K_{income} = 1.2 - 0.033 \times$ (per capita income/1,000). Note that this coefficient takes the value of zero at per capita income of dram 36,634, at which point it becomes a disqualifier.

The rest of the coefficients are binary filters or disqualifiers (that is, their value can be either 0 or 1):

- $K_{car} = 0$ if the household owns a motor vehicle.
- $K_{business} = 0$ if any member of the household is a participant (shareholder) of a limited-liability company or enterprise, is a shareholder or depositor of a trust or cooperative or engages in formal entrepreneurial activities.
- $K_{real\ estate} = 0$ if any member of the family acquires real estate.
- $K_{customs} = 0$ if any member of the family pays customs duties on imports or exports.
- $K_{electricity} = 0$ if the electricity consumption of the family during summer months exceeds the specified maximum threshold.
- $K_{phone} = 0$ if the amount of the family's average intercity telephone bills within any three consecutive months of a given year exceeds the specified maximum threshold.
- $K_{assessment} = 0$ if a social worker making a home visit assesses the family as ineligible.

Source: Based on Nikitin, forthcoming.

---

gradually reduced over time, from 36.01 at inception to 33.01 in 2007 to 30.01 in 2008 (Nikitin, forthcoming). If the household's score qualifies it for the family benefit, the amount of the monthly transfer includes a basic benefit of dram 8,000, plus a supplement for children, which depends on the number of children in the household and the vulnerability score (see table 4.7).

By 2013, the Armenian Ministry of Labor and Social Issues was evaluating the formula with support from the World Bank and could consider switching to a regression-based formula.

Table 4.7 FBP Supplements per Child, by FBP Score and Number of Children, Armenia, 2008

Dram

Household eligibility score	Three children or less	Four children or more
30.01–35.00	5,000	6,000
35.01–39.00	5,500	6,500
39.01+	6,000	7,000

Source: Based on information provided by Ministry of Labor and Social Affairs, Armenia, adapted from World Bank 2011.
Note: FBP = Family Benefit Program.

Narrowing the Target Group with Additional Eligibility Criteria

In addition to the welfare status, some countries use additional criteria to refine the definition of their target groups. These criteria may be applied in two ways: (a) as categorical filters and (b) as formula or eligibility threshold adjustments. Categorical filters can be positive (including specific categories) or negative (excluding specific categories) and are used to delimit the target group(s) of the programs based on demographic, health, or occupational criteria. The formula adjustments (discussed above) represent usual customizations of the eligibility formula to ensure the program includes specific (vulnerable) groups or to provide higher benefits for such groups by attaching different weights to, or setting different eligibility thresholds or benefit levels for, different subgroups of the poor—in most cases those considered deserving or most vulnerable.

Four countries included in the pool of case studies use such additional criteria; Albania and the Kyrgyz Republic use filters, and Armenia and Bulgaria use formula adjustments (table 4.8). The Kyrgyz Republic uses categorical filters to target its Unified Monthly Benefit only to families with children, elderly, or disabled. In Albania, where the program was introduced to support the long-term unemployed who are left without unemployment benefits, the program is restricted to those who do not earn incomes from nonfarming activities, capital, or remittances. Thus, in addition to households who have a member abroad, all households with employers, employees, or self-employed in nonfarm activities do not qualify for the MT, which implies that the working poor are excluded from the program.

Eligibility Formulas and Thresholds

In most countries, the eligibility formulas are based on a simple principle: the total family income is compared with a threshold, and all families with an income lower than the threshold are eligible to receive the benefit (provided they pass the asset test and fulfill any additional criteria). The variation among countries regarding how this principle is applied in practice comes from two sources: (a) the definition of income (discussed above) and (b) the definition of threshold(s). The latter can influence the program target group (size and composition) and, for GMI-type programs, the generosity of benefits.

Table 4.8 Other Eligibility Criteria in Means-Tested Programs

Country and program	Use of additional criteria	Groups and categories						
		Occupational	Disabled	All children	Newborn or young children	Orphans	Elderly	Single parent
Albania: NE (Ndihma (Ekonomike)	Yes, for exclusion of some categories of income earners	✓						
Armenia: FBP (Family Benefit Program)	Yes, by assignment of higher vulnerability scores for specific groups or categories, or for exclusion of some categories by setting a weight of zero	✓	✓	✓	✓	✓	✓	✓
Bulgaria: GMI (guaranteed minimum income)	Yes, for customization of the minimum income for specific vulnerable groups or categories		✓		✓	✓	✓	✓
Kyrgyz Republic: UMB (Unified Monthly Benefit	Yes, as filters or criteria to define eligible groups, or for adjustment of the benefit		✓	✓	✓		✓	
Lithuania: SB (social benefit)	No							
Romania: GMI	No							
Ukraine: GMI	No							
Uzbekistan: BLIF (benefit for low-income families)	No							

Source: Based on case studies.

Two main elements are involved in the design or construction of thresholds: (a) choosing the threshold level and (b) accounting for the family size and composition. Over time, another important decision is (c) the indexation of benefits.

Choosing the Threshold Level with the Guaranteed Minimum Approach. In most of the countries included in this review, the thresholds represent minimum guarantees (guaranteed minimum level of consumption in the Kyrgyz Republic, GMI in Bulgaria and Romania, and state-supported income in Lithuania). The criteria used for choosing the threshold level vary from country to country: in Albania, the initial threshold was linked to the unemployment benefit;[20] in Romania, the threshold was initially established as a function of the intended coverage of the program (the poorest 10 percent of the population); in Lithuania and Bulgaria, the threshold represents an anchor for ensuring consistency between multiple benefits (for example, unemployment benefit, minimum pension, and social pension). In Uzbekistan, according to the ministry's instructions, the threshold is linked to the minimum wage. However, the instructions have only a guidance role, and evidence suggests that the threshold is not necessarily uniform across the country but can vary from region to region, from *rayon* (lowest administrative level) to rayon, or even from mahalla to mahalla.

The eligibility thresholds are generally kept very low in all countries—between 5 and 12 percent of the national average household consumption (see chapter 5). Moreover, in most countries the thresholds of LRIS programs are not adjusted on a regular basis to keep pace with inflation, being updated in some cases at intervals of 4–6 years (Albania, 1998–2004; Bulgaria, 2001–07 and 2007–09; Lithuania, 1998–2005).

One of the factors influencing the threshold levels is the availability of resources and budget constraints, but this is not necessarily the most important factor because the thresholds decreased in real value even during periods of economic growth. Except Romania, no other country reviewed in this study has included indexation with inflation in the legislation, most likely because this approach may limit government flexibility in adjusting expenditures. In Albania, where the threshold should have been adjusted as a function of the unemployment benefit, the indexation was not implemented, and the threshold was frozen for several years despite the increases in the unemployment benefit level. In the second half of the 2000s, the real value of the LRIS benefits decreased significantly in many Eastern Europe and Central Asia countries. At the same time, the thresholds and benefits for other SA programs (for example, child allowances, utility benefits, and social pensions) were increased at a faster pace than those for LRIS programs, leading not only to inconsistencies among various SA benefits (except in Bulgaria and Lithuania), but also to a decrease of the relevance and impact of poverty-targeted benefits compared with categorical benefits.

Accounting for Family Size and Composition. Most programs give higher benefits to larger families or those with more dependents. They use a variety of implicit or explicit equivalence scales or threshold weights and adjustments to ensure the inclusion of, or higher benefit generosity for, specific groups considered most vulnerable. In the Kyrgyz Republic, Lithuania, and Romania, the formula accounts for family size only, whereas in Albania and Bulgaria, it accounts for both size and composition. In the Kyrgyz Republic and Lithuania, a per capita equivalence scale is used: the family income per capita is compared with an administrative threshold per person. In Romania, the threshold (that is, the GMI) is set by family size, using an implicit equivalence scale that assumes significant economies of scale and thus is more restrictive for larger families[21] (figure 4.9).

Albania and Bulgaria use a different thresholds function depending on the family and household composition. As a rule, family members considered more vulnerable are entitled to higher thresholds, whereas the corresponding thresholds for those who are of working age and able to work are lower. In Bulgaria, the thresholds, called "differentiated minimum income" (DMI), are established as a percentage of GMI by categories of persons (table 4.9) and include penalties for children not attending school. For example, the DMI for a single parent with a child up to age 3 years is 120 percent of the GMI (Lev 78 in 2009), but for a single elderly person over age 75 years, it is 165 percent of the GMI (Lev 107.25 in 2009). In Albania, the classification is less complex, differentiating between household members only by age (under working age, at working age, and above working age), with significantly higher thresholds for the elderly.

Indexation of Benefits. Independent of the criteria used to set up the thresholds in the initial stage of the programs, the major challenges related to threshold levels

Figure 4.9 Family Size and Eligibility Thresholds, Romania GMI Equivalence Scale versus Per Capita Approach

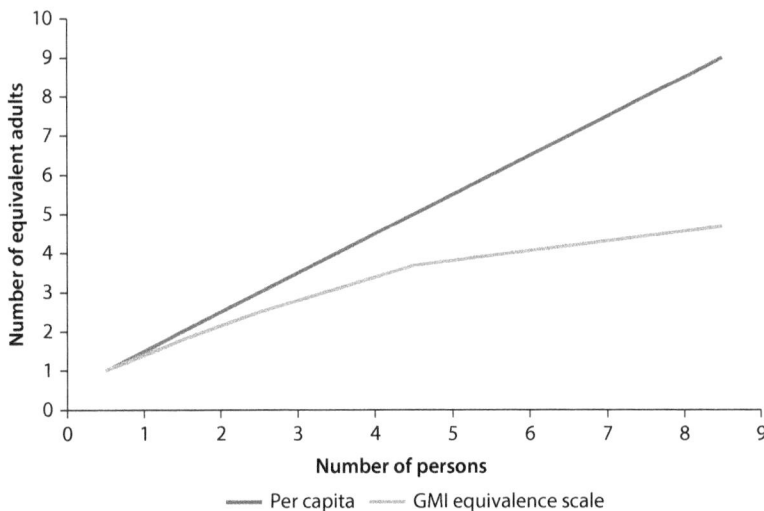

Note: The figure compares Romania's guaranteed minimum income (GMI) approach to a per capita approach.

Table 4.9 GMI Thresholds Differentiated by Individual Characteristics, Bulgaria, 2009

Threshold	Percentage of GMI	Value (Lev)
GMI level	100	65.00
Person over age 75 years, living alone	165	107.25
Person over age 65 years, living alone	140	91.00
Person over age 65 years	100	65.00
Person cohabiting with another person (or persons) or a family; and for each one of the spouses living together	66	42.90
Person up to age 65 years, living alone	73	47.45
Person with permanently decreased working capacity of 50 percent or more	100	65.00
Person with permanently decreased working capacity of 70 percent or more	125	81.25
Child up to age 16 years, and if a student, then until graduation of secondary education, including until graduation of XIII degree of professional high school, but no more than age 20 years	91	59.15
Child between ages 7 and 16 years, and if a student, then until graduation of secondary education, including until graduation of XIII degree of professional high school, but no more than 20 years of age, and if the child has five or more absences of school during the respective month	30	19.50
Nonstudent child between ages 7 and 16 years	20	13.00
Orphaned child; child placed within the family of close friends and relatives or within foster family; child with permanent disability	100	65.00
Single parent caring for child or children up to age 3 years	120	78.00

Source: World Bank 2012b.
Note: GMI = guaranteed minimum income.

are maintaining the real value of the threshold in time and ensuring a reasonable degree of consistency both among various social protection programs and between social benefits (SBs) and labor incomes (to avoid work disincentives, see chapter 5). There are two types of responses to these challenges, which ideally should go together: indexation of the thresholds with the consumer price index and use of a unique anchor for various SA benefits and thresholds.[22] The first approach is used in Romania, and the second is used in Lithuania. In the other countries reviewed here, the threshold levels are updated (or frozen) in a rather arbitrary and contextual way.

During the period of growth between 1998 and 2008, LRIS programs in most countries in Eastern Europe and Central Asia contracted because of two factors: lack of (or insufficient) regular price indexation and the economic growth effect. In a stylized fashion, this is presented in figure 4.10. In the period of growth and insufficient price indexation, the number of beneficiaries of a GMI program would fall despite a constant nominal GMI threshold because inflation was eroding the threshold each year (from Real Threshold T0 to T1, in figure 4.10), and because some of the general prosperity trickled down to the poorest segment of the income distribution (those whose income increases from Real Income T0 to T1, in figure 4.10). The impact of both factors was to reduce the number of eligible beneficiaries, and it was cumulative. In some countries (for example, Bulgaria and Ukraine), the program coverage had shrunk to 1–2 percent of the

Figure 4.10 Why Did GMI Programs Shrink during the Growth Period?

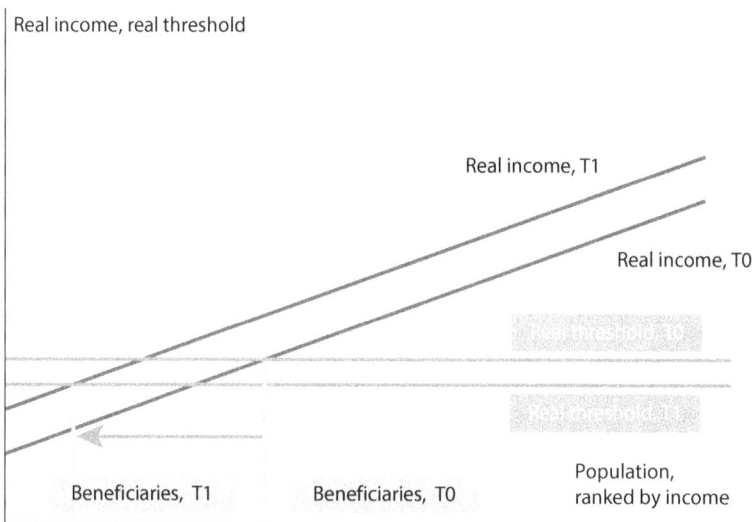

population during 1998–2008. Such low coverage reduces the potential role of the program during crisis time. With the hindsight of the recent period of recession and stagnation in Eastern Europe, governments should consider implementing indexation rules for GMI programs that preserve their automatic fiscal stabilizer role. At a minimum, to counteract a further contraction of the program when growth resumes, governments should index the GMI threshold by inflation or the average growth in incomes (or wages), or both.

Take-Up of GMI-Type Programs. Among LRIS programs, the GMI-type programs are known to suffer from partial take-up. Because their benefit is differentiated by the (per capita or per adult equivalent) income of the beneficiary, take-up tends to be higher for poorer beneficiaries and decreases monotonically toward the GMI level. In fact, the GMI programs have a long history of low benefits, which are not claimed by eligible beneficiaries. Because beneficiaries incur costs to apply for, recertify, and sometimes to cash these benefits, applying to the program is not profitable for those with incomes close to the GMI.

The partial take-up of benefits is well documented in the OECD literature, which notes that take-up rates for all means-tested programs range between 40 percent and 80 percent and GMI programs between 40 percent and 60 percent of those eligible (table 4.10; Bargain, Immervoll, and Viitamaki 2010). The standard methodology of these studies is to compare estimates of eligible beneficiaries derived from household surveys with administrative records of actual beneficiaries.

Tesliuc et al. (forthcoming) reports similar findings for GMI in Romania. Comparing the number of GMI beneficiaries who would be eligible for the GMI based on the 2012 HBS with the actual number of beneficiaries, the authors find

Table 4.10 Some Literature on the Non-Take-Up of Social Assistance

Author(s)	Country	Data	Years	Program*	Selection	Non-take-up rate (%)
Moffitt (1983)	US	PSID	1976	AFDC	Single mothers	55
Blank and Ruggles (1996)	US	SIPP	1986–87	AFDC	Single mothers	30–38
Blank (1997)	US	CPS and admin. data	mid 70s to mid 80s	AFDC	Families with children	10–40
Kim and Mergoupis (1997)	US	SIPP	1976–88–89	AFDC	Working poor	46
Fry and Stark (1989)	UK	FES	1984	Supplementary Benefit (SB)*	All	13–19
Pudney et al. (2003)	UK	FRS	1997–2000	Income Support (IS)	Pensioners	34–35
Bramley et al. (2000)	Scotland	SHCS	1996	Income Support (IS)	All	30–50
Terracol (2002)	France	ECHP	1994–96	Minimum Income (Revenue Minimum d" Insertion)	All	35–48
Neumann and Hertz (1998)	Germany		1991	Social Assistance (Hilfe zum Lebensunterhalt)	All	52.3–58.7
Kayser and Frick (2000)	Germany	GSOEP	1996	Social Assistance (Hilfe zum Lebensunterhalt)	All	62.9
Riphahn (2001)	Germany	EVS	1993	Social Assistance (Hilfe zum Lebensunterhalt)	All	62.3
van Oorschot (1995)	Netherlands	†	1990	Special Social Assistance	All	53–63
Virjo (2000)	Finland	Mail survey (U. of Turku)	1995	Social Assistance (Toimeentulotuki)	n.a.	60
Gustafsson (2002)	Sweden	n.a.	1985, 1997	Social Assistance	All	70–80

Source: Bargain, Immervoll, and Viitamaki 2010.
Note: PSID is the Panel Study of Income Dynamics, SIPP is the Survey of Income and Program Participation, CPS is the Current Population Survey, FES is the Family Expenditure Survey, FRS is the Family Resource Survey, SHCS is the Scottish House Condition Survey, ECHP is the European Community Household Panel, GSOEP is the German Socio-Economic Panel, EVS is the Income and Expenditure Survey for Germany, AFDC stands for Aid to Families with Dependent Children.
* Supplementary Benefit (SB) is the ancestor of the Income Support (IS) in the UK.
† Specific data on Rotterdam and Nijmegen.

a take-up rate of 50 percent in terms of eligible persons, rising to 75 percent when measured in terms of potential benefits claimed. The authors also look at the non-take-up in means-tested programs with flat-benefit formulas and find that the non-take-up is not so severe in these programs as it is in the GMI.

The partial non-take-up has implications for the design of the GMI-type of LRIS programs. If a government has a certain coverage target, it should use higher thresholds taking into account the partial take-up. This approach will increase the amount of transfer (generosity) and the cost (budget of the program), but it will increase the effectiveness of the program by eliminating the typically large exclusion error because of self-selection.

Eligibility Determination: Key Implementation Elements

Eligibility determination involves several activities that can be broadly classified in four stages: (a) outreach of potential beneficiaries, (b) registration and application process, (c) verification of means, and (d) entitlement (benefit award; figure 4.11).

Beneficiaries Outreach

Reaching out to the potential beneficiaries in Eastern Europe and Central Asia is done through multiple channels, including information campaigns and social worker outreach. However the approaches and degree of proactivity vary across countries and with time. Proactive efforts occur in all cases during the very initial stage of the programs, when their launch is accompanied by national awareness and information campaigns about the programs, their rules, and procedures.

In Albania, when the Ndihma Ekonomike (NE) program started operating in 1993, a nationwide public information campaign and active outreach plan had been prepared to reach all potential households in need. A set of programs was aired on the national television station to inform the wide audience about the key elements of the program such as who is eligible, what is the benefit amount, where citizens can apply, and what are the application documents. In addition, labor offices in urban areas played (and still continue to play) an important role in informing and advising unemployed people. Meanwhile, in rural areas, SA offices used family kinships to propagate information.

In Bulgaria, radio, television, and the websites for the Ministry of Labor and Social Protection and the Central Social Assistance Agency inform citizens about

Figure 4.11 Stages of Eligibility Determination Process

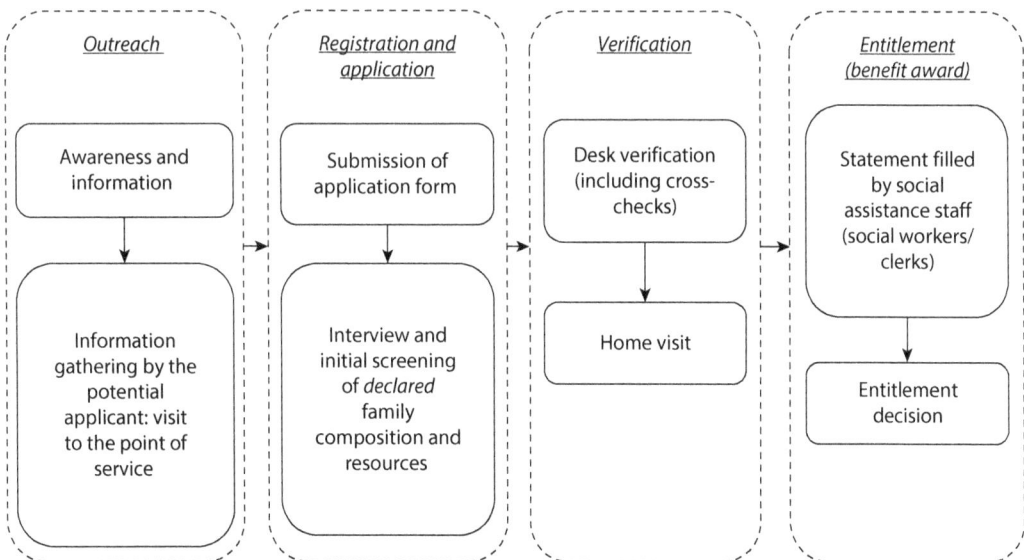

Table 4.11 Methods of Providing Information about the GMI by Type of Locality, Romania

	Locality by size of population					
	Urban, over 30,000		Urban, under 30,000		Rural	
Method	Number	%	Number	%	Number	%
Direct discussions with the town hall clerks	23	92.0	17	81.0	55	79.7
Town hall and Social Assistance Directorate posters	16	64.0	17	81.0	45	65.2
Booklets and leaflets	4	16.0	3	14.3	4	5.8
Designated adviser in the town hall	5	20.0	3	14.3	28	40.6
Other	2	8.0	2	9.5	0	0.0

Source: Romania GMI Evaluation Survey, Local Governments Survey, 2003.
Note: Columns sum to more than 100 percent because local councils were allowed to indicate two methods of publicity. GMI = guaranteed minimum income.

their right to SA. Changes in legislation are broadly announced through press conferences where new provisions concerning the right to SAs are explained. But the cases of active outreach by social workers are isolated and happen more often when they receive information from neighbors or relatives about a person or family who needs SA.

After the launch of a program, the approach is rather passive. Only small (and rather ad hoc) efforts are made by social workers to identify and inform potential beneficiaries. Because the service locations are accessible in most cases, the potential beneficiaries are expected to visit them and receive information about the program. Usually, when the programs mature, the sources of information about the program are the local government employees or social workers, the leaflets and announcements posted at the local service locations, other beneficiaries, and friends or relatives (for the approach used in Romania, see table 4.11).

The lack of periodic information campaigns may affect program performance in multiple ways. The most intuitive one refers to the risk of excluding the poorest, who will not apply for benefits if they are not aware of the programs or criteria. However, not informing the public may have other impacts on program effectiveness as well. In the Kyrgyz Republic, the particularly low ratio of benefit applicants to those receiving benefit entitlements in certain oblasts suggests that the benefit administrators are dealing with a high number of needless inquiries, which could be reduced through improved awareness of eligibility criteria.

Application Process
Individuals and families who consider themselves eligible for the program initiate registration through an on-demand[23] application process. The application process is open; that is, applications can be submitted on an ongoing basis,[24] and the process usually requires more than one visit by the claimant (usually the household head) to the service location. Applying for the benefit involves two main processes: (a) submission of the application form accompanied by supporting documents and (b) an interview. The complexity and length of the process vary from country to country, as well as the costs for beneficiaries, which usually

consist of travel costs, time spent, and costs related to obtaining the required supporting documents (including photocopying or issuance of notarized copies). The application process may represent a barrier to accessing the program when the process is too complex and the transaction costs are high. However, the existing evidence in Eastern Europe and Central Asia seems to indicate that this type of accessibility barrier is an exception.

More significant access barriers are represented by the lack of a national ID (identification document)—an issue that was once common among the Roma population in Romania and Bulgaria—and the lack of a formal domicile or residence. The procedures for the homeless are more cumbersome because the SA offices do not have, in most cases, the required infrastructure to verify if one applicant submits applications in different places. In Romania, for example, the homeless were required to apply to regional offices, which involved high transaction costs for the applicant. For the same reason of avoiding multiple applications, in Albania and the Kyrgyz Republic the claimants who do not have a formal residence or domicile in the locality where they reside de facto are required to apply in the locality of formal residence or submit documents issued from those localities, which, again, may represent barriers for the poor in accessing the program.[25]

In the Kyrgyz Republic, the applicant must visit the Department of Social Protection at least three times to receive the benefit. In the first visit, the applicant has a consultation and receives the list of necessary documents that should be collected and submitted for obtaining the benefit. In the second visit, all information is reviewed and a form is filled out. If all required documents are presented, the benefit will be granted from the first day of the month of the application. In practice, usually a third visit is needed for submission of missing documents.

In Lithuania, to receive the SB a person applies to an SA unit (center) and fills out an application form including all information about his or her family composition, employment status, income, and property. The applicant must fill out the form by himself or herself, but if unable to do so, the applicant will be assisted by an officer. Some municipalities recruit unemployed individuals participating in public works programs to assist in their SA–related work. An officer reviews the form and supporting documents and checks whether all items in the application form are completed. Concurrently, the officer asks additional questions in case of any doubts. Should the applicant fail to fill out all the necessary information or to provide all the documents required for the benefit, the officer hands the applicant a list of missing information or documents. The applicant verifies the correctness of the information, signs the paperwork, and agrees to notify the officer about circumstances for which the SB should be cancelled or recalculated within a period of one month. After copies are made, the original documents are returned to the applicant.

In Albania, to apply for the program, the head of household must visit a local program office and undergo an interview. Staff informs applicants about the range of supporting documents that must be provided and assists in the completion of the application form. Documents required from other public offices are gathered directly by the program office and not the applicant. Applicants must provide information on income from all sources, household composition, assets, housing conditions, employment status of household members, their health status, and children's education status. This is followed by a home visit to validate the information reported by potentially eligible households.

Guidance for the Applicant and Prescreening

In most cases, during a first visit to the service location (SA center, town hall, and the like), the applicant is gathering the necessary information for the application process (eligibility criteria, documents needed, and procedures) from the staff in charge of the program. The applicant is guided through the requirements, steps, and list of documents to be submitted depending on the specific situation. During the same visit, social workers may perform a pre-screening of the applicant, asking questions (for example, about total income, family composition, and assets) to check if the applicant appears to be eligible.

Documents Needed to Support the Claim

The list of documents to be submitted by the applicant varies from country to country, but usually they include proof of (a) family composition, identity, and domicile (for example, identification cards, marriage and birth certificates, school enrollment certificates, and proof of domicile); (b) labor status for the working-age household members (certificates from employment offices); (c) health status (disability certificates if applicable); and (d) income statements (from employers, social insurance, and so on; see table 4.12).

Obtaining all documents may bear costs for the poor, but does not seem to represent a major constraint. In Romania, the median time needed to obtain all documents is about five days, and the median cost involved (transport, notarized copies, and so on) represents about 10 percent of one average monthly benefit per family. In the Kyrgyz Republic, the average time needed to obtain all documents is about two days, whereas the costs are differentiated by area of residence: in rural areas, the average cost is about 15 percent of one average monthly benefit per family, and in urban areas, the average cost is estimated to be higher (about 80 percent of one monthly payment) because of the higher number of certificates to submit and higher transportation costs. In Bulgaria, the applicants obtain copies of the required documents free of charge. If a large number of documents are required or if the documents are complex, this may represent a barrier to accessing the program. In Uzbekistan, about 25 percent of the poorest quintile mentions the number and complexity of documents and forms to be filled out as one of the reasons for not applying for benefits. At the opposite end is Albania, where the applicants must submit only two documents in addition to filling out a declaration with the required information, which is then subject to verification through cross-checks with other institutions and agencies.

Table 4.12 Documents Accompanying an Application for Benefits, Armenia

Document name	Certificate required
Identification	Social passport of family, identity number of passports and birth certificates of all family members
Application statement	Application statement completed by social inspector and signed by applicant
Certificate of family composition, number of family members	In a city: certificate from house management, condominium In a town or village: certificate from self-governance body
Marriage certificate	Copy of marriage certificate
Bill of divorce	Copy of bill of divorce or court decision
Birth certificate for children under age 2 years and from ages 2–8 years	Copy of birth certificate
Certificate of disability (I, II, III group)	Copy of certificate from Socio Medical Expertise Commission confirming disability and certificate from pension-granting body
Certificate from place of learning for students up to age 23 years	Certificate from a university, confirming student's free education
Confirmation of orphanage (one-side, two-side)	Copy of death certificate of parent(s) and certificate from pension-granting body
Certificate of the status of unemployment	Certificate from employment regional center
Confirmation on being an aged pensioner	Certificate from pension-granting body
Confirmation on being pregnant (up to 20 weeks)	Certificate from women's consultation office
Confirmation of being single, disabled pensioner	Certificate from house management, condominium, or self-governance body
Certificate on salary amount	Certificate from place of employment with identification of amount of net salary
Certificate of size of pension (labor, social, and so on)	Certificate from pension-granting body
Certificate of size and type of land, amount of livestock in peasant farm or in personal homestead land	Information included in certificate of family composition provided by self-governance body or condominium

Interview and Screening

The interview takes place in most cases on the same day the documents are submitted, which is usually at the second visit to the service location. During this visit, the information submitted is reviewed, and the social workers ask clarification or verification questions. As a general rule, during the interview the social worker assists the applicant with filling out or finalizing the completion of the application form,[26] and identifies missing documents that must be submitted by the applicant during a possible subsequent visit. The application forms vary in complexity and length (for example, in Lithuania the form has 12 pages, in Romania six pages, and in Armenia three pages). The average duration of an interview in most countries is less than 30 minutes.

The administration and importance of the interview and screening stage differ from country to country. In Lithuania, the social worker decides on the basis of an interview if a home visit to verify the information is needed, especially when inconsistencies are noticed in the documents and application form. In Romania, the interview consists only of checking if the mandatory documentation is provided and the application form is filled out correctly by the applicant. In Uzbekistan, the interview is not carried out by a social worker, but by mahalla committee members. In all countries, a case or file is opened during this stage of the process. The application information is registered electronically only in some of the countries reviewed here. Armenia, the Kyrgyz Republic, and Lithuania are the only countries that register the applications electronically without exceptions[27] and have the individual information merged in a central database. In the other cases, the registration is a mixture (for example, in Romania it is done electronically in some cities but on paper in rural areas and small towns) or only paper (Albania, Bulgaria, and Uzbekistan).

Verifying Eligibility

Eligibility is usually verified in two main steps: (a) a desk verification of the information provided by the applicant and (b) a visit to the applicant's home (social inquiry). Subsequently, the eligibility is assessed.

The desk verification of the information provided by the applicant consists of (a) a thorough check for consistency of the self-declaration of incomes and family composition with the documents submitted by the applicant, and verification of the validity of the documents (presence of stamps, authorized signatures, and so on), and (b) a cross-check of the information with other agencies. This latter activity is performed either manually (based on exchanges of beneficiary lists) or, when the necessary systems are in place, automatically (by directly accessing the databases of other agencies). The cross-checks are not performed in all countries. The Kyrgyz Republic, Romania, and Uzbekistan rely only on the documents submitted by the applicants;[28] the applicants are in charge of collecting and submitting the documents to support their declaration, including lack of incomes from various sources or properties. The capacity to perform cross-checks is important not only because it lowers the costs for applicants (who do not have to collect supporting documents from other agencies), but also because it reduces the opportunities for errors and fraud. In Albania, Armenia, Bulgaria, and Lithuania, the SA staff exchange information with various other agencies and perform the verification based on the information received (box 4.6). However, only Armenia and Lithuania perform real-time computerized cross-checks and only for a subset of the databases.

Home visits (social inquiries) are a second instrument used to verify the information provided by the applicant (especially with regard to assets and family composition) and to assess the household living conditions and the social or health problems that household members may face. Although home visits may seem an expensive and effort-intensive activity, they allow social workers to gain a better understanding of applicants' socioeconomic situation and provide relevant information that cannot be obtained from other sources, especially in rural areas, and, in general, in economies with a high degree of informality. Home visits

Box 4.6 Cross-Checks of Information in Selected Countries

Albania: Every month, based on the list of Ndihma Ekonomike (NE) beneficiaries sent to them by NE offices, the local labor office, tax office, insurance office, cadastral office, real estate property office, vehicle register office, and labor inspection office release attestations regarding whether the listed names of NE beneficiaries are those of their clients.

Armenia: Databases of the ministries and institutions of Armenia are used for cross-checking the following:

• Personal vehicle ownership
• Membership in any association based on the mutual trust, investment, or share in the cooperative, as well as the status of a businessperson
• Amount of electric energy used in summer months
• Average monthly amount of phone usage
• Customs or tax payments on exported or imported goods made by family members

Bulgaria: When processing submitted applications and verifying eligibility, the social assistance (SA) departments request official information from territorial offices of tax administration authorities, employment bureaus, offices of territorial National Social Security Institute (NSSI), and other state and municipal institutions, persons, and legal entities. All these entities are obliged by the Social Assistance Law to provide the requested information within 14 days following a request. More specifically, for the guaranteed minimum income program, the SA departments establish contacts with the following:

• Employment bureaus: information about whether the applicant is unemployed and for how long
• Territorial Tax Administration: verification and additional information about personal and family incomes declared by the applicant
• Territorial NSSI units: cross-check of the insurance status of the person and whether the person receives pregnancy and birth benefits and an allowance for raising a child
• Insurers (employer of the person): cross-check of the information about contracted and insured persons

Lithuania: When the application process is complete, the program officer enters the information in an electronic database and cross-checks the reported information with a range of government databases. Municipalities receive applicant-related information necessary for the award or disallowance of the social benefit (SB) from the State Social Insurance Fund, Center of Registers, Population Register, Land Cadastre, Labor Exchange, Tax Inspectorate, Real Estate Register, Motor Vehicles Register, Ministry of Agriculture (direct payments for crops), and utility companies. The law stipulates that state authorities shall provide municipalities with free information necessary for review of a person's eligibility to receive SB (or any other SA). Municipalities can also buy some information (data or services) required for the above-mentioned purposes from some institutions such as the Center of Registers,

box continues next page

Box 4.6   Cross-Checks of Information in Selected Countries *(continued)*

banks, and post offices on a contractual basis. The Social Assistance Units have direct (electronic) access to the following databases:

• Territorial departments of the State Social Insurance Fund (pension benefit recipients and amounts, employed individuals paying contributions)
• Center of Registers (real estate)
• Population registry

When inconsistencies between self-declarations and information from the databases are noticed, a program officer will make a home visit to verify the reported information and fill out a special home visit form.

---

are a mandatory element of eligibility verification in all countries except the Kyrgyz Republic and Lithuania. In the Kyrgyz Republic, home visits are not mandatory, but the social workers are entitled to perform them; according to administrative data, home visits are carried out in about 40 percent of cases. In Lithuania, the home visits are done only when the benefits are granted on exceptional procedure or when the information provided by the supporting documents is contradictory or considered insufficient by the social worker. In practice, home visits may not happen even when they are mandatory. In Armenia (as well as in other countries), for example, home visits may be skipped because of lack of resources (staff time and transportation cost).

Usually the home visit takes place within two to three weeks from submission of the application[29] and only for those claimants who have inconsistencies in their documents or have already passed the desk review. During the visit, the social worker fills out a standard form on which the final benefit recommendation is based. In some countries (for example, the Kyrgyz Republic, Romania, and Uzbekistan), the home visit is be carried out by a committee, including the social worker and other staff of the local government or members of the local council. Community members as well as nongovernmental organization representatives also can be part of the committee in some cases (for example, in Romania). In addition, interviewing neighbors would not be unusual during the home visit. In most cases, the applicants are informed in advance about the date of the visit, have the right to review the assessment, and are informed about the recommendations.

Home visits have pros and cons. The pros are that in the context of high informality of incomes and assets, as well as in the case of multifamily households, consensual couples, and so on, the home visit allows for a better assessment of the socioeconomic situation of the applicant. The social inquiry can also be the basis for further referrals to other programs and services. In addition, home visits are very useful in the recertification process, allowing for an easy monitoring of the possible changes in family composition, assets, or other socioeconomic characteristics. The main cons are the administrative costs, the possible intrusiveness of the inquiry, and stigma. However, home visits are not necessarily perceived as intrusive or stigmatizing. In Romania, a representative survey of applicants (both accepted and rejected) found that only 5 percent of them felt embarrassed because the committee interviewed their neighbors and about 25 percent found the home visit humiliating, whereas almost 80 percent of respondents had a positive attitude toward the home visit (figure 4.12).

In Bulgaria, the regulatory framework stipulates that within 20 days after the submission of the first and each subsequent application-declaration, the social worker should carry out a social inquiry and prepare a report (a template is given in the Rules for Implementation of Social Assistance Act). The purpose of the social inquiry is to verify the data in the application-declaration by collecting information from different sources (home visit, interview with the applicant, and contacts with other institutions). Using the results of the social inquiry, the social worker makes a proposal for granting or not granting an allowance, its type, and amount. If needed, the social worker includes in the report a proposal for elaboration of an individual project for social integration of the person or family. As a rule, for unemployed people the recommendation is to attend and participate in the program titled "From Social Assistance to Employment." For disabled people, the suggestions are to use various social services aimed at the fulfillment of their

Figure 4.12 Beneficiaries' Assessment of the Usefulness of the Social Inquiry, Romania

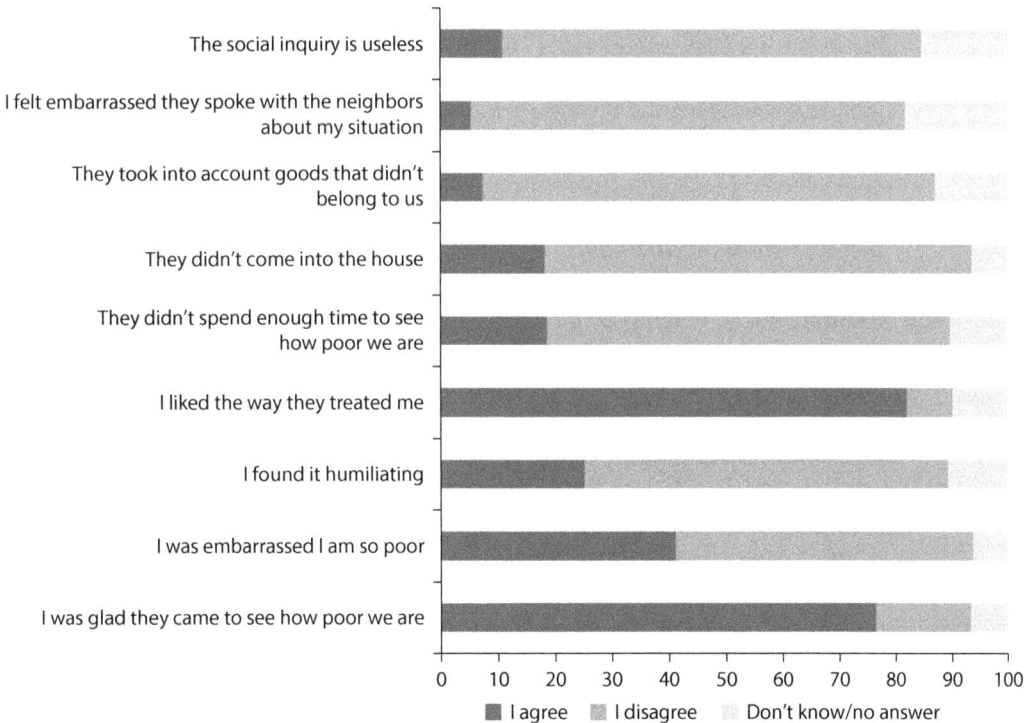

Source: Romania GMI Evaluation Survey, Beneficiaries Survey, 2003.
Note: The statements were chosen in response to the following question: As far as you are concerned, do you agree with the following statements related to the social inquiry?

day-to-day needs and social reintegration. For parents, one of the requirements is to enroll their children in school, if they have school-aged children.

In Romania, the social inquiry–investigation at the applicant's home is meant to ensure the accuracy of the information submitted in the applicant's documentation. The home visit is performed by the staff designated by the mayor's office that handles GMI implementation or by the SA department staff. The home visit must be announced in advance to the applicant. The SA staff performing the home inquiry can use information provided by (at least) two individuals who are knowledgeable about the socioeconomic condition of the applicant. SA staff may be accompanied by other staff from the mayor's office or local council, as well as other representatives of public institutions or nongovernmental organizations. In the case of multiple families within one household, SA staff is required to perform an individual social inquiry for each family or single person.

The social inquiry report format is standardized, provided by the Methodological Norms. However, there is no manual or specific instruction regarding the social inquiry procedures. The social inquiry report includes information on the following: family composition and structure (names, ages, and occupation); housing (owned, rented, surface, number of rooms, assets, and cleanliness); family income (including the income shared with and by other household members if there are additional families within one household); system and type of heating (district or own, type of fuel, and so on); record of assets owned by the family (land, real estate, mechanized vehicles, and other); family members' health status; special needs for the family as assessed by the SA staff; beneficiary preference for cash or in-kind benefits; other observations of the social worker, including a recommendation to grant the benefit or not and the justification if the recommendation is negative. The form must be signed by both the social worker and the applicant.

Benefit Award (Entitlement)

Using the results of the verified MT, the social worker assesses eligibility and recommends a benefit award or rejects the application. When programs are implemented by local governments, the benefit award may be subject to local councils' approval. The local councils' role and importance in the entitlement decision varies from country to country. In Uzbekistan, where the targeting mechanism is community based, the mahalla committees play a very important role, because they review each file and decide eligibility. In Albania, the local council decides on each case based on the recommendation of the social worker. In the Kyrgyz Republic, the *aiyl okmotu* (local government) committee must recommend eligibility, but it cannot make the final decision, which is made by the rayon (municipal) department of social protection after supplementary cross-checks are performed at the rayon level. Romania's GMI is the decentralized program in which the local council is not involved in the benefit-award decision, which is made by the mayor.[30] When service delivery is ensured by the ministry branches (that is, in Bulgaria), the local councils are not involved. In Bulgaria, the social worker's recommendation is reviewed and endorsed by the director of the

(Municipal) Social Assistance Directorate. In Armenia, the final decision is made by (the head of) the Social Service Agency after the list of eligible applicants has been reviewed and approved by a Social Assistance Council.[31]

Although consistent information across countries is not available, the rejection rates vary from about 25 percent in the Kyrgyz Republic (2004)[32] and Romania (2003),[33] 30 percent in Albania (2005), and 45 percent in Armenia (2002) and Uzbekistan (2004) to as much as 60 percent in Bulgaria in recent years. The reasons for rejection vary considerably from country to country. In Albania, 15 percent of applications are rejected because of budget constraints, 10 percent are rejected on the basis of verification of information through cross-checks and home visits, and another 5 percent are rejected because of ineligibility. In the Kyrgyz Republic the main reason for rejection is nonfulfillment of eligibility criteria[34] and incomplete files (16 percent) followed by verification through home visits (4 percent). In Romania, about 17 percent of applications are rejected because of ineligibility, 6 percent because of the findings during the home visits, and about 2 percent because of incomplete files.

Updates, Recertification, and Exit

All programs in Eastern Europe and Central Asia require beneficiaries to declare any changes in their income, assets, occupation, and family composition as soon as they occur. In addition, a regular recertification is performed for each beneficiary at given time intervals. The approach to recertification and the time intervals vary from country to country. Usually recertification consists of just a visit by the beneficiary to the SA office and completion of an abridged application form or a declaration stating the occurrence or not of any changes in the welfare status or family composition. This application or declaration must be accompanied by updated documents and certificates, but in most cases not all the documents submitted with the initial application are required. In case of changes in household composition or welfare status, the beneficiaries are asked to fill out a full application form, and their eligibility status and benefit level are reassessed. The recertification process can include mandatory home visits, home visits only if the beneficiary declares a change in the eligibility criteria, or no home visits at all.

The recertification is the responsibility of beneficiaries. If they fail to submit the declaration and accompanying forms, they are suspended from the program for a short period (a grace period of up to four months), and then excluded. By design, in some countries (for example, the Kyrgyz Republic) beneficiaries should receive a notification before the recertification deadline in order to prepare their documents. In practice, however, this rule is not enforced, and notifications are rather random.

In general, the frequency of recertification may vary from three months to one year (table 4.13). Albania is one exception to this rule, requiring a monthly visit by beneficiaries to the NE offices—more as a mechanism of increasing the opportunity cost for beneficiaries and reducing the risk of paying benefits to

Table 4.13 Frequency of Recertification and Updates of Beneficiary Information

Country	Recertification cycle	Cross-checks	Mandatory update of (selected) documents	Home visits required for updates or recertification
Albania	Monthly	Monthly	Annually	Yes; every 6–12 months (less frequent if income is unlikely to change)
Armenia	Annually (can be semestrial, quarterly in specific cases)	Monthly	Annually	Yes; annually (but not for all cases, because of staff shortages)
Bulgaria	Annually	Annually	Annually	Yes; annually
Kyrgyz Republic	Annually (can be semestrial, quarterly in some cases— especially in urban areas)	No	Annual	No; only at the initiative of the implementation unit
Lithuania	Quarterly (less frequent if incomes are not likely to change)	Quarterly	Quarterly (less frequent if incomes are not likely to change)	No; only at the initiative of the implementation unit
Romania	Annually (quarterly for proof of registration with employment offices)	No	Annually	Yes; every 6 months (or at the initiative of the implementation unit)
Uzbekistan	Quarterly	Quarterly	Quarterly	Yes; quarterly

Source: Based on case studies.

those who migrate abroad. However, a high frequency of recertification is increasing the workload of staff and thus the administrative cost of the program, although the evidence regarding its effectiveness is not documented. In practice, in some countries the frequency of recertification varies by groups of beneficiaries (though not necessarily following formal regulations). In the Kyrgyz Republic, recertification is done more often (every three to six months) in urban areas, where the opportunities of employment are higher. In Lithuania, municipalities are entitled to allow for a recertification period longer than three months but less than a year. The social workers may decide on the frequency of recertification based on profiling of the beneficiary (for example, in cases where the social worker estimates that the family composition or income is likely to remain unchanged, or in the case of the disabled and the elderly).[35]

The duration of benefits in most of the Eastern Europe and Central Asia countries is unlimited, as long as the eligibility criteria and conditions are fulfilled. Most countries have no exit strategy other than requiring those beneficiaries who are able to work to register as job searchers with the public employment services. One exception is Bulgaria, which, starting in 2006, introduced successive reforms to the duration of benefits for the beneficiaries who are able to work by imposing a time limit of 18 months in 2006, 12 months in 2007, and 6 months in 2008.[36] The beneficiaries can reenroll after one year from the forced exit. In Romania, the local governments adopted a different strategy in practice by transferring the GMI beneficiaries to public works programs. At the end of the public works programs, the beneficiaries could apply again for the GMI (which increased costs of both program administration and beneficiaries). In a few countries (Albania and Uzbekistan), the programs, by design, do not have time limits, but in practice beneficiaries are often rotated out because of budget constraints: at the end of the recertification cycle, the pool of beneficiaries is partially refreshed by bringing in new eligible households and leaving out some of the households that already benefited for a cycle or more.

Lessons and Areas for Improvements

Most countries in the Eastern Europe and Central Asia region operate LRIS programs whose targeting accuracy compares well to international standards. For many Eastern Europe and Central Asia countries, the most important challenge is to scale up the programs with low coverage without loss of targeting accuracy. This study sheds light on some ways to possibly improve less critical areas in some of these programs such as targeting accuracy, lower administrative costs, or improved governance. These lessons are likely to have value beyond Eastern Europe and Central Asia as well.

Lessons from the eligibility criteria and procedures of Eastern Europe and Central Asia LRIS programs include, in particular, the following:

• *Reduce the gap between the economic and the administrative definitions of income used for eligibility.* To reduce the difference between the economic and the administrative definitions of income, programs should take into account all formal incomes, include presumptive income for hard-to-verify incomes, and avoid income disregards. The most problematic aspect is how to determine the values for presumptive incomes. Here, the best practice is to derive the value for presumptive income from reliable sources (for example, farm models for agricultural income and specialized surveys) or to use the schedule of the tax authorities, when this exists and is reliable. The imputed values for presumptive incomes should be reassessed regularly.

Removing hard-to-verify incomes from eligibility criteria and replacing them with presumptive income rules is likely to generate a virtuous circle. Our case studies have shown that hard-to-verify incomes are rarely declared in full, often not at all. The inclusion of such incomes in the eligibility criteria is unlikely to improve targeting, but will impact negatively on compliance with program rules. Some beneficiaries will fail to report them; administrators will not have the means to detect such cases. Ultimately, the eligibility provisions that include hard-to-verify incomes (or assets) are an invitation to error and fraud. Those who design and administer LRIS programs could, instead, use simple imputation rules that rely on household circumstances that are easily observed or verified.

- *Reduce the gap between reported and true income through cost-efficient documentation and verification.* Even formal incomes could go underreported if the documentation and verification procedures are poorly crafted or absent. The proper documentation for formal incomes simplifies the work of SA workers and makes the process fair and transparent for beneficiaries. Without documentation, certain income sources are not remembered (error) or are underreported on purpose (fraud). In 2010, the introduction of documentation requirements in the means-tested Heating Benefit in Romania was the key factor that triggered a reduction in applications by about 50 percent (Grigoras, Corches, and Tesliuc 2012). Documentation requirements should cover all household circumstances that determine eligibility: incomes, assets, and additional household circumstances that determine the value of presumptive income (for example, registration as sole entrepreneur, taxi driver, and ownership of productive assets and their quantity or quality).

Finally, an important lesson from our case studies is that paper verification, although it has its limits, does work and can produce very accurate targeting results. However, over time it is advisable to move from paper verification to electronic verification of information, via cross-checks.

- *Complement income testing with asset testing, where appropriate.* As shown in this chapter, many Eastern Europe and Central Asia countries use asset filters beyond an administrative income test to restrict access to the program. Sometimes, these filters restrict access not only for the nonpoor, but also for the deserving poor. For example, the filters applied to NE beneficiaries could reduce the number of eligible beneficiaries from the poorest decile to about 8 percent (World Bank 2010). A good asset filter would be one that effectively discriminates between poor and nonpoor applicants (reduces inclusion error without generating large exclusion errors) and that is easy to verify and hard to falsify (when asset ownership information is stored in a public or third-party registry and can be cross-checked). Whether an asset is a good candidate for a filter is country and time specific. The program management should conduct a study before imposing such filters. Finally, to reduce both administrative and client costs, programs should minimize to the maximum extent possible the list of assets that filters beneficiaries. Some assets tend to cluster at the beneficiary level (for example, an old black-and-white television and an old refrigerator; a plasma television and a last-generation refrigerator). It is important to be aware of multicollinearity during testing of different asset lists.

- *Combine means testing with other targeting methods, where appropriate.* As discussed in this chapter, many Eastern Europe and Central Asia countries have successfully combined means testing with self-selection via workfare tests (work for the benefit of the local community, as in Albania and Romania). A comparative review by Coady, Hoddinott, and Grosh (2004) of targeting methods finds that using multiple targeting methods improves targeting accuracy.

- *Set the eligibility thresholds taking into account the intended target group of the program, based on the administrative income defined in the program rules and the factoring in of partial take-up.* Estimating the eligibility threshold of the program based on representative survey data of good quality is sound practice. When information about actual beneficiaries is available, comparing the simulated caseload with the actual one could reveal what portion of the eligible beneficiaries is not applying for the program either because it lacks information or because the household perceives the application costs to exceed the value of the stream of benefits from the program. LRIS programs using GMI formulas are more prone to partial take-up, and this should be taken into account when determining or revising the eligibility threshold.

- *Adjust the eligibility threshold for family size using an equivalence scale that includes some economies of scale.* However, given that poor households have spent a large share of their budget on food, the extent of economies of scale is likely to be low. An adult equivalent scheme with relatively low economies of scale could be appropriate in most Eastern Europe and Central Asia countries.

- *Consider a reasonable recertification period.* Recertifying often may help exclude from the program the beneficiaries whose welfare improved over and above the eligibility thresholds. However, the recertification process imposes significant costs on all current beneficiaries and even can deter some eligible beneficiaries from applying to the program.

- *Index benefits regularly.* Eligibility and benefit formulas need to be kept current; otherwise, the coverage of the target group will erode over time. At a minimum, this approach means indexing benefits with price inflation. Indexing to the value of real wages rather than to inflation will help a program keep a constant place in social policy, avoiding the near policy irrelevance into which some have fallen. Alternatively, programs may shift to more relative poverty concepts, such as aiming to cover the lowest 5 percent of the population or those with incomes below a third or a half of the median income.

- *Ensure an appropriate level of resources—human and material—for smooth implementation and administration of the program.*

Notes

1. This stylized model applies to most LRIS programs in Europe and Central Asia countries, except those using a PMT: Armenia, Georgia, and Turkey. Recently, the Albanian LRIS program is experimenting in moving from MT to PMT.

2. PMTs use a formula combining several (proxy) indicators of welfare, which are easy to observe, measure, and verify. The indicators and formula can be selected and respectively designed, based on empirical models or expert opinion. Across the Eastern Europe and Central Asia region a recent review (2010) of targeted safety net programs found only a few countries (for example, Armenia, Georgia, and Turkey) using a PMT/nonmonetary metric.

3. The undermeasurement still has implications for setting the eligibility threshold or the size of the transfer.

4. Note that this test could detect only the share of beneficiaries who "forgot" to report certain types of incomes, but could not detect the underreporting of income in monetary terms.

5. Such capacity is verifying the information based on administrative and official sources.

6. These can include right-based benefits or emergency social assistance (SA).

7. Other typical hard-to-verify incomes are those from seasonal or occasional work, nonagricultural self-employment, and remittances.

8. After 2009, Romania's GMI program disregarded agricultural income, and instead used a system of asset filters to identify the poor farming households from the medium- and high-income ones.

9. Serbia has a similar approach (see World Bank 2013).

10. For example, anecdotal evidence shows that Roma are discriminated against either by being refused work or by being offered lower wages.

11. In Romania, this approach was adopted in 2006, after the program was reformed.

12. The local rules approach was also used in Romania during the incipient stages of the programs (that is, before 2006).

13. Horizontal inequity refers to the situation when two households with similar poverty status have different probabilities of entitlement (acceptance into the program).

14. Some OECD countries use a wealth eligibility threshold in addition to the income threshold for means-tested benefits. In the United Kingdom, by 2012, this threshold was called "capital condition," and ranged from £8,000 to £23,500, with a modal value of £16,000. Households also benefit from a capital disregard limit, with a modal value of £6,000 (see NAO 2011). Among our six core country studies, Lithuania uses a similar approach.

15. Some countries define them as "basic needs" or "strict necessity needs"; others define them as "minimum standard." The simpler instance of a filter is the ownership status (a binary "variable" with possible values of yes/no); the more complex versions take into consideration "standards" by family type, needs, and the like.

16. The reports are based on qualitative work or authors' interviews in Albania, Armenia, Bulgaria, Romania, and Russia.

17. That is, the program gains the support of the "median voter."

18. When a family member belongs simultaneously to several groups, a weighted sum is computed for that individual.

19. The estimated minimum salary is different from the official minimum wage.

20. After a period of time, it was delinked and set up by government decision.

21. This is an aspect related not only to the political economy or legitimacy of the program (that is, acceptance and support from the population), but also to stereotypes.

Although there are good reasons to assume economies of scale for large families, the Romanian scale is clearly disadvantaging this type of household, which in Romania is predominantly Roma.

22. Linking thresholds with the minimum wage, especially in countries with strong trade unions, may give rise to risks of unpredictable pressures on the budget and is, in general, avoided by most countries. Indexation with a consumer price index ensures that beneficiaries are not expelled from the program even if their incomes do not change, and it maintains the purchasing power of the benefits when the amount is linked to the threshold.

23. This application process differs from that used in other regions (for example, Latin America and the Caribbean), where registration by survey or census, implemented from time-to-time (usually several years between surveys), is more frequent.

24. In some countries, new applications are received only during preestablished periods of the year or month. For example, in Albania the SA centers are organized to receive applications only two weeks per month.

25. In the Kyrgyz Republic, applicants who are living without registration in rented apartments and are registered in other localities can apply on the basis of a certificate issued by the "neighborhood or building committee" and confirmed by two neighbors.

26. In Lithuania, the municipalities recruit unemployed persons in public works programs to assist the applicants with filling out the forms. In Romania, according to beneficiary survey data, about 45 percent of applicants were assisted by social workers in filling out the forms, and about 10 percent were assisted by friends, relatives, or other beneficiaries.

27. In the Kyrgyz Republic, the electronic databases are located at the rayon level; the information from lower levels (rural *aiyl okmotu*, or local government) is sent on paper to rayons.

28. In these cases, cross-checks are not systematic, but they may occur ad hoc at the initiative of staff.

29. The regulations differ from program to program, but most of them fit into the two- to three-week interval.

30. The ministry used this approach to solve the (principal-agent) accountability dilemma. Otherwise, holding the local council accountable for implementation would have led to increased complexity of legal procedures and decreased capacity of enforcement (sanctions).

31. The councils are operating on a voluntary basis at the Regional Social Security Agencies and include the representative of Marzpet (Mayor of Yerevan), the representative of local self-governance bodies, the representatives of Employment and Labor Service Local Offices, Social Insurance Fund Local Offices, Inspections Dealing with Children under the Legal Age, of Regional Departments of Police, and of nongovernmental organizations.

32. Thirty percent were rejected in 2006–07.

33. Forty percent were rejected in the first year (2002) of implementation of the reformed GMI.

34. In most cases, the applicants find out about refusal to be included in the program during the interview with the social workers, that is, before registration of the documents.

35. Again, there are no clear national procedures or regulations with respect to this approach.

36. The measure was highly controversial and subject to mediation and the decision of the European Committee of Social Rights (Complaint No. 48/2008) since it violates the concept of "minimum income guarantee."

References

Bargain, O., H. Immervoll, and H. Viitamaki. 2010. "No Claim, No Pain: Measuring Non-take-up of Social Assistance Using Register Data." IZA Discussion Paper 5355, Institute for the Study of Labor, Bonn.

Blank, R. 1997. "What Cause Public Assistance Caseloads to Grow?" NBER Working Paper 6343, National Bureau of Economic Research, Cambridge, MA.

Blank, R., and P. Ruggles. 1996. "When Do Women Use Aid to Families with Dependent Children and Food Stamps? The Dynamics of Eligibility Versus Participation." *Journal of Human Resources* 31 (1): 57–89.

Bramley, G., S. Lancaster, and D. Gordon. 2000. "Benefit Take-up and the Geography of Poverty in Scotland." *Regional Studies* 34 (6): 507–19.

Coady, D., J. Hoddinott, and M. Grosh. 2004. *Targeting of Transfers in Developing Countries: Review of Lessons and Experience*. Regional and Sectoral Studies. Washington, DC: World Bank.

Council of Ministers. 2005. Decision No. 787/2005 on Determining the Criteria and Procedures of Economic Assistance Levels. Council of Ministers, Tirana, Albania.

Dabalen, A., T. Kiloic, and W. Wane. 2008. "Social Transfers, Labor Supply and Poverty Reduction: The Case of Albania." Policy Research Working Paper 4783, World Bank, Washington, DC.

de Neubourg, C., J. Castonguay, and K. Roelen. 2007. "Social Safety Nets and Targeted Social Assistance: Lessons from the European Experience." Social Protection Discussion Paper 0718, World Bank, Washington, DC.

Fry, V., and G. Stark. 1989. "The Take-Up of Supplementary Benefit: Gaps in the 'Safety Net'?" In *The Economics of Social Security*, edited by A. Dilnot and I. Walker, 179–91. Oxford, U.K.: Oxford University Press.

Government of Romania. 2012. Decision No. 57/Jan 2012 on the Implementation of Guaranteed Minimum Income. Government of Romania, Bucharest.

Grigoras, V., L. Corches, and E. D. Tesliuc. 2012. *Staying Warm in a Cold Fiscal Climate: How the Government of Romania Used PSIA to Reform Its Heating Subsidies*. Unpublished report, World Bank, Washington, DC.

Grosh, M., and P. Glewwe, eds. 2000. *Designing Household Survey Questionnaires for Developing Countries: Lessons from 15 Years of the Living Standards Measurement Study*. Washington, DC: World Bank.

Gustafsson, B. 2002. "Assessing Non-use of Social Assistance." *European Journal for Social Work* 5 (2): 149–58.

Institute for Urban Economics, Independent Institute for Social Policy, and World Bank. 2007. *Improving Social Assistance and Employment Assistance Programs to Combat Poverty: Proposal for a Social Assistance Strategy*. Unpublished report, World Bank, Washington, DC.

Kayser, H., and J. R. Frick. 2000. "Take It or Leave It: (Non-) Take-Up Behavior of Social Assistance in Germany." *Journal of Applied Social Science Studies* 121 (1): 27–58.

Kim, M., and T. Mergoupis. 1997. "The Working Poor and Welfare Recipiency: Participation, Evidence, and Policy Directions." *Journal of Economic Issues* 31 (3): 707–29.

Lokshin, M., and A. Posarac. 2006. *Implementing the Proxy-Means Test System in Georgia.* Unpublished report, World Bank, Washington, DC.

McKay, A. 2000. "Should the Survey Measure Total Household Income?" In *Designing Household Survey Questionnaires for Developing Countries: Lessons from 15 Years of the Living Standards Measurement Study*, vol. 1, edited by M. Grosh and P. Glewwe, 83–104. Washington, DC: World Bank.

Ministry of Labor and Social Issues. 2004. *The Poverty Family Benefit and Lump Sum Assistance Allocation and Payment Terms in the Republic of Armenia: Enforcement Provisions.* Book 2. Yerevan: Ministry of Labor and Social Issues.

Ministry of Labor, Social Solidarity and Family, Romania, and Birks Sinclair and Associates Ltd. 2004. *Evaluation of the Implementation of the Minimum Income Guarantee (Law 416/2001).* Unpublished report (CNTR 012921, DFID, WB), Birks Sinclair and Associates Ltd, Durham, U.K.

Mofitt, R. 1983. "An Economic Model of Welfare Stigma." *American Economic Review* 73 (5): 1023–35.

NAO (National Audit Office, United Kingdom). 2011. *Means Testing.* Report, National Audit Office, London.

Neumann, Udo, and Markus Hertz. 1998. "Verdeckte Armut in Deutschland." ISL Institut für Sozialberichterstattung & Lebenslagenforschung, Forschungsbericht im Auftrag der Friedrich-Ebert-Stiftung.

Nikitin, D. Forthcoming. "Analysis of the Targeting System of Armenia Family Benefit Program." South Caucasus Social Inclusion and Labor Programmatic Technical Assistance, World Bank, Washington, DC.

NILSR (National Institute of Labor and Social Research). 2009. *Main Issues of Armenia's Social Assistance System.* Unpublished report, Yerevan.

OECD (Organisation for Economic Co-operation and Development). 1998a. *The Battle against Exclusion: Social Assistance in Australia, Finland, Sweden and the United Kingdom.* Paris: OECD.

———. 1998b. *The Battle against Exclusion: Social Assistance in Belgium, the Czech Republic, the Netherlands and Norway.* Paris: OECD.

Pudney, S., M. Hernandez, and R. Hancock. 2003. "The Welfare Cost of Means-Testing: Pensioner Participation in Income Support." Paper presented at the Royal Economic Society Conference, Warwick, U.K, April 7–9.

Riphahn, R. T. 2001. "Rational Poverty or Poor Rationality? The Take-Up of Social Assistance Benefits." *Review of Income and Wealth* 47 (3): 379–98.

Terracol, A. 2002. "Analysing the Take-Up of Means-Tested Benefits in France." Unpublished draft, Université Paris 1 Panthéon-Sorbonne, Paris.

Tesliuc, E., V. Grigoras, F. Gerard, and P. Bachas. Forthcoming. "Romania: Ex-Ante Evaluation of the Minimum Social Insertion Income Program." Discussion paper, World Bank, Washington, DC.

Tesliuc, E., P. Leite, and K. Petrina. 2009. *Improving Targeting of Social Assistance Programs in the Ukraine.* Unpublished report, World Bank, Washington, DC.

van Oorschot, W. 1995. *Take It or Leave It: A Study of Non-Take-Up of Social Security Benefits.* Tilburg: Tilburg University Press.

Virjo, I. 2000. "Toimeentulotuen alikäytön laajuus ja syyt. [The extent and motives of non-utilisation of social assistance]." *Janus* 8 (1): 28–44.

World Bank. 2010. "Albania Social Assistance Policy Note, Key Challenges and Opportunities." Social Assistance Policy Note 70032, World Bank, Washington, DC.

———. 2011. *Armenia: Social Assistance Programs and Work Disincentives.* Report 63112-AM, Europe and Central Asia Region, Washington, DC.

———. 2012a. *Project Appraisal Document on a Proposed Loan in the Amount of Euro 38 Million (US$50 Million Equivalent) to Albania for the Social Assistance Modernization Project.* Report 66666-AL, Europe and Central Asia Region, Washington, DC.

———. 2012b. *Bulgaria: Household Welfare during the 2010 Recession and Recovery.* Report 63457-BG, Europe and Central Asia Region, Washington, DC.

———. 2013. *Western Balkans Activation and Smart Safety Nets AAA: Synthesis Note.* Unpublished report, Washington, DC.

———. Forthcoming. "Croatia Public Finance Review: Restructuring Spending for Stability and Growth." World Bank, Washington, DC.

Zalimiene, L. 2006. "Program Implementation Matters for Targeting Performance—Evidence and Lessons from Eastern and Central Europe: Country Study: Lithuania." Unpublished report, World Bank, Washington, DC.

CHAPTER 5

Benefit Levels and Conditions: Balancing Designs to Manage Disincentives to Work

One of the distinctive features of last-resort income support (LRIS) programs in the Eastern Europe and Central Asia region is the guaranteed minimum income (GMI) design used in most countries. This design is the theoretical epitome of narrow targeting, spending just enough but no more than needed to bring all persons in the country to the defined income level. It is also the epitome of a design that imbeds, at least in concept, disincentives to work. This chapter explores what governments are doing to keep work disincentives in check.

Work Disincentives: Theory and Evidence

Incentive compatibility is always an important aspect of the design of targeted income support programs, both technically and politically—with political concerns often intense even when technical concerns have been reasonably well addressed (see table 5.1). Poverty-targeted cash social assistance programs may negatively affect the intensity of the job search efforts of adult beneficiaries and to their acceptance of job offers. First, dependency on benefits and reduced participation in the labor market may lead to the exclusion of prime age beneficiaries from mainstream society. Second, policy makers in some countries are concerned about the effect of programs on the choice between formal and informal sector jobs. Given the size of the informal sector in some countries, income support programs may run the risk of unintentionally increasing the attraction of the informal sector. Third, policy makers have political economy concerns related to the legitimacy and political backing for income support programs. The perception by the general public that income support programs create dependency on state benefits or encourage informality may limit the support for financing such programs. This in turn affects the programs' capacity to provide effective protection against temporary income shocks or chronic poverty.

Table 5.1 Concerns about Targeted Social Assistance Programs

Intensity of job search effort and acceptance of job offers	Labor supply of other household members	Choice between formal and informal sector jobs	Political economy
Income support programs may negatively affect the intensity of the job search effort and the reservation wage, leading to longer unemployment spells.	Income support programs may negatively influence the labor supply of other household members.	Income support programs may run the risk of unintentionally increasing the attraction of the informal sector.	The public may perceive income support programs as creating dependency on state benefits or encouraging informality.

Rigorous empirical evidence on work disincentives in LRIS programs in the Eastern Europe and Central Asia region is quite limited. Two studies have looked at the work disincentive effects in the Albania Ndihma Ekonomike (NE) program and the Armenia Family Benefit Program (FBP). Without further study, one cannot determine which program would yield larger disincentive effects. The Albanian program has much less generous benefits than the Armenian program and stricter activation requirements; Albania's NE is means tested with a 100 percent marginal tax rate (MTR) on earnings, whereas Armenia's FPB is one of the few programs in the region that is proxy means tested and has a much less differentiated benefit structure (a flat-rate benefit per household member for three different bands of need).

For Albania, Dabalen, Kiloic, and Wane (2008), find evidence of work disincentives among urban beneficiaries who are capable of work—especially women. For the group of urban adults who are capable of work, the authors estimate the average reduction in labor force participation rates (that is, the extensive margin). For urban adults who work, the authors estimate the average reduction in hours worked (that is, the intensive margin). The receipt of an average benefit of about lek 2,400 per month is found to reduce labor force participation by 5.8 percent. For those already working, the receipt of an average benefit reduces the hours worked by about 2.7–2.9 hours per week. No such effects are found for the rural sample. The results are compatible with the following theoretical work disincentive model (Moffit 2002b): in urban areas, any additional lek earned reduces the benefit by a similar amount (an MTR of 100 percent), whereas in rural areas, most incomes are derived from agriculture and are presumed or imputed on the basis of assets (land and livestock) owned. A poor or good harvest, for example, would reduce or increase the agricultural output and—if one assumes no impact on local prices—the profits, but would not diminish the benefit. Thus, the disincentive effect is strong in urban, but not rural, areas. To identify the extent of work disincentives, the Albanian study uses a panel approach. A new, rigorous evaluation of the Albanian NE program is planned in the near future (Davalos and Santos 2011).

In Armenia, in contrast, a more recent study has found no work disincentives (World Bank 2011). An evaluation carried out using both descriptive and rigorous empirical evaluation techniques (regression discontinuity) pointed to the absence of labor disincentive impacts from the Armenia FBP. In general, the FBP does not appear to create any disincentives for participation in the labor force, for work effort, or for movement to the informal sector. The profile of FBP beneficiaries revealed that the propensity for inactivity is similar for FBP and non-FBP able-bodied individuals of working age. The analysis of benefit generosity suggests that the amount of the FBP transfer does not compensate for the potential earnings in the formal labor market, nor does it fully cover a family's living expenses. The estimates of program effects obtained by rigorous empirical analyses support the descriptive results and show no significant negative impacts of the FBP on inactivity and informality. The only negative effect of the FBP identified was a reduction in hours worked in the rural sample.

The evaluation also provides valuable insights on the employability profile of beneficiaries:

- Less than half of all members of FBP families are of working age.
- FBP families have fewer able-bodied individuals of working age and a higher dependency ratio than an average Armenian household.
- FBP beneficiaries who are able to work appear to have lower education than similarly defined nonbeneficiaries. Given their lower educational attainment, members of FBP families can be expected to have, on average, lower employability than their nonbeneficiary counterparts.
- Members of FBP families appear more likely to be working part time and in the informal sector. However, FBP beneficiaries' higher probability of working in the informal sector is not likely to be a matter of choice, given that formal workers earn much higher wages than informal workers.

In the absence of more rigorous evidence on final impacts of more programs, we must garner what indications we can from theory and from the magnitudes of factors that influence the presence or size of work disincentives. From a theoretical perspective, a social assistance program could reduce the supply of labor by beneficiaries if the following conditions apply (see figure 5.1):

- *The benefit provided by the program is large enough to allow the beneficiary (and his or her family or household) to "live off the benefit."* A proxy for this factor is the generosity indicator: the ratio of social assistance transfers to the consumption or income of the beneficiary households (ranges from 0 to 1).
- *The social assistance transfers are reduced when the beneficiary's earnings go up.* This occurs when the benefit formula includes an implicit MTR on earnings. Higher values of MTR indicate fewer incentives to work. Positive MTRs are found in all income- or means-tested programs. A simple GMI program that reduces the value of benefits at par with any extra earnings has a 100 percent MTR and would be expected to discourage work. MTRs may rise even higher if entry into the LRIS program confers other benefits, such as free or discounted social insurance, heating benefits, or supplemental child allowances, or they may be less than 100 percent if the benefit formulas are tweaked to "make work pay."

Figure 5.1 Factors Determining the Extent to Which Social Assistance Transfers Cause Work Disincentives and Dependency

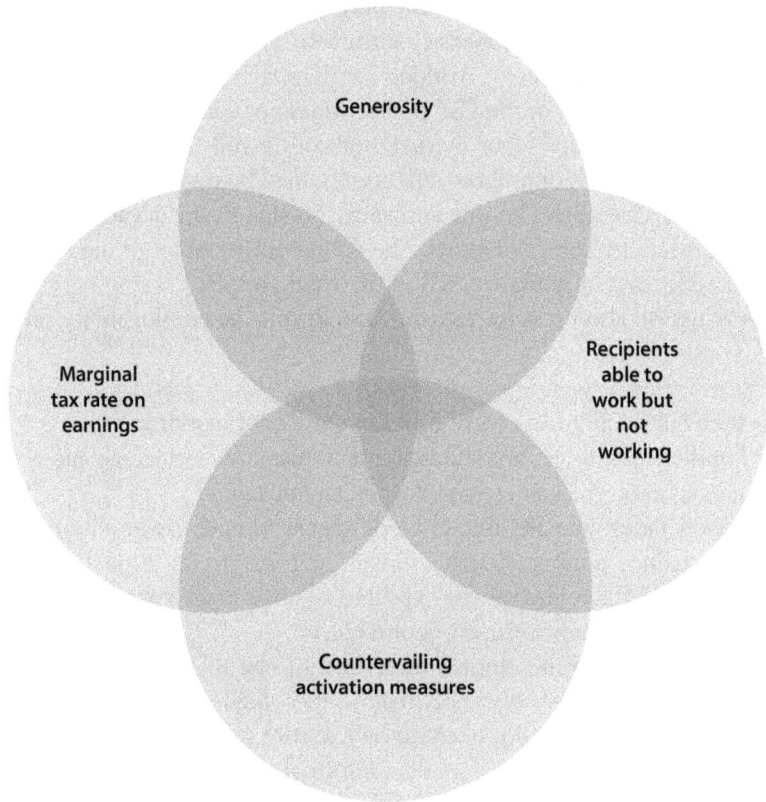

- *The beneficiary household includes members of working age who do not work (as much as expected).* A more formal definition of this group is individuals of working age who are not in employment, education, training, or disabled (the NEETD group). The relative size of the not in employment, education, training, or disabled group will put some bounds on the size of expected work disincentives.
- *No elements of the program design encourage or facilitate work effort.* To counterbalance the work disincentives inherent in the GMI design, almost all LRIS programs in Eastern Europe and Central Asia and in all of the case study countries have activation measures, though of uneven and often dubious effectiveness.

The remainder of this chapter explores each of these factors in turn.

The Generosity and Details of the Benefit Formulas

A basic design question for any social assistance program is how generous its benefit should be. In theory, the benefit level should derive from the stylized model that describes how the program intervention will help achieve the intended outcome of the program. For LRIS programs, the intended outcome is poverty reduction. Hence, the level of benefit or the generosity of the program should be set as a function of the income gap of the target group. According to this argument, providing all beneficiaries with a differentiated benefit that brings their average consumption to the poverty line will eliminate poverty with the lowest budgetary cost. This argument has inspired the type of LRIS program most common in Eastern Europe and Central Asia—the GMI program. In this case, the benefit level is set simultaneously with making the decision about the eligibility threshold. Implementation of the GMI design depends on the capacity of the administration to determine with relative accuracy the income of each applicant family. When family income is difficult to estimate and verify for each family but the poor can be identified with certain precision, a flat-rate benefit proportional to the average income gap of the target group can be used instead. Typically, this type of benefit formula goes hand in hand with the use of proxy means testing to identify the target group. The benefit formulas of all LRIS programs in Eastern Europe and Central Asia tend to fall into one of these two cases, illustrated in figure 5.2.

Benefit Levels

The levels and generosity of the benefits are generally low in Eastern Europe and Central Asia LRIS programs, in most cases ranging from 2 to 9 percent of the average national consumption per capita—from 5 to 31 percent of beneficiaries' consumption. For the six countries listed in table 5.2, the average benefit level contributes to a reduction of the income gap of the population in the pretransfer poorest decile and falls short of eliminating this poverty.

Figure 5.2 Differentiated- versus Flat-Rate Benefits in LRIS Programs

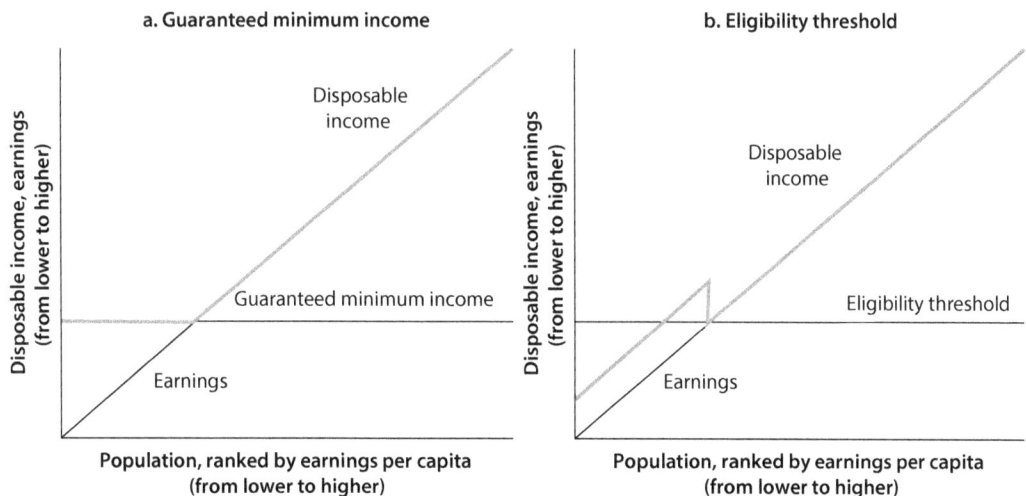

Note: LRIS = last-resort income support.

Table 5.2 Benefit Level and Generosity for LRIS Programs, Selected Eastern Europe and Central Asia Countries

Country	Average transfer[a] per beneficiary (direct and indirect)		Average transfer per beneficiary (% of national consumption per capita)		Generosity (benefits as % of beneficiaries' consumption)			
	2005	2008	2005	2008	Total, 2005	Total, 2008	Poorest quintile, 2005	Poorest quintile, 2008
Albania	464	746	2	3	8	10	12	15
Armenia	2,683	3,986	6	6	17	20	28	29
Bulgaria[b]	22	17	9	4	31	16	43	21
Kyrgyz Republic[b]	32	47	2	2	6	5	11	8
Lithuania	33	96	3	5	14	25	20	28
Romania	35	49	4	4	25	22	31	26

Source: Based on the Household Budget Survey from selected countries and years.
Note: Data are the most recent information available for all countries. More recent information was available in the World Bank's ECA Region Social Protection database, Social Protection Performance Indicators (May 2013 version) for Armenia (2010) and Romania (2009) only. The corresponding generosity indicators for the beneficiaries and the subset of beneficiaries from the poorest quintile were 25.1 percent and 35.6 percent, respectively, for Armenia and 21.5 percent and 24.1 percent, respectively, for Romania. These represent marginal changes compared with the 2007–08 figures.
a. Current local currency, survey estimates.
b. Comparable data are available for 2003 and 2007.

Differentiated Benefits per Household

Most LRIS programs in Eastern Europe and Central Asia, including five of the six countries studied in depth and listed in table 5.2, use a differentiated benefit formula of GMI type. Except for Armenia, Georgia, Turkey, and Uzbekistan, they calculate the benefit levels as the difference between a threshold and the measured total income, by subtracting the actual income (adjusted for family size and composition) from the threshold (minimum guarantee).[1]

From country to country, slight variations or additional rules in implementing this formula exist. For example, in the Kyrgyz Republic, the benefit is paid only for the eligible people in the household (children, the elderly, people with disabilities), and thus the difference between the actual family income per capita and the guaranteed minimum is multiplied by the number of eligible persons (see box 5.1). In Lithuania, the benefit amount is computed as 90 percent of the difference between the actual income and the threshold (the "state-supported income"). In Bulgaria and Romania, the benefit amount is calculated simply as the difference between the threshold and the actual family income. In Albania, the approach is supposed to be similar: households with no employed members (that is, no income sources) are eligible for the full benefit amount (that is, corresponding to the threshold), whereas those households with income-earning members are eligible for a partial benefit that, according to the rules, should be equal to the difference between the threshold and the actual incomes earned. In practice, the exact amount of the partial benefit is subject to the discretion of the authorities implementing the program (the local governments). Local discretion in establishing the benefit level also exists in Uzbekistan, where the benefit amount is not a differential one (that is, the benefit amount does not represent the exact difference between the household incomes and a threshold) but is designed at the discretion of *mahalla* committees (subunits of local governments) within given limits.

Flat-Rate Household Benefits

A few LRIS programs in Eastern Europe and Central Asia offer flat-rate or simpler benefits, for example, in Armenia, Georgia, Turkey, and Uzbekistan. A benefit of this type goes hand in hand with a different welfare metric used to determine eligibility: proxy means testing. For example, the Armenia FBP offers a benefit consisting of a basic amount and a supplement. The basic amount is the same for all eligible families (a flat-rate benefit of dram 8,000; see Nikitin, forthcoming). The supplement depends on the level of the family's vulnerability (determined by score) and the number of children under age 18 years. The supplement is paid for each child under age 18, in amounts differentiated by three bands of vulnerability levels. Families with up to three children and scores from 30 to 35 receive an additional dram 5,000 per child. If the vulnerability score ranges between 35 and 39 or is above 39, the amount is increased by the schedule presented in table 5.3.

Box 5.1 Example of Calculation of United Monthly Benefit in the Kyrgyz Republic

A family from the Kantskyi *rayon* (administrative division) consists of four people: mother, father, and two children ages 10 and 12 years. The parents do not have jobs, and both of them are registered with the employment services. One of their children is an invalid. They have 10 hundred parts of a nonirrigated land plot and 5 hundred parts of irrigated land. The potential income of this family consists of imputed income from the land plot, given the normative value of som 4.6 per month from 1 hundred parts of irrigated land and som 1.2 per month for 1 hundred parts of nonirrigated land. Thus, they have declared the following monetary income when applying for the Unified Monthly Benefit (UMB):

- Som 200 per month as an unemployment benefit of 100 percent for each parent
- Som 225 per month as a social benefit for the invalid child
- Som 35 = (10 × 1.2) + (5 × 4.6) for the imputed land income

The aggregate family income is 200 + 225 + 35 som 460; the income for each member is 460/4 = som 115; and the guaranteed minimum level of consumption is som 140. Therefore the UMB for one child of this family will be 140 − 115 = som 25; the amount of the UMB for the family will be 25 × 2 = som 50.

Source: Kyrgyzstan Center for Social and Economic Research 2006.

Table 5.3 FBP Supplements per Child, by FBP Score and Number of Children, Armenia

Household eligibility score	Three children or less	Four children or more
30.01–35.00	dram 5,000	dram 6,000
35.01–39.00	dram 5,500	dram 6,500
39.01+	dram 6,000	dram 7,000

Source: Nikitin, forthcoming.
Note: FBP = Family Benefit Program.

Maximum Benefit per Household

To limit benefit dependency, Albania and Uzbekistan impose maximum benefit limits per family or household. In Albania, during the first stages of the program, this limit was linked to unemployment benefits (the maximum was set at 2.5 times unemployment benefits), but it was subsequently delinked and is now set by government decision. In Uzbekistan, the maximum benefit level is equal to three times the minimum wage.

Form of Transfer: In Cash or in Kind

Benefits are usually paid in cash, but in some cases (Albania, Bulgaria, Lithuania, and Romania) the regulations permit the (partial) substitution of cash with in-kind transfers by the implementing agencies (that is, social assistance offices). In Bulgaria, the director of the local social assistance department may decide that, when "parents do not take care of their child or the money allowance is used for other purposes," the monthly allowances be paid in kind: for example, in partial or full payment of kindergarten and school fees; as expenses for food in school canteens; for purchase of food products, clothes, shoes, and manuals; and so on. In Lithuania a similar rule is applied, whereas in Romania benefits in kind may be paid at the request of beneficiaries or can be partially substituted with free meals in social canteens (usually in urban areas where such canteens exist).

The predominance of cash benefits in the Eastern Europe and Central Asia region seems an optimal policy choice. International evidence shows that in-kind benefits cost more to deliver than cash benefits, because of higher administrative costs of procuring, storing, and transporting the respective goods and because of losses that occur on the distribution chain. Moreover, when in-kind benefits are inframarginal to the consumption of the beneficiary (when they provide a quantity of the good that is less than the amount that the beneficiary will consume for the given price), they do not bring any increase in the consumption of the respective good (Grosh et al. 2008). Given that commodity markets in the Eastern Europe and Central Asia region are quite fluid, the payment in cash as the default is appropriate.

Complementary Benefits

In some countries, eligibility for the LRIS program provides an entitlement to the benefits or influences of other social assistance transfers. In Albania, beneficiaries are entitled to a fee waiver for the electricity bill (subsidized price).

In Bulgaria and Romania, eligibility for GMI provides entitlement to the heating allowance payable during winter months. In Armenia, Georgia, and Romania, the entitlement to GMI provides health insurance for all family members. In addition, in Romania GMI beneficiaries with children receive higher amounts (top-ups) of family allowance benefits, if entitled to them. In the Kyrgyz Republic, the United Monthly Benefit beneficiaries are given certificates or vouchers entitling them to receive preferential health services and exempting them from various school payments (a 50–100 percent discount for textbook rentals or for school repairs), but evidence of these benefits being granted in practice is scarce. From an administrative perspective, a strong rationale exists for using a well-targeted program to offer complementary benefits to poor beneficiaries, because it saves on administrative costs of delivering the additional benefits and on the private costs incurred in applying for these benefits. At the same time, the fact that these extra benefits are contingent on being eligible for the program and are lost when the income of beneficiaries goes above the program threshold exacerbates the problem of work disincentives, tackled in the next section of this chapter.

Making Work Pay

A mantra of social assistance reform in the past decade or two in countries with well-developed and generous social assistance systems, especially the United Kingdom, the United States, and various Western European countries, is "make work pay." The most sophisticated way of doing so is to reduce the benefit for each dollar earned by something less than a dollar of benefit. Figure 5.3 illustrates program scenarios with one-for-one and one-half-for-one reductions in earnings, using currency names and amounts pertinent to the GMI-type Croatian social benefit program (Tesliuc 2013). The figure contrasts a scenario that guarantees a minimum income level (in the figure, HRK 2,400 for a family of four) to a scenario that continues to guarantee this level but increases the eligibility threshold by half the amount of labor earnings (wages) for all households who move from assistance to full-time or part-time employment. The first scenario is depicted in orange, the second in blue. In the case of the first scenario (a GMI program), irrespective of the earnings up to HRK 2,400, the total household income is HRK 2,400; in other words, any extra earnings up to this threshold reduce benefits one for one. In the case of the second scenario, any additional earnings from employment increase the total income of the household by 50 percent of the amount earned. For example, if one individual resumes employment and earns HRK 2,400, the total income of the household would rise to HRK 3,600. From a static perspective, the make-work-pay program costs more than the GMI program. In this simplified version, it costs twice as much. However, the overall cost of the program depends on the distribution of beneficiaries able to work who are between no work, part-time work, and full-time work. Such dynamic effects would reduce the difference between the two alternative designs.

Figure 5.3 Example of Make-Work-Pay Reform of a GMI Program

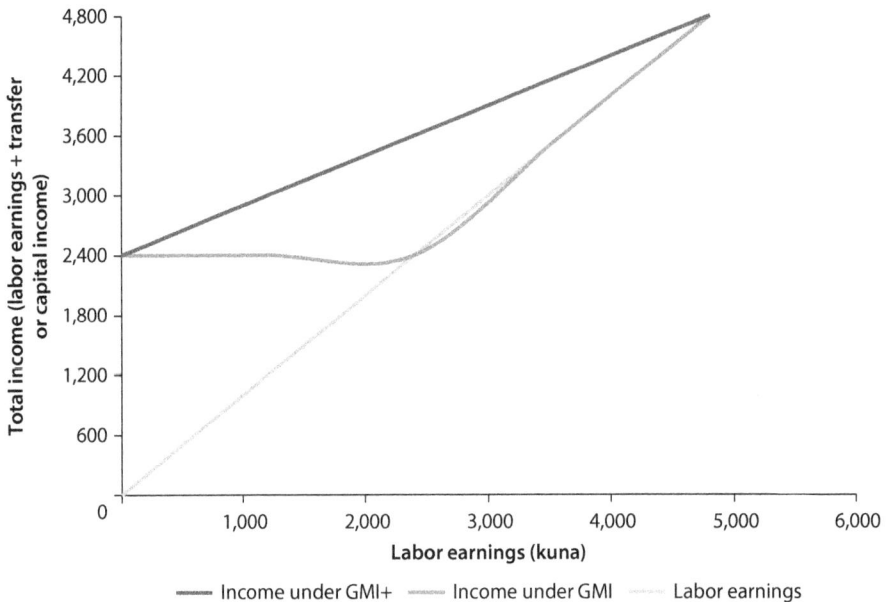

Source: World Bank, forthcoming.
Note: GMI = guaranteed minimum income; GMI+ = a version of a GMI program in which a share of earnings is not taken into account in determining the benefit level, thus reducing the implicit marginal tax on earnings and improving work incentives.

In France, the United Kingdom, and the United States, the benefit formula for the last-resort programs has been modified to reduce the MTR on earnings from 100 percent to a lower level in the manner illustrated in figure 5.3. France's Revenu de Solidarité Active has reduced the MTR to 38 percent; in the United Kingdom, the new Universal Credit program uses an MTR of 65 percent; and in the U.S. Temporary Assistance for Needy Families program, the rates vary across states with a modal value of 50 percent.

As early as 1995, the Romanian benefit formula was tweaked in the direction of making work pay. The presence of a working family member increases the benefit entitlement by 15 percent. This means that, in contrast to other types of additional income that reduce the value of the benefit by an amount equal to the respective income, the additional income from employment is not "taxed" at 100 percent. However, how the 15 percent figure was estimated is not clear, and this "premium" is available only once, regardless how many family members are working. More recently, other newer European Union countries have embarked on such reforms. Hungary modified the design of its regular social assistance benefit so that beneficiaries could continue to receive some benefits for up to six months after getting a job. Similarly, Latvia has introduced a GMI benefit of limited duration that can be received in reduced amounts after getting a salaried job. In the Slovak Republic, the program of reforms to mitigate any adverse impact on incentives to join the labor market included tax policy reforms, active labor market policies, and the social assistance benefit itself.

A simpler way to reduce labor disincentives is to reject a GMI design and use a flat-rate benefit. This structure reduces the work disincentive everywhere except at the "kink" in eligibility around the threshold. Moreover, it reduces significantly the complexity of program administration, thus reducing the risk of error or fraud. For this reason, using or moving toward a simpler benefit formula may be of interest and is the choice made in most countries outside the Eastern Europe and Central Asia region and a few within. At the moment, however, evidence indicating what type of formula is more equitable and effective in maintaining work incentives is lacking.

The actual distribution of LRIS benefits in the six-country study shows a relatively long middle range where the generosity of the programs using a GMI-type benefit is rather flat (figure 5.4). Because benefits are pretty similar for most beneficiaries, shifting to a flat-rate benefit for each adult equivalent would not alter too much the amounts transferred but could induce a positive change for work incentives and simplify administration.

Time Limits

Time limits are an even blunter way of limiting the work disincentive. This feature has not been used in the Eastern Europe and Central Asia region,

Figure 5.4 Cross-Country Differences in the Generosity of LRIS Benefits

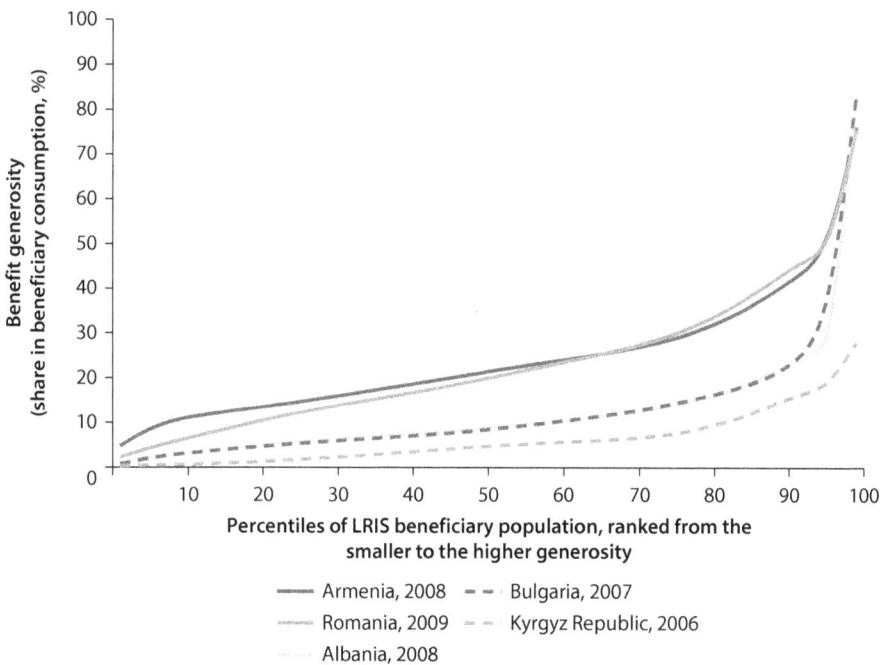

Percentiles of LRIS beneficiary population, ranked from the smaller to the higher generosity

— Armenia, 2008   – – Bulgaria, 2007
— Romania, 2009   – – Kyrgyz Republic, 2006
— Albania, 2008

Source: Based on Eastern Europe and Central Asia Social Protection Expenditure and Evaluation Database, Social Protection Performance Indicators.
Note: LRIS = last-resort income support.

Income Support for the Poorest · http://dx.doi.org/10.1596/978-1-4648-0237-9

except for a brief period during which Bulgaria limited the time beneficiaries could receive GMI benefits. As of July 1, 2006, the maximum duration of eligibility for GMI for able-bodied working-age beneficiaries was limited to a maximum period of 18 months. Upon losing the GMI benefit, former participants were eligible to enroll in remunerated employment and training programs but could not reapply for the GMI benefit until after 12 months of break in benefit receipt. The policy measure was enforced beginning January 1, 2008, resulting in a substantial drop in beneficiaries from around 60,000 to below 50,000 within just two months. The duration of GMI receipt was further reduced to 12 months as of July 1, 2008. In August 2009, the European Committee of Social Rights found the policy measure to be in violation of Bulgaria's obligations under the European Social Chapter. The time limits were eliminated in 2011.

The Presence of Nonworking Adults in Recipient Households

The concern over labor disincentives is an issue only for households with members who can work but who are not doing so. The first screen is age: children and the elderly are not expected to work. Most societies, though not all social assistance programs, deem active pursuit of education or training an acceptable alternative to work. The norms for other beneficiary groups are changing. Whereas a few decades ago, women, especially mothers of minor children, were not expected to work, with the gradual rise in women's participation in the labor force throughout the income spectrum, increasingly women receiving social assistance are expected to work. People with disabilities are generally not expected to work in analyses of social assistance, though the social inclusion movement and activation processes may encourage it. Because LRIS programs are tightly targeted to households with low earnings, they tend to assist those households with fewer than average expected workers.

In LRIS programs, the majority of working-age adults are either working or not expected to do so. The share of working-age NEETD adults in the total adult population of LRIS programs is, however, significant. In the subset of countries illustrated in table 5.4, it varies between one-third and around one-half of the total number of adults.

Because LRIS programs are a small part of larger social assistance systems in Eastern Europe and Central Asia, the number of NEETD adults in LRIS programs tends to represent a small proportion of the total number of adults able to work who are benefiting from any type of social assistance. In Romania, for example, 42 percent of adults in households who receive benefits from the GMI programs are NEETD; for the full panoply of social assistance programs, the share of NEETD is 22 percent of working-age beneficiaries. However, the absolute numbers are much smaller: 194,000 NEETD for the GMI program, compared with 1.8 million for social assistance as a whole.

LRIS beneficiaries often have low employability, which must be taken into account in setting expectations. In Armenia (World Bank 2011); Kosovo, the

Table 5.4 Share of Working-Age NEETD Adults in LRIS Programs, Selected Eastern Europe and Central Asia Countries

Country	Year	Total population (thousands)	LRIS program coverage[a] (%)	Share of adults (ages 15–64 years) in LRIS program (%)	Share of NEETD adult beneficiaries in total LRIS adult beneficiaries (%)
Armenia	2009	3,268	11	48	44
Croatia	2010	4,225	5	68	34
Romania	2009	19,043	4	63	42
Macedonia, FYR	2009	2,100	6	65	55
Serbia	2010	7,260	3	63	36
Montenegro	2009	620	4	61	34
Kosovo	2009	1,800	10	56	64

Sources: World Bank 2011, 2013, forthcoming.
Note: LRIS = last-resort income support; NEETD = not in employment, education, training, or disabled.
a. Based on administrative data or survey data (when administrative data not available).

former Yugoslav Republic of Macedonia, Montenegro, Serbia (World Bank 2013); and Romania (Tesliuc et al., forthcoming), social assistance beneficiaries who can work were found to have worse outcomes in the labor market (lower employment rates and higher unemployment rates). However, such rates were partly explained by higher barriers to employment than those experienced by the general population (lower level of education, larger share of out-of-school youth, and higher caretaking duties).

In Romania, for example, Tesliuc et al. (forthcoming) looked at NEETD adult recipients of social assistance from the poorest quintile. An important finding was that the size of the NEETD group was higher than the number of registered unemployed (6.3 percent compared with about 4 percent in 2013). The study found that most NEETD adults could be classified in eight groups (see table 5.5). One-third of the NEETD are relatively closer to the labor market, another third would require more intensive activation services to raise the likelihood of their employment, and a final third face high barriers to employment that may make helping them achieve sufficient autonomous incomes quite difficult. The profiling exercise generated a few relatively homogenous subgroups that could be helped through different measures, depending on their distance to the labor market. The two largest groups— educated, unemployed, urban men and married, middle-age, rural women— often have education and previous work experience and are relatively close to the labor market. Job search assistance and short training courses could be particularly effective in helping them. The groups comprising inactive youth are often much farther from the labor market and usually face low human capital as a main challenge. Offering vocational and apprenticeship programs for these subgroups is crucial. However, these groups often face additional barriers for labor market entry because of their minority status and number of children requiring care.

Table 5.5 Types of NEETD Beneficiaries from the Poorest Quintile in Romania, Ranked by Their Distance to the Labor Market, 2012

Group	Size of the NEETD group, first quarter		Probability of employment[a] (%)	Recommended activation measure
	Number of persons	Percent		
Educated, unemployed, urban men	151,000	24	56	Retraining, job counseling
Married, middle-age, rural women	114,000	18	52	Child care, retraining, part-time work
Uneducated, idle youth	110,000	17	38	Human capital
Young, rural, family women	70,000	11	42	Child care, part-time
Single, Roma youth	63,000	10	41	Integration, human capital
Educated, rural unemployed	50,000	8	70	Job search assistance, entrepreneurship
Urban, Roma, family women	44,000	7	31	Integration, child care
Young, urban couples	32,000	5	40	Job services, human capital
Total	634,000	100		
% of total active population	6.3			

Source: Tesliuc et al., forthcoming.
Note: NEETD = not in employment, education, training, or disabled.
a. Probability of employment (self-employed and employee) of bottom-quintile individuals is shown as predicted by a probit model on their group characteristics. This provides an indicator for the distance to the labor market and probability of employment.

An attempt to force the activation of long-term, hard-to-serve beneficiaries in Bulgaria during 2009–10 did not produce the intended results, underscoring that factors other than disincentives embedded in social assistance are important in leading people into NEETD status (see box 5.2).

Links to Activation Measures for LRIS Participants

By design, the programs in Eastern Europe and Central Asia have strong incentive compatibility components (see table 5.6), although no strong evidence indicates the effect of these components. (That is, do they really reduce potential disincentives to work or succeed in improving employability?) In addition to household income (poverty status) in determining and maintaining program eligibility, an important element of all programs is represented by a set of conditions and requirements with which household members must comply. The main type of such requirements, present in all countries, is related to the (so-called) activation measures. They are targeted to adult beneficiaries able to work and are meant to link beneficiaries with employment services and to avoid dependence on benefits by encouraging the beneficiaries to remain active in the labor market. In addition to this type of condition, some countries include conditions and incentives meant to enhance the human capital of school-age children in beneficiary households, who are required to enroll in school.

The policy niche or extent of coverage of the LRIS programs influences the need for and possibly the success of potential activation measures. Across the

Box 5.2 The Impact of Sudden Benefit Removal on Activity of Former Guaranteed Minimum Income Recipients in Bulgaria, 2008

In January 2008, the government shortened time limits in the program and began enforcing them more strictly, resulting in a drop in participation from around 60,000 to just below 50,000 in just two months. The rationale for the measure was that the buoyant labor market created an opportunity to remove employment disincentives in the social assistance system and to move people off benefits and into work.

A survey of the initial cohort of affected beneficiaries conducted by the National Statistical Institute in April 2008 confirmed their highly vulnerable profile. Almost 60 percent of the affected beneficiaries had primary education (four grades), had less than four grades of education, or were illiterate. Close to two-thirds of the affected beneficiaries were between 21 and 40 years of age, while one-third were between 41 and 60 years of age. Close to two-thirds of the surveyed population resided in rural areas, where the demand for labor is limited. The majority of affected beneficiaries were Roma (63 percent), regionally concentrated in the Plovdiv/Pazardjik and Vidin regions.

About 70 percent of those who lost their benefits because of the change in time limits remained unemployed three months after the stoppage of the guaranteed minimum income (GMI) support—despite a situation of overall high labor demand. Just over 15 percent were formally employed, while the rest worked in the informal sector, were self-employed, or took temporary employment.

About a quarter (27 percent) of the affected beneficiaries stated that they had not looked for jobs after they stopped receiving GMI support. They pointed to several reasons: lack of qualifications, low pay offered or a higher reservation wage, family reasons (child care), and long distance to travel between the offered job and the place of residence. Not looking for a job does not seem to be driven by the receipt of other forms of social benefits. Barriers also include apparently insufficient activation support by employment offices. Despite early identification of beneficiaries and the preparation of individual action plans, many former beneficiaries reported that they were left to search for jobs on their own. Another reason for the low activation rate is the low share of those who were offered participation in programs for subsidized employment or training: only about 12 percent of the respondents stated that they had been given such options, and only two-thirds of those who received offers participated.

Source: World Bank 2009.

Table 5.6 Employment-Related Requirements and Incentives

Country	Registration with employment services	Work requirements	Earnings disregards	Other income-generation-related conditions and filters
Albania	Yes	Yes	No	Applicants who refuse agricultural land are not eligible for benefits.
Armenia	Yes	No	No	No

table continues next page

Table 5.6 Employment-Related Requirements and Incentives *(continued)*

Country	Registration with employment services	Work requirements	Earnings disregards	Other income-generation-related conditions and filters
Bulgaria	Yes	Yes	No	Applicants who refuse agricultural land (ownership or lease) are not eligible for benefits.
Kyrgyz Republic	Yes	No	No	No
Lithuania	Yes	Yes	No	No
Romania	Yes	Yes	Yes	No

Source: Based on World Bank data.

Eastern Europe and Central Asia region, LRIS programs play either a residual role (with population coverage between 1 and 5 percent) or a broader and more meaningful role in poverty alleviation (when population coverage exceeds 10 percent of the population). The programs with small coverage tend to have a high density of hard-to-employ beneficiaries (for example, Bulgaria, Lithuania, and Romania), who are harder to activate. The larger programs (for example, Albania, Armenia, and the Kyrgyz Republic) have a sizable share of NEETD adults, including a larger proportion of NEETD adults with good employment prospects.

Registration with Public Employment Services and Requirement to Accept Employment and Training Offers

Registration with the public employment service (PES) of unemployed LRIS beneficiaries who are able to work is mandatory in all six case-study countries. Once registered, beneficiaries are required to not refuse employment or training offers provided by these services; in the case of refusal, they lose the entitlement,[2] and in most cases they also lose the right to reapply for a given period of time (for example, one year in Bulgaria). The registration condition must be fulfilled before enrollment in the program[3] by all working-age adults in the family or household with some exceptions that usually include people with disabilities, caregivers, pregnant women, single parents raising children below school age, or youth enrolled in education.

The working-age beneficiaries who can work must submit periodically a certificate or other proof that they have not refused any job, employment program, or training offer and are still registered with the PES. The certificate must be obtained by the beneficiary during periodic visits to the PES, when he or she may be offered employment or training. The required frequency of renewing and submitting the certificate to social assistance offices varies from country to country and does not necessarily overlap with the program recertification cycle.[4] When a beneficiary fails to submit the certificate on time, the family or household is sanctioned by being suspended from receiving the benefit (as in Albania, Armenia, Lithuania, and Romania). When the renewed certificate is submitted, the household is reenrolled in the program. In most cases, if the beneficiary fails to submit the certificate for two consecutive months (or cycles), the household is excluded from the program and must apply again. If the employment status of the beneficiary changes, he or she is obliged to inform the social assistance office, and the file is reassessed. In addition, in some countries (for example, Albania and Romania) regular (usually monthly) updates of the beneficiaries' employment status are obtained directly by the social assistance office from the PES by exchanging lists of beneficiaries.

In theory, registration with the PES serves as proof that beneficiaries are actively seeking work or trying to increase their employability through participation in training or qualification programs. Little evaluation evidence exists to support definitive statements, but one may wonder whether, in practice, the requirement to register with the PES is effective in improving employment outcomes for LRIS recipients. The existing assessments of the PES in Eastern Europe and Central Asia point to constraints. First, in most cases, the PES is understaffed (Kuddo 2009) and not well connected to employers, which implies the agencies do not have adequate resources to assist hard-to-serve beneficiaries. Second, the scant evidence on PES service delivery points to creaming off the easiest to place in Romania (Rodríguez-Planas and Jacob 2009), while in Bulgaria the time spent in an interview with hard-to-serve beneficiaries to elaborate an individual plan is estimated at 15 minutes (Shopov 2012).[5] Third, although the requirement is applied to all beneficiaries able to work,[6] it is relevant mostly for the urban ones because the PES, usually located in cities or towns, seldom has job or training offers that can be attended by rural beneficiaries.[7] Moreover, the PES does not always perceive the safety-net beneficiaries as being typical clients, and because these beneficiaries usually have multiple employability constraints and are hard to serve, the PES has no incentives or capacity to provide them with services. In Romania, for example, only 4 percent of the GMI beneficiaries who registered with the PES received training or job offers (Ministry of Labor, Social Solidarity and Family, Romania, and Birks Sinclair and Associates Ltd. 2004).

Wage Subsidy Programs

Only two countries (Albania and Bulgaria) of the six case-study countries are implementing targeted programs aimed at improving access to jobs or employability of LRIS beneficiaries. In both cases, the programs consist of subsidized employment, and in the case of Bulgaria, this is complemented by training.

Albania has in place two programs: (a) a wage subsidy program that pays employers the equivalent of four monthly minimum wages when hiring long-term NE beneficiaries for at least one year (World Bank 2010); and (b) a special wage subsidy scheme for specific categories of unemployed women registered under the NE, such as those older than age 35 years, and disabled. During the first year of the contract, this category receives 75 percent of all contributions and four monthly salaries; during the second year of the contract, the benefits increase to 85 percent of the contributions and six monthly salaries; and during the third year, it is supported with 100 percent of the contributions and four monthly salaries. However, the performance of these measures has not been evaluated.

In 2003, Bulgaria introduced the program "From Social Assistance to Employment" with the declared objectives to (a) generate (temporary) employment and social integration of unemployed persons who receive social benefits and (b) increase the employability of persons within the program. The program provided subsidies, including salaries and social contributions, for employing long-term unemployed social assistance beneficiaries (or those eligible for benefits) for a period of at least nine months. In addition, the social assistance beneficiaries participating in the program could access literacy and vocational courses combined with part-time employment. Priority was given to long-term unemployed persons (registered with the employment bureau for more than 24 months) receiving social assistance benefits for more than 18 months, members of a family with children in which both parents are unemployed, and unemployed single parents receiving social benefits. The program participants could be hired by local governments and by state, private, and nongovernmental organizations as long as they were engaged in nonprofit, socially beneficial activities. In general, the work consisted of typical community service activities, including small ecological or communal projects (from establishment of green recreational spaces to cleaning, reforestation, protection of cultural sites, and so on) and social services (for example, assistance to persons with disabilities). The employers were required to apply for the program by submitting a project. Registration, evaluation, and approval of the projects was done by the employment agency. The agency's local units (employment offices) were responsible for (a) selecting and referring beneficiaries to employers; (b) organizing and financing the literacy courses and vocational training; and (c) monitoring and supervising the program.

A midterm evaluation[8] of the program covering 2003–04 indicates that the program's effect was rather mixed. The study found positive effects on length of unemployment (on average, the program reduced by half the unemployment duration of a participant) and increased self-confidence and job-search motivation of beneficiaries, and positive results for the local communities (creation and maintenance of public goods, including social services). However, the overall effect on employment was rather small (8 percent), and the net impact was estimated to be negative. The evaluation also found that the program did not increase the chances of participants to find a regular job, attributing this failure to the low levels of training provided before or during employment under the project, as well as to a possible lock-in effect (that is, the tendency of participants to stay in subsidized employment). In addition, the evaluation found some evidence of displacement effects, in particular in the public sector (about 14 percent of the projects would have occurred even in the absence of the program, meaning that employment for those projects would have been created anyway). Some of the evaluation's main conclusions were that the training component should be strengthened and the composition of employers carrying out projects under the program should be changed in favor of private sector and nongovernmental organizations (where some of the negative impacts were less evident).

Work Requirements: Community Services and Workfare

The LRIS programs in Albania, Bulgaria, Lithuania, and Romania include workfare requirements for working-age able-bodied beneficiaries who are not otherwise employed, conditioning the receipt of benefits on participation in community services (works) programs organized by local governments (figure 5.5). Such requirements are meant to respond to several objectives. First, by introducing an opportunity cost for those beneficiaries active in the informal labor market as well as for inactive ones, these requirements are an important self-selection mechanism; second, they contribute to increasing legitimacy and support for the program by attenuating the belief that beneficiaries are lazy and that social benefits create a culture of passivity; and third, they contribute to maintaining or improving community assets (small local infrastructure, public facilities, and so on). The responsibility for organizing and supervising community work requirements usually lies with the local governments.[9] Community works programs usually consist of small-scale environmental programs (including landscaping or cleaning of parks and public spaces), public works (including rehabilitation or maintenance of local roads), or provision of social services (including support for the elderly).

The regulations regarding work requirements vary from country to country. In Bulgaria, beneficiaries are required to perform (at least) five days of community work per month if they are not already participating in programs initiated by the employment services. Albania has no minimum or maximum number of days, but the legislation stipulates that the work should be remunerated according to the minimum wage. In practice, this means that beneficiaries cannot be asked to perform more hours of work than would be covered by the benefit amount, or the local governments should top up the benefits from their own budget if extra hours of work are required. In Romania, since the 2006 reform, the rules are similar: the amount of work required should be proportional with the benefit

Figure 5.5 Romanian Community Works: Type of Activities

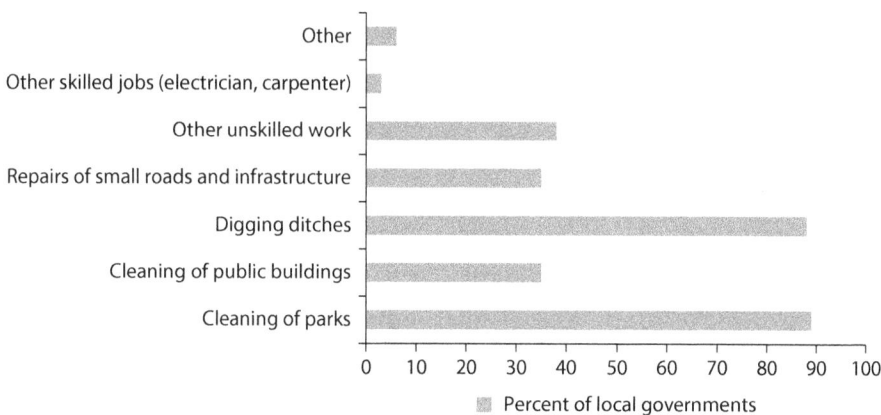

Source: Calculations based on the Romania Guaranteed Minimum Income Survey, 2003, Department for International Development and World Bank.

Income Support for the Poorest • http://dx.doi.org/10.1596/978-1-4648-0237-9

amount, assuming a salary per hour based on the minimum wage, but the maximum number of community work hours is set at 72. The categories of beneficiaries exempted from registration with the PES are also exempted from the community work requirement.

The sanction for noncompliance or refusal varies from country to country. In most countries, the whole family is suspended from benefits in the respective month; however, in some cases (for example, Romania), the local governments allow more flexibility by suspending only the noncompliant family member from the calculation of the benefit rather than sanctioning the entire family. An important lesson learned in the case of the Romanian GMI was to carefully define the exemptions from the work requirement. In the early stages of the program, when the conditionality was first implemented and exemptions were not clearly defined in the regulations, about 20 percent of beneficiaries under 40 years of age complained about not being able to comply with the work requirement because of lack of child care facilities.

In practice, community works are not always easy to implement. First, they require some administrative capacity to plan, organize, and supervise the works. Depending on the complexity of the works, these activities require resources (staff and time) that add to the administrative cost of the program. Second, even if in most cases the works are labor intensive, they require basic tools, equipment, and materials that are not always available in poorer communities. As a result, not all communities are able to organize community works in a systematic and regular manner. However, evidence based on qualitative research in Albania and Romania shows that, when organized, the results are considered positive by both local governments and beneficiaries. Community works are viewed as activating beneficiaries, even if for a short time; helping filter beneficiaries; and improving community infrastructure and social services.

School Enrollment and Attendance Requirements and Incentives

Opportunities for promoting links of cash social assistance to human capital have not often been tapped in Eastern Europe and Central Asia. Within the region, a conditional cash transfer–like program exists in 4 of 30 countries: Bulgaria, FYR Macedonia, Romania, and Turkey. Started in 2001, the Turkish program was the earliest one and the most closely modeled on that of Latin America. It has shown results in increasing secondary enrollment despite relatively low benefit levels (Ahmed et al. 2007). The Bulgarian GMI includes both school attendance and health and vaccination conditions. Monitoring data for 2010–11 show about 1–2 percent noncompliance. Romania operates an FBP that targets the poorest quintile; since January 2011, benefits for school-age children have been conditioned on the children's school attendance. Lessons learned from these programs will be useful to understand the constraints and opportunities for enhanced use of coresponsibilities in Eastern Europe and Central Asia and to shape the future regional agenda.

Higher school enrollment rates in Eastern Europe and Central Asia may explain in part why the LRIS programs have few links to education or health services, but a gap in enrollment still exists for children living in poor households. For some of the countries, the explanation is that this requirement is included in other social assistance cash transfers, such as family or child allowances, which are prevalent in the region and cover larger shares of the population. Bulgaria and Romania, for example, feature such conditionality in their means-tested family allowances (which are more generous than the GMI), although in the case of Romania it is not rigorously enforced. In Bulgaria, in addition to setting requirements, the program uses incentives for poor parents to enroll their children by applying a smaller GMI coefficient (percentage) for a child who is not enrolled; this means a lower threshold for the whole family and thus a lower benefit or even noneligibility for the program.

Outside Eastern Europe and Central Asia, many countries have conditioned cash transfers on school attendance to provide incentives for higher school attendance and possibly higher education outcomes or on health checks and immunization. Ample evidence indicates these approaches can be successful (see, for example, Fiszbein and Schady 2009).

Conclusion

Theory tells us that the GMI programs of Eastern Europe and Central Asia are at risk of significant work disincentives, but the very scant empirical evidence is mixed and so is the extent to which proximate factors that would cause work disincentives are present. However, this concern is clearly present in the political discourse around LRIS programs in many countries.

Benefit levels in the LRIS programs represent about 26–29 percent of the income of the poorest quintile, which is clearly insufficient to replace work effort but possibly a helpful top-up to income. As we saw in chapter 4, the eligibility thresholds and thus implicitly the benefit levels are on the low side in many countries, and further lowering thresholds and benefits is not a sensible course in general.

The past experience of programs in Eastern Europe and Central Asia shows that although the GMI type of formula has its advantages and in most countries is working perhaps better than might be expected, this approach may not be always the most effective. Countries may want to modify the approach to reduce either the difficulties of establishing eligibility and benefit levels or the potential work disincentives, or both. The countries with relatively small informal sectors and high levels of documented (that is, easy to verify or cross-check) incomes, assets, and family composition could experiment with time-limited earning disregards or in-work benefit bonuses that would decrease the MTR from 100 percent to 70 percent or even to 50 percent. These changes would reduce the disincentives to work built into formulas that tax 100 percent of earned incomes and will probably have only marginal implications on program cost, although they would increase the complexity of benefit formulas. The countries with larger informal sectors would probably be better off choosing simpler benefit formulas, with a limited number of benefit levels, instead of using a differentiated approach. Simpler formulas are easier to administer (reducing errors and administrative costs) and could enhance the work response of beneficiaries who can work.

The share of LRIS recipients who are working-age NEETD adults is not overwhelming, but it is high enough to suggest that the activation agenda needs to be taken seriously. Activation policies are common in countries in Eastern Europe and Central Asia and at the forefront of policy attention these days. An unfinished agenda clearly exists in providing support that is effective rather than merely mechanical, and the problem will in general be harder for recipients of LRIS programs than for other groups. There are challenges in assessing the prevailing barriers to work faced by the particular target population of social assistance beneficiaries and in identifying the appropriate measures or support services to overcome these barriers in a cost-effective manner. Delivering the right type of intervention to hard-to-serve social assistance beneficiaries will require a certain integration and coordination between social assistance and active labor market programs, as well as adjustments in the roles, responsibilities, and functioning of public agencies to ensure the pertinence and relevance of their interventions within these particular groups. This is likely to imply a different structure of incentives for the various institutions and organizations involved in policy making and service delivery, improved infrastructure (for example, management information systems and one-stop shops), and additional or different human resources at the program level (for example, caseworkers). Such an agenda is in its infancy in most Eastern European and Central Asian countries.

Notes

1. Some countries (such as Bulgaria and Romania) still use flat-rate benefits for other types of means-tested programs, such as means-tested child and family allowances. In this case, the benefit amount depends only on the number of children and not on the income gap. The main difference between a flat and a differential benefit is the implicit "taxation" of any additional revenue (that is, the actual household incomes). In the case of GMI programs, any additional earnings beneficiaries receive lead to a decrease of the benefit amount (that is, the transfer declines as the actual income approaches the threshold, therefore implying a high MTR imposed on low incomes). In the case of family allowances in Bulgaria and Romania, the benefit amount is the same (flat benefits) regardless of actual earnings, as long as the family's income is lower than the threshold.

2. In Lithuania, noncompliance may lead to replacing the cash with an in-kind transfer.

3. In Bulgaria and Lithuania, the beneficiaries should have been registered with employment services for six months before applying for the GMI and the social benefit, respectively, with some exceptions (such as for recent school graduates).

4. Certificate renewal or submission is required at three months in Albania, Lithuania, and Romania, six months in the Kyrgyz Republic, and one year in Armenia. See recertification later in this chapter.

5. See also Kuddo (2012) for a review of PESs in developing countries.

6. Except in Albania, where the requirement applies only for urban beneficiaries.

7. Public works employment programs represent an important exception.

8. See de Koning, Kotzeva, and Tzvetkov 2007. The evaluation did not have an experimental design, being an ex-post evaluation based on a cross-section survey. Still, it used a "nonexperimental control group." Despite the flaws in sampling and comparability of the treatment and control group, the evaluation is indicative of the program's effect.

9. In large cities, it lies with a specialized department or staff, different from the one implementing the LRIS program.

References

Ahmed, A. U., M. Adato, A. Kudat, D. Gilligan, and R. Colasan. 2007. "Impact Evaluation of the Conditional Cash Transfer Program in Turkey: Final Report." International Food Policy Research Institute, Washington, DC.

Dabalen, A., T. Kiloic, and W. Wane. 2008. "Social Transfers, Labor Supply and Poverty Reduction: The Case of Albania." Policy Research Working Paper 4783, World Bank, Washington, DC.

Davalos, M. E., and I. Santos. 2011. "Albania Ndihma Ekonomike: Reform to Better Target the Poor, Pilot Impact Evaluation Design." Presentation, Social Assistance Modernization Project, World Bank, Washington, DC, December 6.

de Koning, J., M. Kotzeva, and S. Tzvetkov. 2007. "Mid-Term Evaluation of the Bulgarian Programme 'From Social Assistance to Employment.'" In *Employment and Training Policies in Central and Eastern Europe: A Transitional Labour Market Perspective*, edited by J. de Koning, 103–31. Amsterdam: Dutch University Press.

Fizsbein, A., and N. Schady. 2009. *Conditional Cash Transfers: Reducing Present and Future Poverty*. World Bank Policy Research Report. Washington, DC: World Bank.

Grosh, M., C. del Ninno, E. Tesliuc, and A. Ouerghi. 2008. *For Protection and Promotion: The Design and Implementation of Effective Safety Nets*. Washington, DC: World Bank.

Kuddo, A. 2009. "Employment Services and Active Labor Market Programs in Eastern European and Central Asian Countries." Social Protection Discussion Paper 0918, World Bank, Washington, DC.

———. 2012. "Public Employment Services, and Activation Policies." Social Protection Discussion Paper 1215, World Bank, Washington, DC.

Kyrgyzstan Center for Social and Economic Research. 2006. *Program Implementation Matters for Targeting Performance—Evidence and Lessons from Eastern and Central Europe: Country Study—Kyrgyz Republic*. Unpublished report, World Bank, Washington, DC.

Ministry of Labor, Social Solidarity and Family, Romania, and Birks Sinclair and Associates Ltd. 2004. *Evaluation of the Implementation of the Minimum Income Guarantee (Law 416/2001)*. Unpublished report, Birks Sinclair and Associates Ltd., Durham, U.K.; Department for International Development (U.K.), London; and World Bank, Washington, DC.

Moffit, R. 2002a. "Economic Effects of Means-Tested Transfers in the U.S." *Tax Policy and Economy* 16 (1): 1–35.

———. 2002b. "Welfare Programs and Labor Supply." NBER Working Paper 9168. National Bureau of Economic Research, Cambridge, MA.

Nikitin, D. Forthcoming. "Analysis of the Targeting System of Armenia Family Benefit Program." South Caucasus Social Inclusion and Labor Programmatic Technical Assistance, World Bank, Washington, DC.

Rodríguez-Planas, N, and B. Jacob. 2009. "Evaluating Active Labor Market Programs in Romania." *Empirical Economics* 38 (1): 65–84.

Shopov, G. 2012. *Implementing Activation and Graduation Measures for Social Assistance Beneficiaries—Bulgaria: A Review of Experiences.* Unpublished report, World Bank, Washington, DC.

Tesliuc, E. 2013. "Croatia: Improving the Effectiveness of the Social Assistance System." Background paper for the Croatia Public Finance Review, World Bank, Washington, DC.

Tesliuc, E., V. Grigoras, F. Gerard, and P. Bachas. Forthcoming. "Romania: Ex-Ante Evaluation of the Minimum Social Insertion Income Program." Discussion paper, World Bank, Washington, DC.

World Bank. 2009. "Mitigating the Impact of the Economic Crisis on the Poor." Social Safety Net Reform Policy Note 68711, World Bank, Washington, DC.

———. 2010. *Social Safety Nets in the Western Balkans: Design, Implementation, and Performance.* Report 54396-ECA, Europe and Central Asia Region, Washington, DC.

———. 2011. *Functional Review of the Ministry of Labor, Family and Social Protection in Romania.* Unpublished report, Washington, DC.

———. 2013. *Western Balkans Activation and Smart Safety Nets AAA: Synthesis Note.* Unpublished report, Washington, DC.

———. Forthcoming. "Croatia Public Finance Review: Restructuring Spending for Stability and Growth." World Bank, Washington, DC.

CHAPTER 6

Control and Accountability in LRIS Programs

Management information systems (MISs) are the administrative backbone of all social assistance programs, indeed so central to their functioning that program implementation is hard to discuss without discussion of MISs. They are all the more important where links are being made between programs, as is increasingly the case in Eastern Europe and Central Asia, because eligibility for last-resort income support (LRIS) programs conveys other benefits, such as social health insurance or heating or child allowances, or conveys responsibilities, such as registration for public employment services or labor activation programs. The complex eligibility and benefit formulas of guaranteed minimum income (GMI) programs in Eastern Europe and Central Asia make the programs highly prone to error, fraud, and corruption (EFC), thus calling for strong control measures.

In recent years, some islands of excellence have appeared in the area of management of information and development of mechanisms and institutions to reduce error and fraud in LRIS and other social assistance programs. This section reviews these experiences and attempts to draw lessons for the other countries that are still in their infancy in these areas.

Management of Information

A good MIS might be considered the backbone of a well-functioning social assistance program. It can provide services to the program at every step in the service delivery chain: identification and enrollment of potentially eligible beneficiaries; storage of beneficiary information in a database system; validation or checks of eligibility through cross-checks with other databases or registries; derivation of lists for payment purposes; production of reports to inform policy making; registration of complaints and follow-up; and case management (see table 6.1).

Commonly, an MIS is developed for each LRIS program. However, some MISs extend beyond a given social assistance program to provide an integrated database of beneficiaries for most or all of the social assistance programs in a country,

Table 6.1 Typical Modules of an MIS for LRIS Programs

Module	Content
Eligibility	This module is used to determine which families are eligible for the program. It provides system functions for data entry, validation, and creation of a database with information for program beneficiaries, including the following: (a) family demographics; (b) education; (c) employment; (d) dwelling, utility, and durable goods; (e) household assets; (f) social protection benefits received; and (g) income sources. This information, along with paper documentation, can be verified by cross-checking it against other government databases. The beneficiary database typically contains active as well as former beneficiaries (who have exited the program). Maintaining this information allows generation of reports and statistical analysis for current and historic scheme activity.
Benefit level	This module uses the information supplied by applicants and the eligibility rules of the program to determine whether an applicant is eligible or not and his or her benefit level. For the Armenia Family Benefits Program, for example, this module computes the household poverty score based on household consumption and income characteristics. For the Romania GMI, it computes the reported per capita income of the household, applies different asset filters (exclusion criteria), and then computes the benefit level as the difference between the household-specific GMI and per capita income.
Payments	This module provides a number of functions to accomplish the complete payment business process. The process begins with identification of households eligible to receive the monthly payment. The database stores active as well as inactive beneficiaries. A listing of families and payment amounts detailing specific payment items as well as identification information is generated and submitted both to the payment agency for review and approval and to the payment agents (post offices, banks, and treasury).
Reporting	Operational reports are designed and developed to support the administrative, financial, and management processes and activities of the program. These reports typically include listings of active beneficiaries at local government, regional, and national levels; monthly, quarterly, and annual payments; and beneficiaries by age groups, by gender, and in general, by any classification based on stored data. The reports could also include statistical data as required by users.
Monitoring	This module generates program performance information, including beneficiary enrollment increase or decrease, payment and use of program funds, families that exited the program, estimated poverty reduction impact, and so on.
Case management and complaints	This module enables frontline units to collect and process various types of events, requests, and related communication with beneficiaries as they submit complaints or problems associated with service delivery from the program. The MIS maintains an interactive case management database to manage individual beneficiary cases that require a follow-up or action by program. Issues presented by beneficiaries may concern payments, errors, service quality, family changes, questions, and even reports of fraud or misuse of program funds.

Source: Adapted from World Bank 2012.
Note: GMI = guaranteed minimum income; LRIS = last-resort income support; MIS = management information system.

thus allowing checks to be made and easy identification of complementary services. Examples of system-wide social assistance MISs are found in Armenia, Croatia, Romania, and Ukraine.

For most of the 1990s and 2000s, the LRIS programs in Eastern Europe and Central Asia relied mainly on paper-based MISs and, as chapter 2 indicates, achieved overall good program performance. However, countries and program administrators were more and more aware of the limitations of the paper-based MISs and began to move to electronic systems. By the mid-2000s, not all countries had electronic registries of beneficiaries at each administration level, and even fewer had systems integrating all program components or processes from registration to benefit award, cross-checks, payments, appeals, or compliance with conditions. In some countries, such as Albania, Bulgaria, the Kyrgyz Republic, and Romania, the information at local levels is stored on paper, particularly in rural areas. That information is usually sent to the next administrative level, where it is registered in electronic databases (except in Albania, where the information stays on paper). The complexity and structure of the registries vary from country to country, but countries are relatively uniform in using the data only to produce payrolls or basic reports. The information flows usually focus on two types of information: payments and caseloads. Furthermore, beneficiary registries are usually not integrated or linked with other databases (except in Armenia, Lithuania, and recently Romania), thus preventing performance of automatic cross-checks.

A number of factors have stimulated the move toward electronic MISs, including the falling cost of information and communication technology (ICT), the growing demand for accountability, and a greater realization of the benefits of an electronic MIS. A move to an electronic MIS has four advantages:

- *Reduces transaction costs to beneficiaries.* Electronic MISs can reduce the private costs of beneficiaries associated with eligibility determination or recertification. Documentation required for eligibility criteria poses a high time cost by the beneficiary in obtaining the certifications and complying with this requirement, compounded by the obligation by all family members to appear physically to certify and sign. These costs can be reduced if the program MIS is either a part of, or communicates with, other public databases that can supply some of this information already stored elsewhere and thus free applicants of the need to reproduce it.

- *Reduces transaction costs to government.* An electronic MIS can also improve the process of verification of information supplied by beneficiaries by reducing the cost and extending the scope of information cross-checks across different public databases. For example, the Ndihma Ekonomike (NE) program in Albania uses a complex system of cross-verification of information in paper-based systems, relying on exchanging letters with different agencies that hold information on formal incomes, assets, or family composition. This process works but is only partial, takes significant administrative resources, and has a significant response time. Cross-checking through manual verification sometimes takes more than the allowed 10 days, resulting in the beneficiary not receiving the benefit until the following month. Moving toward an electronic MIS would reduce the response time, increase the coverage of the cross-checking process to the whole caseload, and transform this effort from an ad hoc response to a routine process.

- *Facilitates planning, budgeting, oversight, monitoring, and evaluation.* Paper-and-pencil systems make production of statistics and reports and aggregation of information needed to constantly track program performance and identify trouble spots in a timely fashion difficult and time consuming.

- *Helps reduce the level of error and fraud in the program by reducing substantially the cost of detecting irregularities in eligibility status.* Evidence from the Organisation for Economic Co-operation and Development (OECD) shows that increased use of data matching allows social protection administrators to identify data mismatches across public databases, and to target scarce detection resources (for example, fraud investigators or social inspectors) on those cases with the highest probability of error or fraud. A cost/benefit analysis of the data-matching activity of the Department for Work and Pensions in the United Kingdom estimated that for every pound (£) invested in data matching, the automated system identifies £24 of irregularities (NAO 2008). This highlights the point that investment in ICT can be cost-effective in the longer run (NAO 2006). ICT is thus becoming an increasingly important enabler for improving governance not only by reducing the risks of EFC, but also by improving access to information and facilitating beneficiary feedback. Some of the countries in our sample—Armenia, Lithuania, and Romania—have already made significant steps in this direction.

Two country cases—Albania and Romania—illustrate the complex process of transitioning from a paper-and-pencil MIS to an electronic one and offer a number of lessons for other programs, agencies, or ministries that are embarking on this process.

Albania
After years of operating a paper-and-pencil MIS, Albania embarked on developing an electronic MIS in 2012, encompassing the two largest social assistance programs in the country: NE and disability allowances. The timing of this change coincides with a significant parametric and administrative reform of the NE program, aimed at improving its targeting accuracy and coverage (program design), as well as its business practices (program implementation). A key factor behind the decision to move to an electronic MIS was an increased awareness of such a system's benefits by the management team of the ministry. Under the old system, large amounts of information were collected at local levels, but only a fraction of this information—in summary form—was passed to the regional and national levels. This lack of complete information limited the capacity of the central level to use such information

to improve the program or to exercise oversight and control over the frontline units. The new system makes all this information accessible to all levels.

The MIS will be developed in modular fashion, starting with a few functions and then adding more modules, each contributing to program efficacy and efficiency, as well as to the transparency of a program. In the first phase, the MIS will support eligibility determination, recertification, payments, and basic reporting. In the second phase, the MIS will expand to cover budget preparation and execution, monitoring and evaluation, appeals and complaints, identification of suspicious cases that could be affected by error or fraud, and case management. Figure 6.1 illustrates the business functions of the MIS for the NE for each of the three stages.

Figure 6.1 Modular Approach in Developing an MIS for Ndihma Ekonomike, Albania

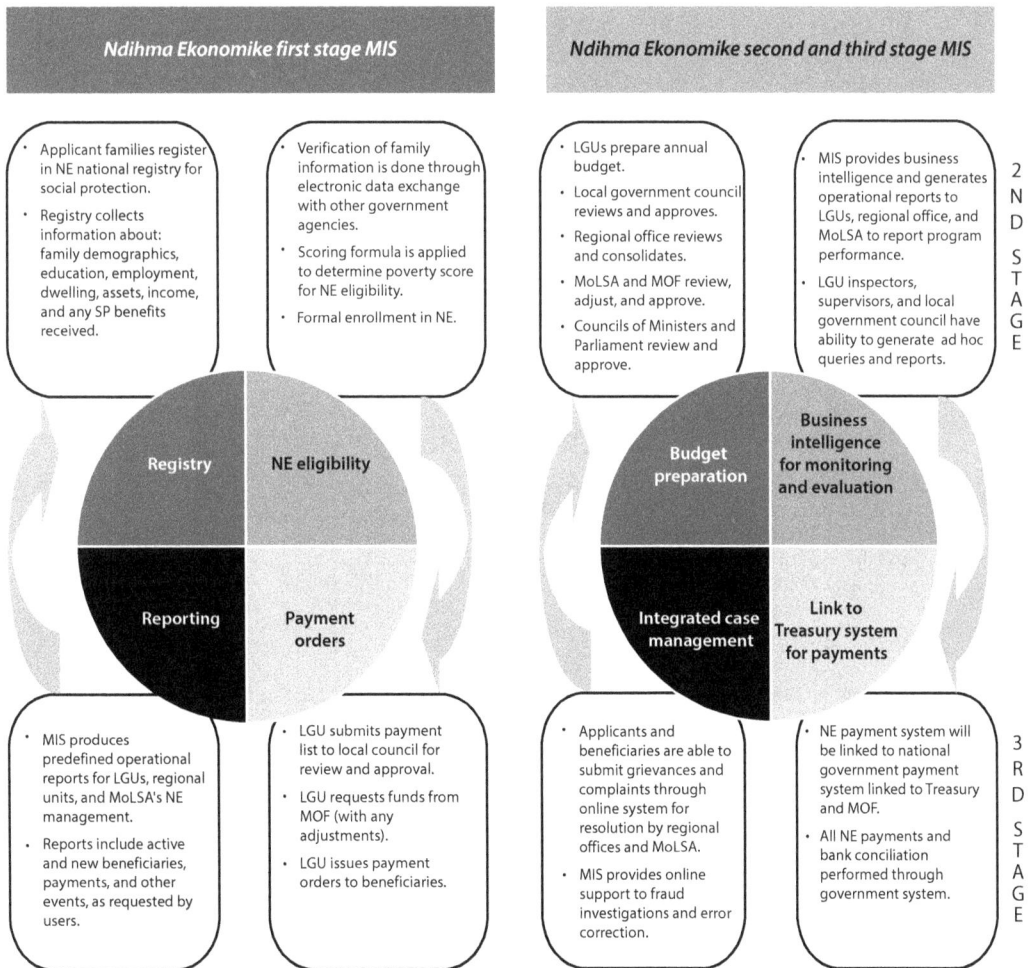

Source: Adapted from World Bank 2012.
Note: LGU = local government unit; MIS = management information system; MOF = Ministry of Finance; MoLSA = Ministry of Labor, Social Affairs, and Equal Opportunities; NE = Ndihma Ekonomike; SP = social protection.

Romania

In the case of Romania, an MIS was first developed to cover some of the largest (but not all) social assistance programs; only later did it incorporate the LRIS program (the GMI program). The Romanian MIS for social assistance programs, called SAFIR, was developed during 2007–08, piloted in two counties in early 2009, then rolled out nationally in the second part of 2009 (figure 6.2). Since mid-2009, SAFIR has operated with more than 500 users from all National Agency for Social Benefits and Inspection (NASBI) county-level offices (40 units in total). The key business functions of the initial MIS focused on eligibility, recertification, and payments. In terms of program coverage, the 2009–10 SAFIR covered six family support programs, consisting of different types of benefits for

Figure 6.2 An Integrated Social Assistance MIS, Romania, 2012

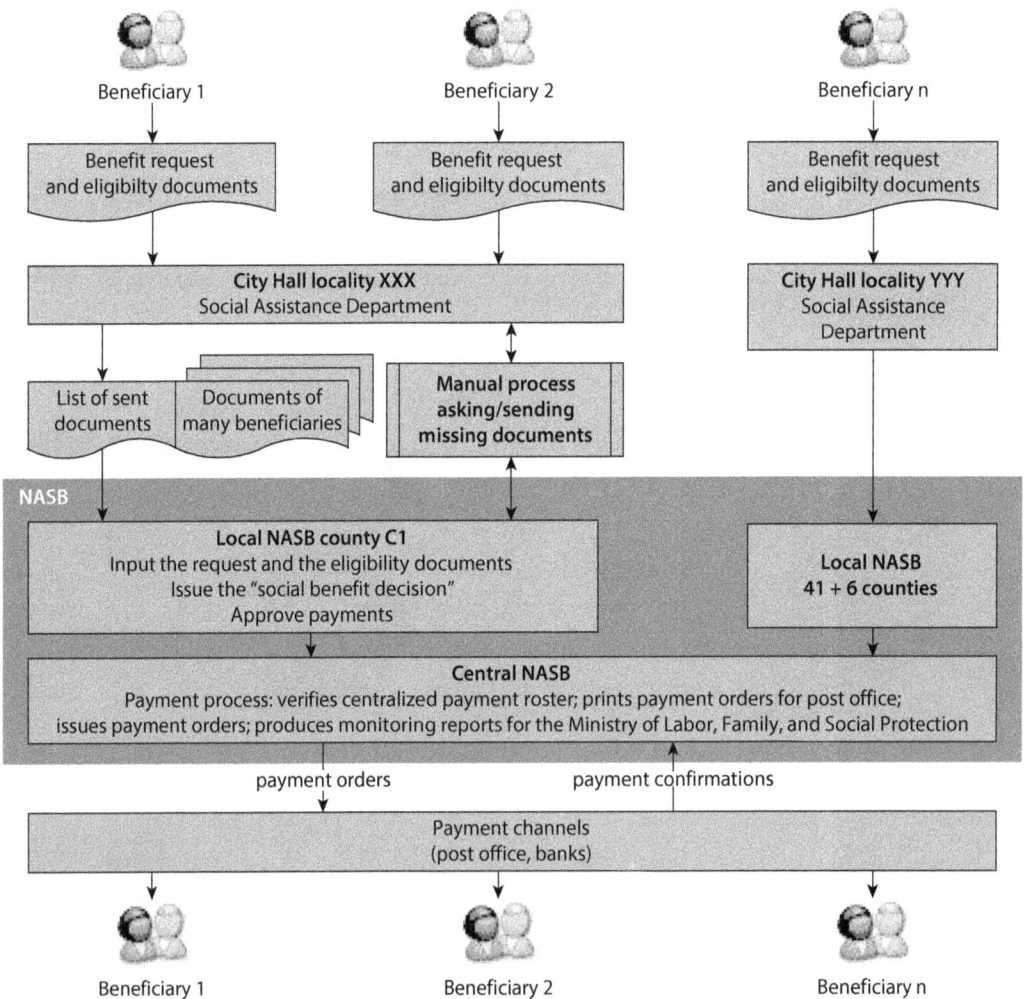

Source: Based on Chiricescu 2013.
Note: NASB = National Agency for Social Benefits.

children and child care (the largest in terms of number of beneficiaries and spending), but left out three significant programs (heating benefits, GMI, and disability allowances). In terms of geographical coverage, the MIS covered the central agency plus 40 regional branches (based on administrative jurisdictions called *judeţe*), but did not include the frontline units (about 3,200 social assistance departments operated by local governments or city halls, which collect applications and information on eligibility). Applications for social assistance programs are made in the frontline units and physically shipped to the regional social benefit agencies a number of times per month. Each regional social benefit agency covers about 80 frontline units. Once in the MIS, beneficiaries are paid through a network of banks and the post office. In figure 6.2, the units served by the MIS are represented in the blue area (labeled NASB [National Agency for Social Benefits]).

During 2011–12, the Romanian MIS expanded in terms of both program coverage and business functions. In January 2011, SAFIR took over the claims and payment processing for the GMI program. The decision-maker module, covering reporting and monitoring, was expanded. And to support the work of the social inspectors who have started to verify compliance with program rules in five large social assistance programs, including the GMI, beneficiary records have been cross-checked with other databases (for example, wages, pensions, unemployment benefits, and agricultural subsidies) to detect potential errors or fraud. Finally, to ensure that the information collected by SAFIR is accurate—a staggering one terabyte of data as of 2012—the NASB is launching a data audit, during which a third-party firm will compare the information from paper-based applications with the information in SAFIR from a representative sample of files to identify the quality of the administrative data as well as the extent and the likely causes of data inaccuracies.

According to the Social Assistance Reform Strategy adopted in 2011, NASBI's MIS will gradually expand to include all large social assistance programs (such as disability allowances and heating benefits) by 2015. Plans exist to extend the outreach of the MIS to frontline providers; to add new business modules (to cover appeals and complaints, to support the work of the Social Inspection team through a stronger referral system, and to profile clients in terms of propensity to be associated with error or fraud); and to strengthen existing ones (for example, cross-checking beneficiary information with a growing number of other public databases and improving the reporting functions to become a full-fledged performance monitoring system). At the same time, plans exist to simplify the process of applications for social benefits, including the GMI, by reducing some of the information requests required from beneficiaries and instead using the information already stored in other public databases.

The development of the Albanian and Romanian MISs for social assistance programs offers a number of lessons. First, no MIS is ever "ready"; it is always a work in progress. After the initial development in 2009, the Romanian MIS had to be updated yearly, to accommodate changes in program parameters and to add new programs or new business modules. Similarly, the Albanian MIS was developed in steps, with few core modules developed in the first phase and other modules in a second phase. Second, using the MIS information and improving the quality and accuracy of that information follow each other in a virtuous circle. The demands for information from operational and policy-level management have expanded over time, and with them the database administrators have detected and corrected codes that were inadequate (that is, different coding for the same variable across regions) or aberrant values resulting from poor data entry or other causes. Finally, adequate technical support for maintenance and development is a prerequisite for efficient use of an MIS.

Reducing Error, Fraud, and Corruption in LRIS Programs

In most developed countries, the ministries or agencies that implement social protection programs devote significant resources to ensure that benefits reach the right beneficiary, in the right amount, and at the right time—in other words, to combat error, fraud, or corruption in the benefit system (see box 6.1). Such investments in institutions and mechanisms that prevent, detect, deter, and monitor the level of EFC tend to pay off. Without such investment, the system is vulnerable to abuse, public money is wasted, and the trust in the social protection administration diminishes.

In contrast, the reduction of the level of EFC in LRIS (or social assistance) programs is a relatively recent policy priority in some of the countries in Eastern Europe and Central Asia. The issue was relatively neglected throughout the 1990s and 2000s. During that period, most countries focused on developing their LRIS programs and improving their key parameters (eligibility criteria, recertification, links with social services, and introduction of behavioral conditionalities, especially work requirements for able-bodied beneficiaries). A few islands of excellence appeared only in the late 2000s, for example, in Albania and Romania, with the development of dedicated units to check program compliance, separate from the internal audit departments. At the time of writing, in 2013, this agenda spanned a larger cluster of countries (including Armenia, Croatia, Moldova, and Ukraine), but not all.

Across the Eastern European and Central Asian countries surveyed in this book, we observed two models of tackling EFC. Under the first model, the integrity of the benefit system is part of the internal audit department. As a general function, the audit department provides assurances about the system's integrity, including the capacity of each social assistance program to pay the right beneficiary, the right amount, at the right time. In terms of size, the audit departments are relatively small, with about 10–20 auditors. Armenia, Bulgaria, and the Kyrgyz Republic are examples of countries where the EFC agenda is one element of audit team responsibility. Under the second model, a specialized team checks program compliance and refers to the prosecutorial branch those cases raising suspicion of fraud or corruption. Albania, Croatia, Moldova, Romania, and Ukraine have such teams, labeled "social inspection." The size of these teams ranges from small (Croatia with about 10 social inspectors; Moldova with 30)

Box 6.1 International Experience in Reducing Error, Fraud, and Corruption

LRIS programs, irrespective of their main targeting mechanism (means or proxy means testing), have complex eligibility and recertification requirements that make them prone to EFC (see figure B6.1.1). By *fraud*, we mean the intentional violation of rules—that is, when someone deliberately makes a false statement or fails to provide truthful and complete information that affects eligibility status or benefit level. By *error*, we mean the unintentional violation of benefit rules. A distinction is made between *official error*, which is due to a staff mistake and results in payment of benefits to someone who is not entitled or in payment made at a wrong level, and *customer error*, which occurs when a customer inadvertently provides incorrect information. Similarly, *beneficiary* fraud should be distinguished from *corruption*, which commonly involves political manipulation (for example, registering potential beneficiaries for clientelism purposes to garner political support), bribery of staff to unlawfully obtain program benefits, and so on.

Figure B6.1.1 Definitions of EFC

Note: EFC = error, fraud, and corruption.

The risk of EFC is also high across the higher-income and middle-income countries where a reasonable measurement process is in place. OECD experience shows that within the social protection system, means-tested social protection programs had the highest fraud and error rates (5–10 percent), followed by unemployment benefit and disability pension programs (1–2 percent; NAO 2006). Old-age pensions had the lowest rates (0.1–1.0 percent). For example, in the United Kingdom in 2010, means-tested benefits had a combined under- and overpayment rate of about 5–7 percent, compared with less than 0.5 percent for old-age pensions or other simpler, categorically targeted programs.

box continues next page

Box 6.1 International Experience in Reducing Error, Fraud, and Corruption *(continued)*

Means-tested programs have high levels of error and fraud because some applicants underreport their income when eligibility is determined. Income underreporting is often associated with income sources that are poorly documented (informal incomes) and hard to verify. Moreover, many beneficiaries fail to report changes in circumstances (changes in income, assets, and family composition) that affect their eligibility or their level of benefit, or both. The generosity of the benefit and the income stream gives an incentive to an ineligible person to defraud the program. This opportunity is larger when the program does not request regular recertification or when sanctions are absent or not properly enforced.

The inherent complexity of LRIS programs also makes them prone to error. Errors occur because of excessive staff caseloads, inadequate support and training of case managers and team coaches, and breakdown or override of internal controls. An inadequate administrative system triggers error when there are failures of payment or information technology systems, problematic information management, and inadequate monitoring or reporting procedures. Finally, the complexity of benefits and rules confuses administrators and benefit claimants.

However, a higher relative rate of payment irregularities in LRIS programs is a rather small price to pay, compared to the fiscal savings that are gained when categorical programs are replaced by poverty-targeted ones. The introduction of poverty targeting in a categorically or geographically targeted program could reduce caseloads significantly, as illustrated in figure B6.1.2. The number of beneficiaries who do not comply with the program rules could be, overall, in the same order of magnitude; in relative terms, this means a substantially higher error and fraud rate for means- or proxy-means-tested programs. However, in absolute terms, the difference is significantly smaller compared to the fiscal savings that could be reaped through poverty targeting. In the landscape of social assistance programs in Eastern Europe and Central Asia, LRIS programs have a small budget because they target their benefits narrowly—to the poor.

Figure B6.1.2 Level and Share of Funds Lost to EFC, by Administrative Targeting Method Used

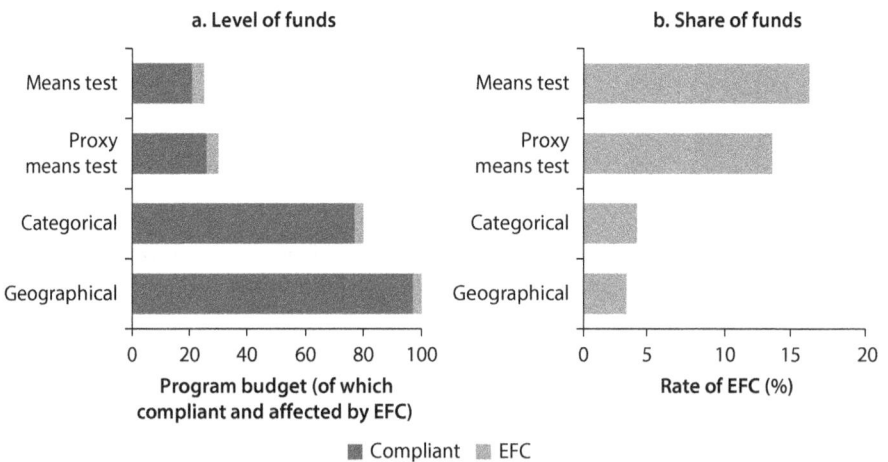

Note: Figure assumes constant level of EFC across type of programs. EFC = error, fraud, and corruption.

box continues next page

Box 6.1 International Experience in Reducing Error, Fraud, and Corruption *(continued)*

Another international lesson on combating EFC in social protection programs is that some level of EFC is unavoidable. No program is immune to error or even some degree of fraud or corruption, but having solid mechanisms to measure, prevent, detect, and deter EFC helps. The use of multiple instruments can strengthen the system. Adequate program control and the introduction of incentive-based systems (with appropriate rewards and penalties) are particularly important when implementation is decentralized. No ready-made solution exists, and programs are not isolated within a country and reflect the character of the government's overall governance agenda.

Nonetheless, evidence indicates that EFC can be reduced in programs that have invested in robust measurement and monitoring systems. In the U.S. food stamp program, the error rate was 8.4 percent (1999–2003), with a declining trend toward 4 percent recently, because of actions taken to improve program compliance at the state level and a system of performance-based incentives that penalize the states with the highest error rates and reward those with the lowest rates. In the United Kingdom, the overall fraud rate in the social protection system was halved from 2000 to 2010, after the implementation of a comprehensive EFC reduction strategy.

Source: van Stolk and Tesliuc 2010.
Note: EFC = error, fraud, and corruption; LRIS = last-resort income support; OECD = Organisation for Economic Co-operation and Development.

---

to moderate or large (Romania with about 300 social inspectors; Ukraine with about 2,000). The first model is internally focused: it typically checks a small sample of cases and proposes solutions (regulatory, organizational, or human resource measures) aimed at resolving the problems that have been detected. The second model is externally focused and proactive and could lead to a higher rate of irregularities detected and remedied. This second model is closer to international best practice (NAO 2006).

Evidence of the effectiveness of different approaches is scarce and, where it exists, relatively recent. Reviews of the EFC mechanisms in the Kyrgyz Republic, Romania, and Ukraine (van Stolk 2008a, 2008b; van Stolk and Fazekas 2010) offer a diverse regional picture. In the Kyrgyz Republic, the small size of the audit department and its broad terms of reference have not made EFC a key policy priority. The detection work is reactive, the auditors learning after the fact when EFC have occurred.[1] In Ukraine, despite the large number of social inspectors, the detection rate is very low. Institutional arrangements may be at fault; that is, social inspectors are part of the local offices and subordinated to the head of the local office, and they cannot effectively perform their control functions or decide on their work program.

Contrasting Romania's and Ukraine's experience in combating error and fraud in the social assistance system, including the LRIS program, could provide important lessons for the other countries in the region on how to build capacity in this area and what to avoid.

To protect the benefit system against fraud and error, the Ukrainian Ministry of Social Policy has put in place a complex and well-staffed system, aimed at preventing, detecting, deterring, and monitoring the level of overpayments. At the center of this system are the Internal Audit Department and the Social Inspection functions. The ministry and its territorial units used 1,515 social inspectors to check the validity and accuracy of benefit applications. About 60–70 percent of the workload of a social inspector relates to income-tested programs (including GMI and housing subsidies) and child grant and child allowance programs; the additional work is inspections for local programs. In terms of quantity, the volume of resources (staff) invested in detection in Ukraine compares favorably with, for example, that of the United Kingdom, another country that operates a large number of income-tested programs, and is about 13 times more generous than in Romania.[2]

The same risk factors that are present in all social protection systems affect the social assistance system in Ukraine. For example, Ukraine operates a number of complex social assistance programs that are inherently prone to EFC (such as the GMI, the means-tested family allowances, and the housing and utility subsidy). It also operates generous programs with high benefit levels, infrequent recertification requirements, and eligibility circumstances (for example, for disability allowances) that are difficult for social assistance staff to verify. In addition, some overly generous programs such as birth grants can trigger identity theft by beneficiaries or program staff, or both.

However, the institutions and mechanisms that should protect the benefit system against EFC are rather weak. On paper, Ukraine has a large number of social inspectors working in the local welfare offices. However, the social inspectors' EFC detection rate is one of the lowest in the region: the overall rate of social inspections is high, but the results in terms of detections are low. Social inspectors have a prevention function (ex ante control) that operates through home visits. In 2007, they visited about 22.3 percent of the caseload. The rate of denial of applicants based on home visits was about 15.8 percent of cases inspected (about 3.5 percent of total benefit applicants). Social inspectors also have a detection function (ex post control). They check about 42.5 percent of the current caseload for the accuracy of the information on income and assets (through a combination of requests for information and home visits). The number of subsequent detections through random checks is much lower, between 1.2 and 2.3 percent of total inspections, or 0.3–0.5 of total benefit claimants (see figure 6.3).

In contrast, most OECD countries would see a 20–30 percent rate in detecting overpayments in their second-stage inspections (in-depth verification of eligibility circumstances that goes beyond simple checks of documentary evidence) as an effective use of resources. This rate is achieved by the following:

• Profiling clients at the outset of the benefit claim and targeting those most at risk of receiving benefits for which they are not eligible
• Gaining better intelligence through tip-offs from the public and more systematic data matching
• Providing professional training and managing the caseload of investigators

Figure 6.3 Negative Correlation of Rate of Error Detection via Social Inspections to the Share of Applications Checked, Ukraine

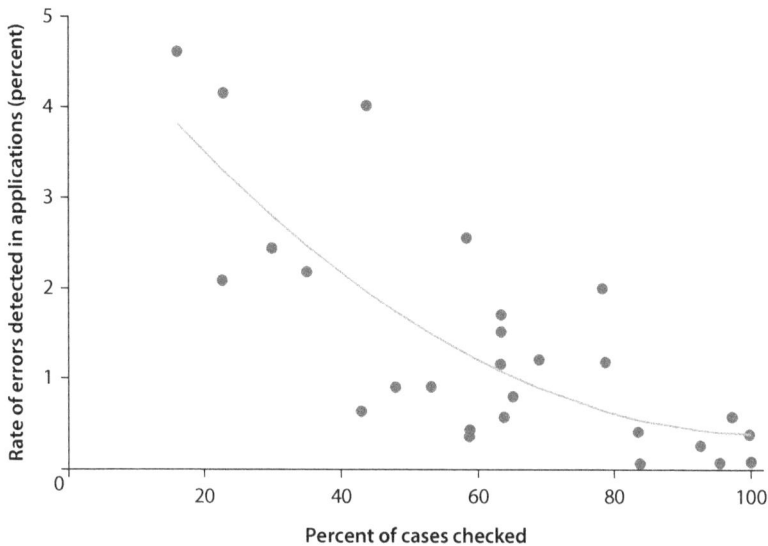

Source: Tesliuc, Leite, and Petrina 2009.
Note: The data points represent the 27 *oblasts* (administrative divisions) of Ukraine.

- Making the functions of fraud investigators more narrowly targeted on specific inspection tasks (mostly second-stage inspections)
- Setting performance targets, such as number of overpayments identified per *oblast* (administrative division) or number of inspections carried out per oblast

Thus, in Ukraine the inspection regime is comprehensive, but fraud and error are detected in only a small portion of the inspections. The system of social inspections seems to be geared to verifying as many applications as possible rather than taking a more risk-based approach to inspections. This strategy does not seem to work. Across the 27 oblasts of Ukraine, the error detection rate was negatively correlated to the percentage of cases being checked (figure 6.3). Possibly, the target for the share of applications checked should be lowered (to 10–30 percent, as is the norm in some OECD countries), and staff should have more time for thorough reviews for each case. This negative correlation raises the question of effectiveness and whether the inspections are appropriately targeted. Rather than inspections being comprehensive, intelligence gathering should be comprehensive and used to inform where inspections should take place.

A number of reasons exist for the low effectiveness of the social inspection work in Ukraine. First, there are institutional issues. The social inspectors are subordinated locally, and their job description and mandate are managed by the local director of the local welfare offices. This institutional arrangement is very problematic; asking a staff member subordinated to the local director to check other staff members (and implicitly, the management capacity of the head of the local welfare offices) inevitably creates tensions within the unit and between the local welfare office and the Ministry of Social Policy (the financier of the transfers). Under such an institutional setup, the social inspector is often asked to perform tasks other than those of verification of claims or ex post verification of beneficiaries. Second, the social inspectors have a poorly defined job description. Their actual work combines inspection tasks (for example, performing home visits or ad hoc inspections) and social work tasks (for example, solving appeals and complaints and doubling as a social worker at times). Third, the social inspection team is poorly managed under the current institutional setup. The inspectors do more social work than inspection work; their job is focused on a few social assistance programs and only a few benefit-processing tasks within each program. They lack an end-to-end approach to fighting EFC.

Thus, Ukraine is likely losing significant amounts of money because of ineffective institutions and mechanisms to combat EFC in the benefit system. The capacity of the system to prevent or detect fraud is low, and the penalty for error and fraud is also low. Thus, the cost of defrauding the system is rather small (low probability of detection and weak recovery and sanction policy), whereas the benefits are a plus and, for some programs, very high. An illustrative example highlights why improving the capacity of the social protection system to reduce EFC is important for Ukraine. The overall spending for social assistance is about 3 percent of gross domestic product (GDP). Taking a rather conservative EFC rate of 5 percent of the benefit stream places the total cost of EFC in social assistance programs at about 0.2 percent of GDP, more than Ukraine is currently spending on the whole GMI program.

Romania offers an interesting contrast with a much smaller social inspection team that has generated significant savings across the social assistance programs by using a strategic approach to develop the mechanisms and institutions to combat EFC. The effectiveness of the social inspection work was significantly boosted by the availability of a strong MIS (as discussed previously).

The reduction of EFC in social assistance programs became a clear priority in Romania by 2010. One key factor that brought the need to reduce EFC to the forefront of the social assistance agenda was the need to contain social assistance spending during the global crisis (which hit Romania in 2009), after a period of steep increase in social assistance spending during the golden growth decade (1998–2008). From 2005 to 2010, the relative cost of social assistance spending doubled, from 1.5 percent of GDP to 3.0 percent of GDP, without a proportional reduction in poverty or improvement in human development outcomes. This increase was underpinned by an increase in the generosity of existing programs and an expansion in the number of programs, without a corresponding increase in the number of staff members at the front lines or their training or an improvement in the administrative support services. The policy emphasized processing an increasing number of payments rather than safeguarding the benefit system. All these factors could have contributed to deterioration in program compliance and an increase in the rate of irregularities in social assistance programs. Moreover, the basic institutional arrangements put the social assistance system at risk of high EFC. Local governments were responsible for determining eligibility, while the central government financed these entitlements, generating a typical principal-agent problem of differing objectives. The central administration made few systematic efforts to monitor or control the compliance of the local governments. In this environment, the social assistance benefits were a cash injection to the local economy with zero costs for the local governments' budget in the absence of adequate controls and sanctions. Compliance could have deteriorated, and a widespread perception existed that this was the case.

Romania created a special body to check program compliance in social services and cash benefits in 2007, the Social Inspection, based on a French model. This new body has a dedicated staff of about 300 persons, selected from experienced benefit claim staff who also received special training. Their main focus was to review whether social service providers met service standards. During 2008–09, the Social Inspection ventured only once into the field of social assistance benefits to carry out an inspection of the GMI in 2008.

By 2010, the Romanian government took a strategic approach to curb EFC in the social assistance system:

- It changed the priority of the Social Inspection work from social services to cash transfers (the latter amounting to about 90 percent of the total spending).
- Within the social assistance programs, it focused the investigative effort on five high-risk social assistance programs,[3] including the GMI program. These programs amounted to more than half the social assistance spending.
- The Social Inspection team was asked to review compliance with regulations in all local government units and, often, for all active beneficiaries.

The inspections carried out during 2010–11 were large-sample compliance reviews. In the case of the GMI, 100 percent of the beneficiary files were reviewed through documentary checks and, if EFC was suspected, were followed up by home visits, employer interviews, and other in-depth investigations. For a review of the 195,000 GMI beneficiary files, the inspection lasted about three months. When irregularities were detected, in about 8.5 percent of the cases, the inspectors indicated remedial measures and sanctions; the implementation of these recommendations was followed up in two to three months. Similar with findings elsewhere, the irregularities found in the GMI inspection were due to the underreporting of income or assets by beneficiaries or the differences in the amount of the assistance units in cases where more than one family shares a dwelling. The inspectors had a difficult time reviewing compliance with program requirements for community work, registration with the public employment office, and compliance with payment of taxes and fees. All these require coordination and dialogue with the employment office and tax authority.

The inspection of the GMI program in Romania in 2010–11 produced a number of positive results. Through suspension or elimination of the beneficiaries who did not supply required documentary evidence or who underreported their welfare status, the inspection generated fiscal savings and improved targeting performance, which lasted well beyond the life of the inspection (see figure 6.4). Based on household budget survey analysis, figure 6.4 illustrates the share of GMI beneficiaries in each (national) per capita income quintile. According to program rules, compliant households should belong to the poorest quintile. The inspection occurred in the third quarter of 2010, which marked a low point in terms of targeting accuracy. After the inspection (including here the period of follow-up in the fourth quarter of 2010), a larger share of (remaining) program beneficiaries are among the poorest 20 percent of the population. Possibly because of the deterrence effect of the social inspection, targeting accuracy improved again in the first quarter of 2011.

Surprisingly, the inspections found that the level of irregularities in the GMI program was low compared to the other means-tested or risk-prone programs (see table 6.2). The relatively low rate of irregularities in the GMI program could in part be due to some design features that help prevent EFC from entering in the program (the presence of self-targeting elements, such as work requirements for able-bodied beneficiaries and mandatory registration with the public employment office, and the frequent recertification period) or at least discourage it (such as the implementation of an earlier thematic inspection). In contrast, the other programs offered higher benefit levels (especially the child-raising benefit and the disability allowance) for a longer period of time (without or with less frequent recertification), thus affording a higher benefit for defrauding the system. For two other programs, the institutional arrangements were poorly designed and facilitated EFC. Both the disability allowance and the

Figure 6.4 Improvement in Targeting Accuracy after Inspection of GMI Program, Romania

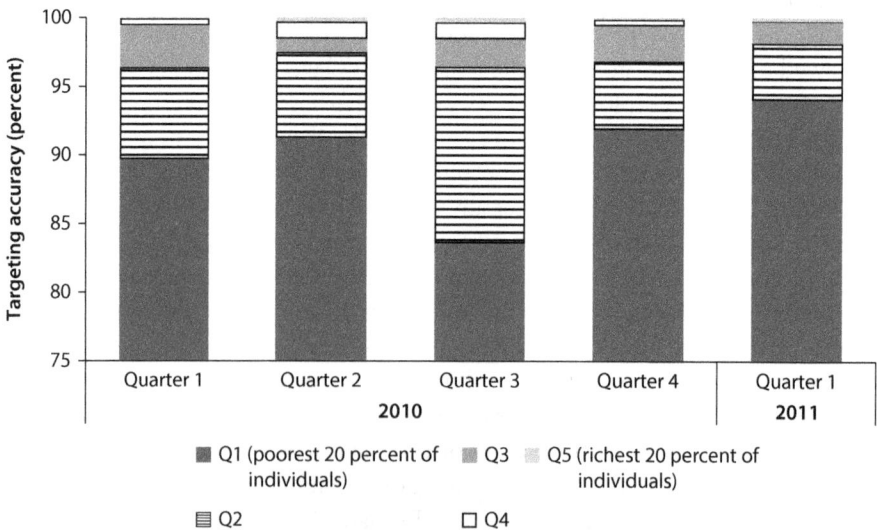

Source: Ministry of Labor, Family, and Social Protection, Romania 2012.
Note: GMI = guaranteed minimum income; Q = quintile.

Table 6.2 Results of Thematic Inspections, Romania, 2010–11

Program	Files checked (number and % of total)	In-depth investigations (%)	Irregularities detected (%)
GMI[a]	195,090 (100)	—	8.7
Heating benefits[a]	417,520 (30)	—	17.6
Family benefits[a]	10,855 (small)	100	35.9
Child-raising benefits[b]	184,180 (100)	0.1 (home visit, employer visit)	10.0
Disability allowance[b]	241,000 (30)	21	Hard to interpret

Source: Ministry of Labor, Family, and Social Protection, Romania 2012.
Note: GMI = guaranteed minimum income; — = not available.
a. Means-tested programs.
b. Categorical, income-replacement programs.

heating benefit program were implemented in a decentralized fashion and were not managed transparently through the MIS (which performs a number of eligibility checks for the programs it covers). In addition, the lack of program inspections in the past created the perception that the cost of defrauding the system is low. Overall, the inspections confirmed the findings of a series of targeting assessments of the GMI program that indicated the large majority of the GMI beneficiaries were honest. The inspection results also offered indirect proof that the complex eligibility requirements and combination of targeting methods do help in selecting the poorest beneficiaries from the population.

The census-like inspection provided a baseline figure on the level of irregularity in the GMI program and helped the Social Inspection develop a risk profile of the beneficiary pool and the frontline units. Annual reviews of the GMI program began in 2012 and will continue, but on a sample basis and using the risk profile (a larger proportion of beneficiaries will be inspected in the high-risk groups compared with the rest). At the end of each inspection, the team summarizes the legal and regulatory aspects that are difficult to comply with or check and makes recommendations to improve the program's regulatory framework. At the time of writing, these recommendations included implementing a more effective and equitable sanction and recovery policy; improving the investigative powers of the social inspectors (including measures aimed at protecting the privacy of beneficiaries); relying more strongly on referrals coming from cross-checking the information on beneficiaries with similar information held in other public databases; and developing risk profiles based on analytic models.

A number of lessons can be derived from OECD and Eastern Europe and Central Asia experiences. To be successful, countries should put in place a strategic approach to reduce EFC in the LRIS program and all other risk-prone social protection programs. This approach includes providing adequate resources for compliance checks (social inspection); carrying out inspections across all high-risk social assistance programs, including LRIS; reducing the marginal cost of detection of irregularities by investing in data matching (cross-checking applicant information with similar information available in other public databases); and improving the cost-efficiency of the EFC detection process by developing analytically based risk profiles.

The need for a strategic approach is further illustrated by the contrasting experiences of the Romania and Ukraine social inspections. Having one resource in abundance is not sufficient to guarantee good results, if the other elements of the system to prevent, detect, and discourage EFC are not in place. In Ukraine, the ratio of inspectors to caseload was 13 times higher than in Romania, but the detection results were very low. The high level of staff members working as social inspectors did not compensate for institutional failures (placing the staff members under the authority of the local welfare offices); for the lack of adequate training, investigative powers, and appropriate sanction policy; or for not having the support of an MIS.

Transparency and Redress of Grievances

Transparency and redress of grievances allow households to bring errors or perceived errors to the attention of an official and have them corrected or explained. Mechanisms to handle appeals and grievances have three goals: (a) to resolve concerns according to program rules; (b) to do so at a low cost to both the clients and the program; and (c) to be and be perceived as accessible, simple, transparent, fair, and prompt.

On paper, all the LRIS programs reviewed incorporate strong transparency provisions. Applicants should be informed in writing of the outcome of the means test and their eligibility status. They should also be informed of the amount of benefit they are entitled to receive or be notified of the reasons for rejection together with information on the appeal process. In Lithuania, Romania, and the Kyrgyz Republic, applicants must be given notice in writing or by phone about benefit award or rejection. In Lithuania, the applicants are expected to be informed of the outcome within one month and to receive a notification indicating the reason for rejection and information on the appeals procedure.

However, the regulations regarding notification of beneficiaries are not enforced in all countries. In Romania, according to 2003 GMI beneficiary survey data, about 13 percent of those rejected were not aware of the reasons for rejection. Many beneficiaries (43 percent in rural and 25 percent in urban areas) did not even know the benefit amount they were entitled to receive. In most cases (72 percent in rural and 51 percent in urban areas), the municipality's decision was not given to the applicants in writing, and even if they did receive a written notification, the amount to which they were entitled was not always specified. With respect to information on the manner in which the amount was calculated (that is, transparency), only about half the written notifications (45 percent in urban and 57 percent in rural areas) contained this information.

Providing beneficiaries with little information regarding entry and exit criteria or entitlement levels seems to be common in many social assistance programs of Eastern Europe and Central Asia. This may be due to not only the lack of regular information campaigns or channels to obtain information on the rights and obligations of beneficiaries, but also the complexity of eligibility criteria. Although beneficiaries are supposed to receive a clear explanatory notice on the level of benefit or the reasons for suspension or eligibility termination, in practice this is not a systematic occurrence. Local governments, which in most cases implement the programs, may need more support from the national level in communicating eligibility requirements to potential beneficiaries, because administrative and financial capacity, as well as incentives, vary across municipalities.

With respect to appeal procedures, the programs' regulations are not always clear, and in most cases applicants are not aware or informed of where they should submit their complaints or what steps to take. As a result, appeals are submitted to a variety of offices. In Albania, for example, appeals are submitted to mayors or other local officials' offices, to the line ministry offices at the regional or central level, or to courts. Complaints can be entered through appointments or by letters. However, no statistics exist concerning appeals or number of complaints.[4]

Grievance redress mechanisms[5] are important for mitigating exclusion errors and for monitoring corruption (Basset et al. 2012). In most social assistance programs in Eastern Europe and Central Asia, the formal institutions and channels that capture and provide redress for beneficiary complaints or grievances related to beneficiary selection, service delivery, or other program functions are still underdeveloped. Most social assistance programs do not have clear procedures for grievance redress, and beneficiaries are not informed about the existing channels for filing appeals and grievances. Moreover, in many countries around the world, program-specific grievance redress mechanisms are increasingly being built into the MISs to allow improved tracking and monitoring of complaints received, as well as reporting by types of complaints and providing feedback to improve the functioning of the program (Silva Villalobos, Blanco, and Bassett 2010). A similar approach should be considered in Eastern Europe and Central Asia, as social assistance programs and systems develop their MISs.

Lessons Learned

For most LRIS programs in Eastern Europe and Central Asia, a number of critical areas of the governance agenda are in their infancy. A large number of LRIS programs do not yet have modern MISs, have not embarked on safeguarding the program from error or fraud, and have thus far underinvested in modern grievance mechanisms.

We acknowledge that many of the LRIS programs were well run even absent modern MISs or institutions that combat error and fraud. For almost two decades, many of these LRIS programs have scored high in terms of targeting accuracy compared with programs in other regions of the world and have succeeded in delivering on their basic function: to provide income support to their country's most destitute population.

During the 2010s, a few countries have moved decisively to modernize their LRIS programs, often as a process of modernizing their whole social assistance system. In social protection, most countries have modernized first their pension systems and then their labor market policy and unemployment systems, leaving social assistance and social services for later. Pensions and labor market were first-order priorities, given their implications for fiscal sustainability and growth agendas. Now it is time for the modernization of the social assistance systems, including LRIS programs. LRIS programs have a lot to offer to this agenda, because they have consistently been islands of excellence in a number of areas (for example, know-how on how to target and the use of process, targeting, and impact evaluations).

Given the inherent, unavoidable risk of EFC in LRIS programs because of their eligibility criteria, each country should develop at least a minimal capacity to reduce error and fraud. These efforts could generate savings beyond the resources required to strengthen the capacity of the line ministry in general, and its detection unit in particular, especially if they are spread over other social protection programs that also pose a clear risk of EFC. An EFC focus in the LRIS program, or across the broader set of social assistance or social protection programs, could improve both the targeting accuracy of LRIS programs and program compliance.

The 2010s offer an opportunity for the Eastern Europe and Central Asia region in terms of improving the governance of the LRIS and, more broadly, social assistance programs. Countries are at different levels of development on this agenda, but many are experimenting with moving toward modern MISs, improving and expanding their MISs, and putting in place institutions to reduce error and fraud or grievance mechanisms. Disseminating the successful examples or promising pilots could help other countries leapfrog to a modern and effective control and accountability system. The recently established community of practice on social assistance in the Eastern Europe and Central Asia region could facilitate this process.

Notes

1. One of the largest irregularities detected by the audit department was a case of payment fraud, in which a post office worker who was responsible for distributing benefits at the local level took the money and left for Kazakhstan.

2. The United Kingdom uses about 3,000 fraud investigators to check the claims of 12 million beneficiaries, of a population of 61.7 million (as of July 2007). The caseload–to–social inspector ratio is about 4,000 to 1. In Ukraine, the social protection system serves about 30 million beneficiaries, of a total population of 46.3 million (as of July 2007). The caseload–to–social inspector ratio is about 2,000 to 1. In Romania, about 300 social inspectors serve about 8 million beneficiaries (households and single persons), of a population of about 19 million. The caseload–to–social inspector ratio is about 27,000 to 1.

3. The five programs considered at higher risk of EFC were three means-tested programs (GMI, heating benefits, and family benefits), the child-raising benefit (an income-replacement program that paid 85 percent of the previous wage for stay-at-home parents during the first two years of their child's life), and the disability allowance program.

4. See the Albania case study earlier in this chapter.

5. These are also known as complaint-handling mechanisms.

References

Bassett, L., S. Gianozzi, L. Pop, and D. Ringold. 2012. "Rules, Roles, and Controls: Governance in Social Protection with an Application to Social Assistance." Social Protection and Labor Discussion Paper 1206, World Bank, Washington, DC.

Chiricescu, S. 2013. "The Management Information System of the Agency for Social Benefits and Inspections: Past, Present and Future." Unpublished paper, World Bank, Washington, DC.

Ministry of Labor, Family, and Social Protection, Romania. 2012. "Reducing EFC in Social Assistance in Romania." Presentation of the Minister of Labor, Family and Social Protection, Romania, Washington, DC, March.

NAO (National Audit Office, United Kingdom). 2006. *International Benchmark of Fraud and Error in Social Security Systems*. Value for Money Report, London.

———. 2008. *Department for Work and Pensions: Progress in Tackling Benefit Fraud*. Value for Money Report, London.

Silva Villalobos, V., G. Blanco, and L. Bassett. 2010. "Management Information Systems for Conditional Cash Transfers and Social Protection Systems in Latin America: A Tool for Improved Program Management and Evidence-Based Decision-Making." Social Protection Unit, Human Development Department, Latin America and the Caribbean Region, World Bank, Washington, DC.

Tesliuc, E., P. Leite, and K. Petrina. 2009. "Improving Targeting of Social Assistance Programs in the Ukraine." Unpublished report, World Bank, Washington, DC.

van Stolk, C. 2008a. *Tackling Benefit Fraud and Error in the Kyrgyz Republic*. Unpublished report, World Bank, Washington, DC.

———. 2008b. *Tackling Benefit Fraud and Error in the Ukraine*. Unpublished report, World Bank, Washington, DC.

van Stolk, C., and M. Fazekas. 2010. *Tackling Error, Fraud and Corruption in Romanian Cash Benefits*. Unpublished report, Washington, DC.

van Stolk, C., and E. Tesliuc. 2010. "Toolkit on Tackling Error, Fraud and Corruption in Social Protection Programs." Social Protection Discussion Paper 1002, World Bank, Washington, DC.

World Bank. 2012. *Project Appraisal Document on a Proposed Loan in the Amount of Euro 38 Million (US$50 Million Equivalent) to Albania for the Social Assistance Modernization Project*. Report 66666-AL, Europe and Central Asia Region, Washington, DC.

CHAPTER 7

Administrative Costs

As we have seen throughout this study, last-resort income support (LRIS) is a complex program to implement, demanding adequate administrative structures. Two of the issues that surround all narrowly targeted programs, but are perhaps especially relevant to minimum income guarantee programs, are how much the program costs to administer and whether the expenditures on administration yield good value. This chapter illustrates how to measure such costs and spells out the potential uses of the cost information for program policy makers and program managers. We hope the information contributes to a more widespread adoption of cost monitoring for LRIS and other social assistance programs in the Eastern Europe and Central Asia region.

Few countries and program administrations in Eastern Europe and Central Asia routinely measure, track, and analyze administrative costs of their LRIS and other social assistance programs. In contrast, such information is routinely available in most developed countries and occasionally can be obtained in regions where there is a stronger emphasis on program evaluation, such as Latin America and the Caribbean (Caldes, Coady, and Maluccio 2006; Lindert et al. 2007) and Sub-Saharan Africa (Hodges, White, and Greenslade 2011).

The scarcity of data on administrative costs of LRIS programs is due to a number of factors. First, the measurement process is quite complex, because the service delivery chain comprises different levels of government (central, regional, and local) and each unit operates more than a single program. Moreover, budgeting of administrative costs is not done by program but by administrative unit, and the overall program administration has no unique source of financing—in particular when program administration is decentralized. Second, insufficient knowledge of the methodology exists to quantify the administrative costs at the program level. Third, there is limited understanding of the usefulness of administrative cost information for monitoring and evaluating the program.

Measuring Administrative Costs

The administrative costs of an LRIS program include all expenditures on the resources required to run the program; in our case studies, the resources are the costs incurred to select and pay the beneficiaries of the program. They include direct, variable costs whose magnitude depends on the number of beneficiaries in the program. Here we include the costs incurred to select beneficiaries from the pool of applicants, make payments to beneficiaries, recertify them, or verify whether they have complied with coresponsibilities (for example, whether beneficiaries who are able to work are actively looking for work). They also include direct, fixed costs, such as the costs of designing and planning the program, informing potential beneficiaries about the availability of the program, providing oversight and controls, and implementing monitoring and evaluation. And, in the case of programs that are administered jointly at local and regional levels, they also include overhead costs.

Administrative costs are only a part of the total cost of designing and implementing an LRIS program. Other elements of costs include private costs, as well as social or incentive costs (see Grosh et al. 2008). Private costs are the monetary and time costs incurred by beneficiaries in accessing LRIS benefits. These costs are incurred when applying, complying with coresponsibilities, recertifying, and cashing in the benefits. Social costs are associated with the stigma of participating in a program for low-income households or the eventual social tension that may arise in the communities where the program is in place. Incentive costs occur when the program diminishes the work effort and hence the earnings of beneficiaries, when it encourages dependency, and when it displaces other sources of household income such as remittances. Among these costs, the information on administrative costs is more frequent, not least because measurement of administrative costs is simpler. In the rare cases where all elements of the costs of the LRIS programs are available, administrative costs are found to be an important element of total costs. Thus, measuring, analyzing, and tracking the administrative costs are important functions for any LRIS or, more broadly, any social assistance program.

To generate information on the level of administrative costs and its structure, this report draws from a series of background studies that have produced snapshot estimates of the administrative costs of a subset of mature, relatively well-targeted LRIS programs. Measuring the administrative costs of these programs was not always straightforward, and attempting to break down the costs by program functions was even more challenging. It required detailed budget data and often imputations, assumptions, or special data collection exercises to decide how to allocate the costs of systems and staff members who work on more than one function or program.

The approach used to obtain more accurate estimates of the administrative costs for this study relied on multiple sources of information. The main data source consisted of a survey implemented at each level of program administration. The samples were not representative in all countries, and ex post corrections could not be done in the case of opportunity samples (for example, Bulgaria and the Kyrgyz Republic). The data collection method consisted of a mix of self-administered questionnaires and phone interviews—meaning that in most cases, respondents completed questionnaires with help from program staff members over the phone. This method was complemented by face-to-face interviews and administrative data collection, in particular at regional and central levels. Table 7.1 summarizes the data collection methods and instruments by country.

Table 7.1 Data Collection Instruments, by Country

Country	Data collection instrument
Albania	• Questionnaires in 28 municipal and communal Ndihma Ekonomike (NE) offices were selected out of the total 385 NE offices (the selection was stratified by region and locality). • Questionnaires were used in 4 regional State Social Service (SSS) administration offices (of 12 offices at national level). • One questionnaire was used in the SSS central administration. • Structured interviews were used in the tax offices and labor offices in two regions. • Structured interviews were used in the Ministry of Labor and Social Affairs and the Ministry of Finance.
Armenia	• Questionnaires were used in 26 regional social services agencies (RSSAs): 12 from Yerevan and 14 from other *marzer* (regional governments); at least one RSSA per *marz* (regional government); two RSSAs per marz were surveyed in *marzer* with high caseloads. • Questionnaires were used in the health and social departments of all 10 *marzer* and the Yerevan municipality. • One questionnaire was used in the line ministry. • Administrative data collection was used from the line ministry and payment agencies.
Bulgaria	• Questionnaires were used in 3 regional social assistance directorates (RSADs) and their 12 subordinated local social assistance directorates (SADs) (most SADs provide services in more than one municipality). The survey covered about 8 percent of the SADs and 11 percent of the RSADs. • One questionnaire was used in the central Social Assistance Agency. • Interviews and administrative data collection were used in the line ministry.
Kyrgyz Republic	• Questionnaires were used in seven *oblasts* (administrative divisions), seven *rayons* (lowest administrative divisions), and seven towns and *aiyl okmotus* (local governments). The selected *rayons* were those located in the *oblast* center. Each *rayon* selected an *aiyl okmotu* with more reliable telephone and fax communication. • Questionnaire interviews were used in all six payment centers. • Interviews and administrative data collection were used in the line ministry.
Lithuania	• Questionnaires were used in all 60 municipalities. The response rate was 65 percent (that is, information was received from 39 municipalities). • Interviews and administrative data collection were used in the line ministry.
Romania	• Questionnaires were used in 80 local governments from 26 counties (of 42). The response rate was 85 percent (that is, 68 questionnaires were returned with complete information). The sample was stratified by region, locality type, and number of guaranteed minimum income applications. • Questionnaires were used in the 42 deconcentrated directorates of the Ministry of Labor, Family, and Social Protection (County Directorates of Dialogue, Social Solidarity, and Family), and 40 completed questionnaires were returned. • One questionnaire was applied in the line ministry.

The questionnaires collected two types of information: (a) expenditures such as gross wages by categories of staff; operational costs, including travel, office supplies, equipment maintenance; and so on; and (b) time allocation tables structured by social assistance programs and by activities grouped into functions. The data on operational costs were also collected according to activities and functions, where appropriate.

Six large categories of activities and functions were identified for the purposes of this study: (a) program design, planning, and coordination; (b) eligibility determination and recertification activities; (c) information to clients, public relations, and appeals; (d) payment of benefits; (e) maintenance of beneficiary databases; and (f) audits, monitoring, and evaluation. Identification of those functions was done through literature review, analysis of program design and regulations, interviews with program administrators, and feedback from pilot surveys in each country. Despite best efforts, countries could not always be fully compared with each other by the activities included under each function. The country research teams had to make choices in the field based on interviews with officials, and thus, in some cases, a few activities slipped from one category to another. The tables summarizing the activities of each category by level of administration are presented in annex 7A for four countries: Albania, Armenia, the Kyrgyz Republic, and Romania.

The administrative costs by activity were calculated as a sum of three components. The first was spending on operational costs that could be assigned to activities (for example, travel for home visits; fees for payments, travel, and per diem in the case of audits and monitoring by social inspectors; and printing of applications for determining eligibility). The second component was staff cost, calculated by multiplying the staff's gross wages (and employers' social contributions) by the share of time devoted to that activity in a year as obtained from the time allocation tables (that is, the time allocated for that activity as a share of the total working time of all employees involved in program implementation). The final component was expenditures on unassigned operation costs (for example, office supplies and utilities), which were allocated to activities by multiplying the total unassigned operation costs by the share of time allocated to that activity from the time allocation table.

Once the total administrative cost of an LRIS program is computed, the information must be presented in a set of indicators to ensure comparability across different programs and countries, or even across different subdivisions within the same program. In the operational literature, the most frequent indicators used to characterize the level of administrative costs and to track them include the cost-transfer ratio (CTR) and the average cost per beneficiary per period (for example, month). The CTR measures the cost of making a one-unit transfer to a beneficiary. It is measured as an index and represents the share of administrative costs in total program budget (administrative costs plus cash transfers). With some caveats (see next paragraph), this indicator could be useful in international benchmarking. To track the level of administrative costs across programs in the same country or for the same program over time, one can use the average costs per beneficiary per period. For international comparison, one can express this indicator in an international currency, using current exchange rates or adjusting for purchasing power parity.

Interpreting and comparing administrative costs and, in particular, targeting costs across countries can be problematic. The simplest way to look at administrative costs and their efficiency is by computing the share of administrative costs in total program expenditures, or the CTR, that is the cost of making a one-unit transfer to a beneficiary. However, many features of a program influence this measure,[1] including the maturity and coverage of the program; the size and type (cash or in kind) of the transfer; and other design elements such as the targeting method, frequency of recertification, the type of payments system, and so on. A program with more generous benefits will have—other things being equal—a lower share of administrative costs than a similar program with smaller transfer amounts per beneficiary.

Likewise, a pilot or start-up program will have a higher CTR than a mature program because of the fixed costs (for example, large up-front expenditures for systems such as purchase of equipment, design of systems, and definitions of procedures), which are high in the first stages of implementation but not strictly proportionate to program size. Finally, administrative costs do not depend only on the actual size or coverage of a program, but also on the number of applicants, or take-up rate, which actually determines the administrative effort devoted to interviews, verification of beneficiaries' self-reported incomes, cross-checks, and so on.[2]

Administrative Costs of Eastern Europe and Central Asia LRIS Programs

The share of administrative costs in the total budget of the program (CTR) for the LRIS programs covered in this study ranges from 2.2 percent (in Armenia, 2006) to 16.2 percent (in Bulgaria, 2007), with most programs clustering between 7.0 and 10.0 percent (table 7.2).

Table 7.2 Administrative Costs of LRIS

	Albania 2005	Armenia 2006	Bulgaria 2004[a]	Bulgaria 2007[a]	Kyrgyz Republic 2006	Lithuania 2005	Romania 2003[b]	Romania 2005
Total program cost (%)	100	100	100	100	100	100	100	100
Of which (%)								
Benefits	92.8	97.8	90.1	83.8	90.7	93.5	89.1	92.9
Total administrative cost	**7.2**	**2.2**	**9.9**	**16.2**	**9.3**	**6.5**	**9.9**	**7.1**
Cost-transfer ratio	0.078	0.023	0.109	0.193	0.103	0.069	0.109	0.077

Source: Based on World Bank administrative costs surveys.
Note: This table is based on a series of country surveys of administrative costs developed by the authors. LRIS = last-resort income support.
a. In Bulgaria, the survey was implemented using the same methodology in 2004 and 2007.
b. In Romania, a similar survey was implemented in 2003, but without taking into account the administrative costs at the central level. The cost-transfer ratio of 9.9 percent in 2003 is slightly underestimated.

The figures in table 7.2 are relatively difficult to interpret in the absence of additional information regarding program characteristics such as program size, maturity of the program, generosity of benefits, targeting mechanism, and so on. The high share of administrative costs in Bulgaria in 2007, for example, is explained by a significant drop in the number of beneficiaries (from 220,000 in 2004 to 130,000 in 2007), because of more restrictive eligibility criteria, simultaneously with a high demand for the program reflected by the high number of applications (350,000 in 2007). The drop in the number of beneficiaries has increased the share of fixed administrative costs in the CTR, while the high application rate has not reduced the variable costs as much. Similarly, the decrease in the share of administrative costs in Romania from 9.9 percent in 2003 to 7.1 percent in 2005 is probably explained by the maturity of the program—2003 was the second year of program implementation following a major reform (a new start with new rules, after the old program was phased out by 2001). Caldes, Coady, and Maluccio (2006) measured a similar downward trend for the CTR of Mexico's PROGRESA,[3] where the CTR declined from a high of 1.34 during the first year of program operation to 0.32, 0.09, and 0.05 in the second, third, and fourth year, respectively, of operation.

Armenia represents an outlier, with a very low share of administrative costs (2.2 percent in 2006). A few features of the Armenian program—Family Benefit Program (FBP)—might explain this low figure (see table 7.3). First, the FBP has higher coverage and generosity compared with most of the other programs, which implies a higher spending on benefits and consequently a lower share of administrative costs. Second, recertification is usually done less often (once a year) than in other programs, and home visits are not performed for all applicants. Also, the FBP employs fewer staff members than other programs with similar coverage. Compared to Albania, the number of staff members in the regional services centers is 10 percent lower. Compared to Romania,

Table 7.3 Targeting Performance Indicators for the LRIS Programs with Cost Assessments

Country and year	Total population of households	Total coverage of households (%)	Q1—Poorest quintile (individuals)[a]			
			Coverage (%)	Targeting— distribution of beneficiaries (%)	Targeting— distribution of benefits (%)	Generosity (%)
Albania, 2005	732,855	17.1	37.7	50.3	46.7	11.8
Armenia, 2006	813,678	15.9	42.3	55.7	56.8	32.6
Bulgaria, 2004[b]	2,895,315	7.6	14.1	77.7	83.0	43.5
Bulgaria, 2007	2,623,086	5.0	13.0	70.4	74.2	23.6
Kyrgyz Republic, 2006	1,317,121	7.7	25.2	38.5	46.9	9.4
Lithuania, 2005	1,355,452	6.2	9.5	67.6	64.4	20.4
Romania, 2005	7,365,336	5.3	20.7	81.6	83.1	30.5

Source: Based on World Bank analysis using the Household Budget Surveys of each country and year.
Note: LRIS = last-resort income support; Q = quintile.
a. Survey estimates.
b. Survey estimates of Q1 coverage, targeting, and generosity are from 2003.

which in 2005 had a ratio of approximately one staff member to 100 beneficiaries, on average, the corresponding figure for Armenia was about one staff
member to 200 beneficiaries.

Our estimates indicate that, excluding outliers, the share of the total administrative costs of LRIS programs in Eastern Europe and Central Asia ranges between
7 and 10 percent of the programs' total costs—which, given the targeting performance of the programs (table 7.3), seems to be reasonably low and to represent
efficient spending. The median value of the CTR ratio is around 9 percent.

How does the CTR for LRIS programs in Eastern Europe and Central Asia
compare with other programs in developing countries? Overall, quite well.
According to Grosh et al. (2008), the median CTR ratio for LRIS programs is
slightly higher than for conditional cash transfer and public works programs, but
significantly lower than for food and fee-waiver programs (see figure 7.1). For
international benchmarking, Grosh et al. (2008) observe that for mature, well-
targeted cash and near-cash programs, the CTR ratio clusters between 8 and
15 percent of program costs. A CTR lower than 8 percent could indicate underdeveloped administrative functions, though it may also imply significant economies of scale or an extremely generous program. CTRs in excess of 15 percent
could indicate a waste of administrative resources.

Our empirical assessment has shown that the share of resources used to
administer mature, well-performing LRIS programs is relatively low. This finding
contrasts with some of the expectations in the theoretical literature on targeting,

Figure 7.1 Share of Administrative Costs in Program Budget
Median value by type of program, selected programs

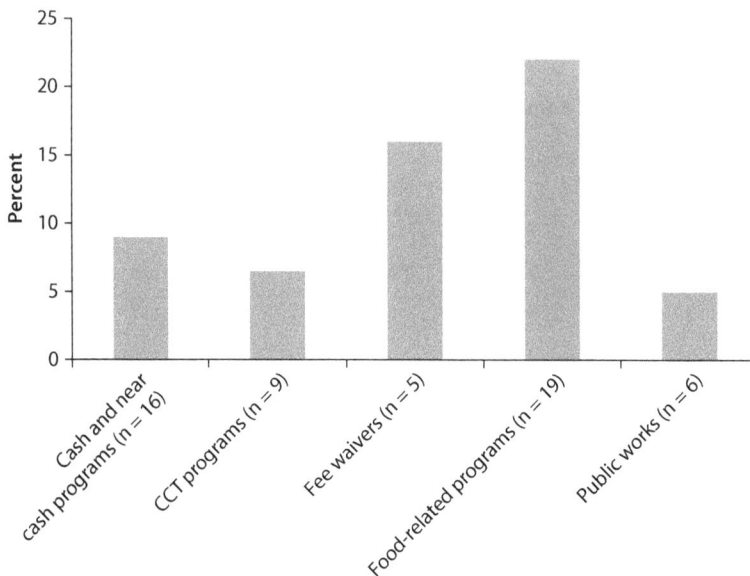

Source: Grosh et al. 2008.
Note: CCT = conditional cash transfer; n = number.

which anticipate such costs to be higher given the complex eligibility requirements associated with means testing. Our findings indicate that the countries in our sample have found a good balance between the investments in the administrative functions of the program and the program's targeting outcomes.

Structure of the Administrative Costs of LRIS Programs in Eastern Europe and Central Asia

Different institutional arrangements are reflected in the distribution of these costs by administrative level (see figure 7.2). Armenia tends to concentrate key functions such as eligibility determination and payment at the central level, and ministry-level costs account for the largest share of administrative costs. Countries with more decentralized settings, notably Albania, Lithuania, and Romania, incur the bulk of administrative costs in the frontline, local-level units.

The distribution of administrative costs by program function does not generate a common pattern (see table 7.4). However, in most cases, the cost of eligibility determination and recertification was the highest share in the total administrative cost of the programs. Exceptions from this rule were Armenia and the Kyrgyz Republic where this category of expenditure ranked second and third, respectively. In both Armenia and the Kyrgyz Republic, one of the highest costs was incurred by the payment of benefits, which in these countries, at the moment of the survey, was done exclusively through post offices. In the other countries, where the payment was made either in cash at the social assistance office (Albania and Romania) or through a mix of banks and post, the cost associated with the payment of benefits was significantly lower. In Lithuania, payments were also being done in kind, which probably explains the higher administrative cost.

Figure 7.2 Share of Administrative Costs by Administrative Level

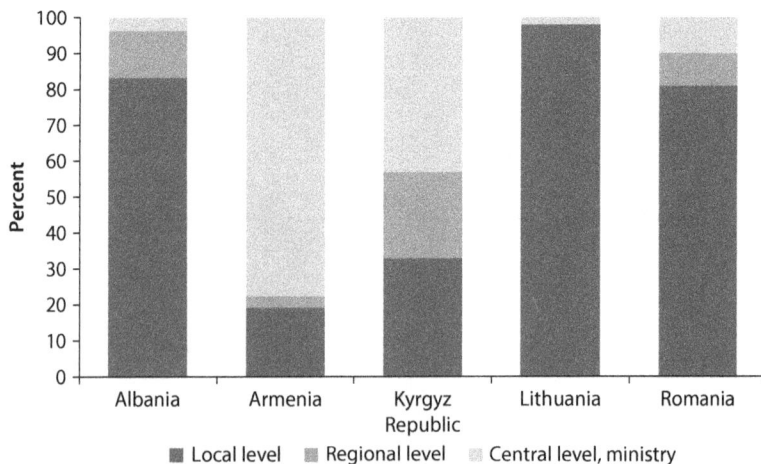

Source: Based on World Bank administrative costs surveys.

Table 7.4 Structure of Administrative Costs
Percent

Structure	Albania 2005	Armenia 2006	Bulgaria 2004	Bulgaria 2007	Kyrgyz Republic 2006	Lithuania 2005	Romania 2005
Total administrative cost	100.0	100.0	100.0	100.0	100.0	100.0	100.0
Design, planning, and coordination	1.4	3.4	13.3	11.8	3.6	6.9	4.3
Provision of information to clients, public relations, and appeals	0[a]	16.6	0[a]	0[a]	15.3	13.4	17.6
Eligibility determination and recertification	69.8	17.9	52.5	51.6	17.7	27.9	49.2
Maintenance of databases of beneficiaries	6.1	6.3	11.4	11.4	6.6	13.0	3.6
Payment of benefits	6.5	53.2	2.8	3.2	32.7	15.2	10.0
Audits, monitoring, and evaluation	16.1	2.7	13.8	14.9	24.1	23.6	15.3
Other	0	0	6.2	7.2	0	0	0

Source: Based on World Bank administrative costs surveys.
a. Costs are distributed across other functions, included mainly in determination of eligibility.

Answering the question "Is targeting cost effective?" is even more difficult, because the cost of targeting is not easy to define and to separate from other costs that would be incurred by the program in the absence of targeting. Ideally, one needs to separate the marginal cost of targeting, that is, those elements of costs that would not be encountered in programs using simpler targeting methods, such as by category or geography. The time spent verifying self-reported levels of income is clearly a targeting cost, but registration procedures and databases of participants will be needed even for universal programs. Intake interviews and supporting databases are indeed more complicated and costly for programs with complex targeting criteria. Nevertheless, it is difficult to estimate and impute the cost share corresponding to the increase in complexity because of targeting. In this report, we have approximated the marginal cost of targeting with the costs associated with eligibility determination and recertification.

The share of targeting costs in total administrative costs is not higher than 50–60 percent in any country but Albania (see figure 7.3). Relative to the total administrative cost, spending on targeting is higher in Albania and Bulgaria (more than 50 percent) and lower in Armenia and the Kyrgyz Republic (less than 20 percent, see table 7.4). In Albania and Bulgaria, this cost category may be overestimated because it includes activities related to outreach and information to clients, such as dealing with complaints and appeals, which in these countries were not reported separately.

Contrary to expectations, a high cost of home visits as a share of targeting cost does not seem to be the rule across countries. This cost can mean more time allocated to desk verification and cross-checks compared to home visits, but it may also mean a high transaction cost associated with cross-checks because of the weak endowment with information technology systems.

Figure 7.3 Targeting Costs: Composition and Share in Total Administrative Costs

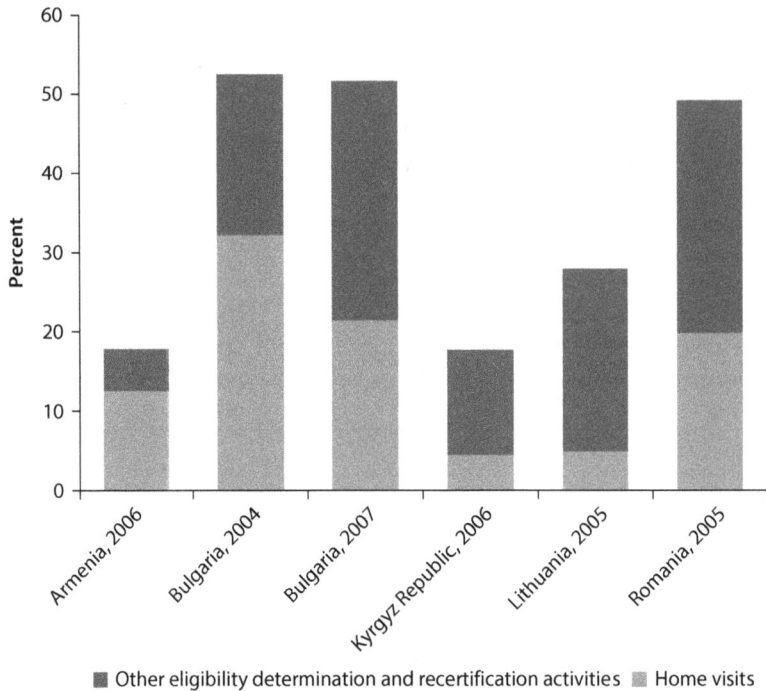

■ Other eligibility determination and recertification activities   ▨ Home visits

Source: Based on World Bank administrative costs surveys.

Does Means Testing Pay Off?

Given that means testing involves additional (marginal) administrative costs compared to, for example, categorical or geographical targeting, are these costs compensated by the additional benefits derived from improved targeting accuracy? If one takes into account existing CTR and cost structure for the LRIS programs examined in this chapter, the answer is unambiguously yes.

Consider, for example, a median LRIS program with a CTR ratio of about 10 and a share of targeting costs in total costs of about 50 percent. A categorical program will have a lower CTR of only 5 percent. However, a lower CTR does not indicate a more effective program in combating poverty. For a concrete example of the categorical program, assume the benefit per capita is 90 units, targeting costs are 5 units, and the other administrative costs are another 5 units. Also assume that about 40 percent of the children in the country are poor, for example, 2 million of 5 million children. This stylized situation is illustrated in figure 7.4, which shows the cost structure of a categorical child allowance program and a means-tested child allowance program. For the means-tested program, the ratio of total administrative costs to total costs (BDEG/ADEH) is higher than for the categorical program

Source: Grosh et al. 2008.

Figure 7.4 Conceptualizing Administrative Costs

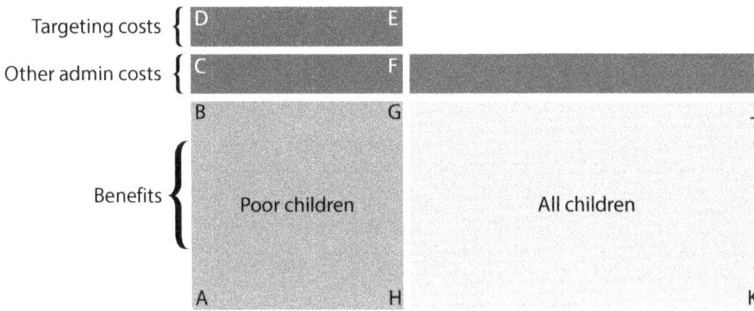

Note: admin = administrative.

(BCIJ/ACIK), but the extra administrative costs of targeting (CDEF) is just a fraction of the savings in benefits paid to the nonpoor children under the categorical program (HGJK). Using the stylized parameters, the targeting costs would amount to 10 million units (5 units × 2 million children). However, the additional targeting costs would save about 285 million units of program costs, including 270 million units of transfers to nonpoor children (90 units × 3 million children) and 15 units of additional administrative costs (5 units × 3 million children). The benefit-to-cost ratio is 27–1. In reality, the ratio will be somewhat lower because there will be inclusion error in the means-tested child allowance program; however, the benefit-cost ratio will remain in the same order of magnitude.

The factual experience of these programs seems to confirm that investment in targeting yields improved performance. Figure 7.5 plots the share of benefits accruing to the poorest 20 percent (targeting performance) against the CTR, as reported in the CTR table in annex 7B. Spending an additional US$0.05 on eligibility determination and recertification for each US$1.00 spent on benefits may improve the share of benefits going to the poorest by 10 percentage points. Interestingly, the cost of audits and monitoring, although relatively significant in most countries, does not seem to correlate with improved targeting performance, which may imply that the audit and monitoring functions of the programs covered in this study were weak at the time of measurement, as discussed in chapter 6.

Monitoring and Evaluating Administrative Costs

Currently, few countries in Eastern Europe and Central Asia regularly monitor the level and composition of administrative costs per program. However, this situation is about to change. The demand for accountability presses program managers to quantify and improve cost efficiency and cost effectiveness.

**Figure 7.5 Correlation between the Share of Program Benefits Reaching the Poorest
Quintile and the Cost-Transfer Ratio**

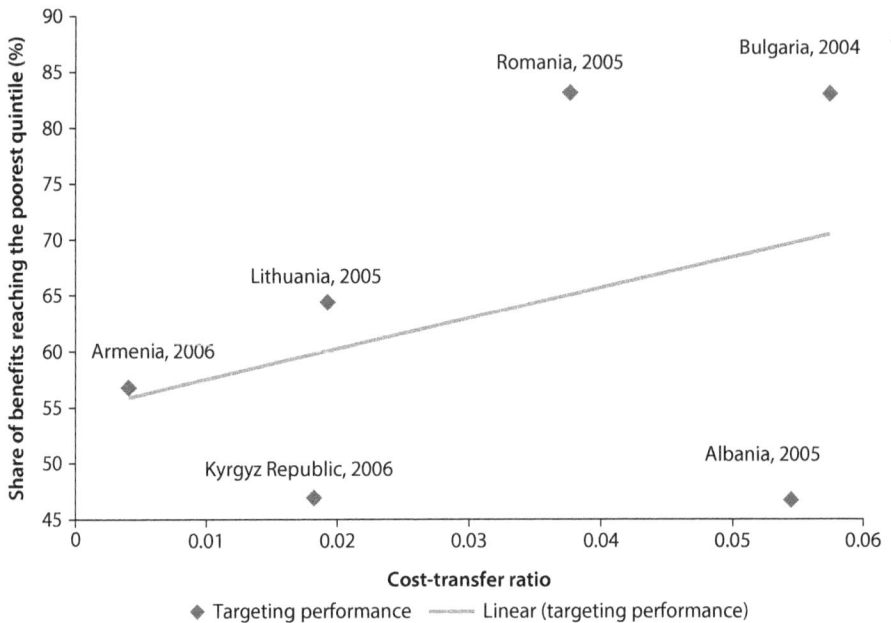

Source: Based on World Bank data.
Note: CTR = cost-transfer ratio.

The information on administrative costs is a critical element for such a type
of program evaluation.

Why is it important to monitor the level of administrative costs at the program and country levels? The regular monitoring of such costs, by institutional-
izing a monitoring system similar to the one-off exercise carried out for this
report, could help program managers adjust their administrative costs to an
efficient level. Disaggregated cost information by regional or frontline units could
reveal not only sources of possible cost reduction, but also underinvestments in
program administration. Such analysis could easily identify differences in the cost
of paying benefits across different payment modalities or providers. The disper-
sion of such costs across frontline units could spot both good and bad performers
and start bringing the poorly performing units toward the median. Or it could
highlight specific manual tasks requiring a large input of labor that could be
computerized.

At country and program levels, the best indicator to track progress is the
administrative cost per beneficiary, and the indicator eventually may be
complemented by a measure of the private cost incurred by the same beneficiary in accessing the program benefits. Blending administrative and private
costs in a composite indicator is justified, because frequent underinvestment
in administrative costs would raise private costs and vice versa. Such a system

to track the administrative and private costs per beneficiary is currently institutionalized in Romania for the three means-tested programs operated in the country (GMI, FBP, and a seasonal heating benefit). A milestone of the government's social assistance strategy is the reduction of administrative and private costs by at least 15 percent over three years. In addition to the headline indicator of administrative and private costs per beneficiary per month, the system is designed to provide information about the cost structure of both administrative and private costs, thereby helping program managers identify sources of cost savings.

Lessons

An important finding of this chapter is that the cost of moving one unit of benefit to beneficiaries is relatively low in mature, well-run programs in Eastern Europe and Central Asia: about 9 cents for one dollar.

Furthermore, the investment in administrative systems needed for narrow targeting (means testing) appears to be cost effective. Overall, the data on six countries point to a positive relationship between targeting costs and targeting performance. This relationship implies that to operate efficiently, the LRIS programs need appropriate levels of administrative costs to finance all functions of the program. Saving on administrative costs is often not the best option to save on the overall program costs: it may increase the inclusion and exclusion error and may not improve program effectiveness. Given the inherent complexity of administrative costs for narrowly targeted programs over those for categorically targeted programs, the share of such costs for LRIS programs should be expected to be higher. At the same time, the marginal increase in administrative costs per beneficiary associated with means testing is often compensated many times over by the targeting effect—limiting the scope of the program to those beneficiaries who need it most.

To improve program efficiency and effectiveness, Eastern Europe and Central Asia governments should focus on improving the effect of the transfers on the livelihoods of the beneficiaries. In our sample, transfers to beneficiaries represent more than 90 percent of the total budget of these programs: focusing on their efficiency and effectiveness is strategic. These improvements could derive from (a) better eligibility and recertification procedures that improve targeting and reduce error of exclusion; (b) well-designed coresponsibilities that incentivize beneficiaries to increase their labor supply or improve the human capital of their families; or (c) the provision of remedial services that could help poor beneficiaries move up the income ladder. To trigger such improvements, some programs would need more resources (hence higher administrative costs) for functions such as better program planning, monitoring, evaluation, and oversight. Saving on administrative costs is less effective and could be risky; administrative costs represent a small fraction of the total program costs, and underinvestment in critical program functions could lead to a deterioration of the program's inclusion or exclusion error.

Income Support for the Poorest • http://dx.doi.org/10.1596/978-1-4648-0237-9

Annex 7A: Functions and Activities by Levels of Government

Table 7A.1 Albania

Functions or activity groups	Activities by levels of administration			
	Local level	District level	Regional level (RSSS)	Central level
Program design, planning, and coordination	Preparation of request for funds; design and approval of local eligibility criteria		Preparation of proposals regarding bimonthly NE funds distribution based on inspections; preparation of reports regarding problems with NE program and possible improvements; training of SA	**SSS (State Social Services Agency):** Planning of bimonthly distribution of NE funds based on block grant indicators and results from inspections; preparation of reports regarding problems with NE program; drafting of NE program changes and improvements **Line ministry:** Preparation of reports regarding problems with NE program; drafting of NE program changes and improvements **Ministry of Finance:** Yearly preparation of total NE budget; bimonthly release of NE funds
Determination of eligibility and recertification	Request of applicant for NE benefit; interview of applicant and fulfillment of annual or monthly declarations; home visit; checking of information from other public offices like labor office, tax office, and so on; update of information (recertification); monthly meetings of municipal or communal council for determination of beneficiaries	Monthly cross-check of NE beneficiaries from tax office, SII offices, labor office, property register office, prefecture public service office, and so on		
Payment of benefits	Preparation of beneficiaries' payrolls; physical payment of NE benefit from municipal or communal cashiers			

table continues next page

Table 7A.1 **Albania** *(continued)*

Functions or activity groups	Activities by levels of administration			
	Local level	*District level*	*Regional level (RSSS)*	*Central level*
Maintenance of databases of beneficiaries	Registering of main beneficiary's data on computers or registers		Registering of inspection information in computers	**SSS:** Registering of information about NE beneficiaries by municipality and commune every month in computers; processing of data and monthly statistical reporting **Line ministry:** Collection of statistical information from SSS administration and preparation of monthly reports for ministry and INSTAT.
Audits, monitoring, and evaluation	Preparation of statistical reports		Monthly inspection (control of NE beneficiaries' documentation and spot check home visits)	**SSS:** Monthly inspections by Inspectorate Department; analysis of information; periodic meetings on NE performance; training of NE regional inspectors **Line ministry:** Monthly inspections by inspectorate and audit departments; monitoring of main NE program indicators; preparation of sectoral reports on poverty indicators; monitoring of main financial indicators **Ministry of Finance:** Monitoring of NE program expenses (both benefit expenses and administrative cost)

Source: Kolpeja 2005.
Note: INSTAT = Institute of Statistics; NE = Ndihma Ekonomike; RSSS = Regional State Social Service; SA = Social Administrator; SII = Social Insurance Institute.

Table 7A.2 Armenia

Functions or activity groups	Activities by levels of administration		
	Ministry level	*Regional level (marzpetaran)*	*RSSA level*
Program design, planning, and coordination	Development of draft legal acts and regulations to improve the legislation of FBP administration Monitoring of adopted legal acts implementation Development of monthly financial request forms for family benefits and lump-sum assistance and their provision to relevant agency Coordination of activities related to assignment and payment of family benefits and lump-sum assistance Preparation of monthly reports on FBP Planning, justification, and organization of business trips to marzer to provide methodological and practical assistance to RSSA staff	Budget redistribution for RSSA operation and maintenance by RSSAs Planning, justification, and organization of business trips to regions to local RSSA	
Eligibility determination and recertification activities, other than home visits	FBP data flow: collation of FBP applications data with data from other administrative sources. (Nork Information-Analytical Center) Calculation of FBP vulnerability score and preparation of a list of beneficiary families (Nork Information-Analytical Center) Tendering of announcements for printing applications and discussion of tender Copying of application forms and their delivery to marzer	Invitation and organization of sessions of the Social Assistance Council (in case the council chair is the marzpetaran representative) Participation at the sessions of the Social Assistance Council (in case the council chair is the head of RSSA)	Application data entry Exchange of Information with MLSA Exchange of information with Nork Information-Analytical Center Receipt of FBP payment sheets from Nork Information-Analytical Center Invitation and organization of sessions of the Social Assistance Council (in case the council chair is the head of RSSA) Participation at the sessions of the Social Assistance Council (in case the council chair is the marzpetaran representative) Preparation or participation in preparation of reports on council's decisions and presentation of them to MLSA
Home visits		Planning, justification, and organization of home visits by RSSAs	Planning, justification, and implementation of home visits Preparation of reports on results of home visits

table continues next page

Table 7A.2 Armenia (continued)

Functions or activity groups	Activities by levels of administration		
	Ministry level	Regional level (marzpetaran)	RSSA level
Information provided to clients, public relations, and appeals	Cooperation with councils on social assistance Organization of meetings, seminars, and conferences Collaboration with international and local NGOs dealing with social issues Processing of letters and appeals from applicants and beneficiaries (including preparation of answers to and delivery of such letters) Audiences for beneficiaries and applicants (complaints, and so on) Cooperation with public relations department of the ministry and with media representatives	Processing of letters and appeals from applicants and beneficiaries (including preparation of answers to and delivery of such letters) Audiences for beneficiaries and applicants (complaints, and so on)	Customer service: provision of clarifications and explanations Completion or acceptance of applications and their initial logical control Processing of letters and appeals from applicants and beneficiaries (including preparation of answers to and delivery of such letters) Cross-check of information and request for clarifications if necessary
Payment of benefits			Submission of payment lists to regional treasury office Submission of payment sheets to the paying agency (usually post office) Receipt of payment sheets from the paying agency and entry of data to database Preparation of a payment receipt together with the paying agency and submission to MLSA
Audits, monitoring, and evaluation	Summary and analysis of monthly, biannual, and annual reports on FBP and lump-sum assistance received from RSSAs and paying agencies Control of activities undertaken to restore the right to FBP for households excluded from the FBP system Monitoring, revisions, and audits of FBP system activities and preparation of reports Development of administrative statistics based on data collected through administrative questionnaires, certificates, and other reports	Processing of information received from RSSAs Preparation of monthly reports submitted to marzpet Monitoring, revisions, and audits of FBP system activities and preparation of reports Preparation of reports on council's decisions and presentation of them to MLSA	Preparation of monthly report on FBP applications for marzpetaran

Source: Harutyunyan 2005.
Note: FBP = Family Benefit Program; marz = state; marzer = states; marzpet = governor; marzpetaran = governors; MLSA = Ministry of Labor and Social Affairs; NGO = non governmental organization; RSSA = regional social services agency.

Income Support for the Poorest • http://dx.doi.org/10.1596/978-1-4648-0237-9

Table 7A.3　Kyrgyz Republic

Functions or activity groups	Activities by levels of administration			
	Ministry	Rayon	Town	Aiyl okmotu
Program design, planning, and coordination	Development of draft legal acts and regulations to improve the legislation of UMB administration Monitoring of implementation of adopted legal acts Coordination of activities related to assignment and lump-sum assistance Planning of number of beneficiaries Planning, justification, and organization of business trips to rayons, towns, and aiyl okmotus to provide methodological and practical assistance to staff			
Eligibility determination and recertification activities, other than home visits		Receipt and check of documents from one aiyl okmotu social worker Check of organizations and farms that issued income references Setting of UMB	Receipt and check of documents from one aiyl okmotu social worker Check of organizations and farms that issued income references Receipt of additional documents and prolongation of welfare payment, every 3 months Setting of UMB	Check of collected documents and additional consultation Registration of new applicant; UMB calculation; preparation and registration of documents for setting UMB for one applicant Annual documents renewal for one UMB receiver Performance of work with inspectors
Home visits		Visit to one applicant's home	Visit to one applicant's home	Visit to home
Information provided to clients, public relations, and appeals		Consultation with one applicant Issuance of references (for hospitals, schools, kindergartens) Work with one notification and complaint Preparation of reply to complaint	Consultation with one applicant Issuance of references (for hospitals, schools, kindergartens) Work with one notification and complaint Preparation of reply to complaint Conducting of technical training	First appeal to benefit, consultation for documents collecting Completion of social passports Creation of survey questionnaires Performance of work with most active members of the village (joomat)

table continues next page

Table 7A.3 Kyrgyz Republic *(continued)*

Functions or activity groups	Activities by levels of administration			
	Ministry	*Rayon*	*Town*	*Aiyl okmotu*
		Conducting of technical training Analysis of different information Documents processing Documents receipt Maintenance of work journals Compilation of lists for electric power compensations Registration of archived files Sending of personal files outside of rayon	Participation in meetings Preparation of documents for 12 kinds of welfare for experiment Delivery of suspended documents to archives Maintenance of registration journal Documents processing	
Payment of benefits	Issuance by payment centers and postal offices			
Maintenance of databases of beneficiaries		Sending of notifications to payment centers Summary, processing, and entry of data into computer	Sending of notifications to payment centers Summary, processing, and entry of data into computer	Preparation of other lists Rayon department of social protection Oblast department payment center
Audits, monitoring, and evaluation	Control of end use of money Spot check of household's receipt of money	Check of aiyl okmotu Check of financing and benefits payment in post offices Conducting of inventory with payment center Correction of UMB reports Preparation of gender information by UMB Preparation of different information and data about welfare department	Check of aiyl okmotu Check of financing and benefits payment in post offices Conducting of inventory with payment center Correction of UMB reports Preparation of gender information by UMB Preparation of different information, lists, and data about welfare department	Preparation of lists for employment service Delivery of lists to rayon SP service for confirmation Preparation of reports to rayon SP service Rayon department of social protection Oblast department of social protection Rayon statistical agency, department of social protection of population, NGO

Source: Kyrgyzstan Center for Social and Economic Research 2005.
Note: NGO = nongovernmental organization; SP = social protection; UMB = Unified Monthly Benefit.

Table 7A.4 Romania

Functions or activity groups	Activities by levels of administration		
	Local level	County level	Ministry level
Program design, planning, and coordination		Meetings and seminars conducted with county social assistants	Overall coordination of GMI program Preparation of legislation, improvements, or changes Training of staff at central and regional offices Support to counties and municipalities by phone
Eligibility determination and recertification activities, other than home visits	Examination of file and clarification of various aspects related to the manner of file preparation (interview) Preparation of report and completion of social investigation card as a result of home visit Calculation of benefit to which an applicant family is entitled Drafting of a decision Updating of an application (as a result of modifications in family composition, incomes, and so on) Renewal of an application (after suspension, payment cessation, and so on)		
Home visits	Visit to applicant's domicile		
Information provided to clients, public relations, and appeals	Explanations offered, upon first meeting, to person requesting GMI Assistance in completing an application, if applicable Audiences for beneficiaries and applicants (complaints, and so on) Answering of complaints	Audiences for beneficiaries and applicants (complaints, and so on) Processing of letters from applicants and beneficiaries (including preparation of answers to such letters)	Answering of letters and claims
Payment of benefits	Preparation of lists of beneficiaries for payment Payments to beneficiaries (if applicable)		
Maintenance of databases of beneficiaries	Registration of applications in computer or registry Preparation of beneficiary lists to be sent to other institutions, if applicable		

table continues next page

Table 7A.4 Romania (continued)

Functions or activity groups	Activities by levels of administration		
	Local level	County level	Ministry level
Audits, monitoring, and evaluation	Preparation of monthly reports for the County Directorates of Dialogue, Social Solidarity and Family Inspections by county directorates	Processing and revising of statistical reports received from municipalities Preparation of monthly statistical reports regarding the GMI (including data entry, if applicable) Monitoring-and-guidance trips in the field, to municipalities Drafting of monitoring reports	Monitoring of implementation of adopted legal acts Summary and analysis of reports on GMI received from county directorates Preparation of statistics and reports Conducting of studies and research Conducting of inspections

Source: Pop 2005.
Note: GMI = guaranteed minimum income.

Annex 7B: Breakdown of the Cost-Transfer Ratio (Ratio of Administrative Costs to Total Program Costs), by Elements of Cost

	Albania 2005	Armenia 2006	Bulgaria 2004	Bulgaria 2007	Kyrgyz Republic 2006	Lithuania 2005	Romania 2005
Cost-transfer ratio	0.078	0.023	0.109	0.193	0.103	0.069	0.077
Design, planning, and coordination	0.001	0.001	0.015	0.023	0.004	0.005	0.003
Provision of information to clients, public relations, and appeals	0[a]	0.004	0[a]	0[a]	0.016	0.009	0.013
Eligibility determination and recertification	0.054	0.004	0.057	0.099	0.018	0.019	0.038
Maintenance of databases of beneficiaries	0.005	0.001	0.012	0.022	0.007	0.009	0.003
Payment of benefits	0.005	0.012	0.003	0.006	0.034	0.010	0.008
Audits, monitoring, and evaluation	0.013	0.001	0.015	0.029	0.025	0.016	0.012
Other	0	0	0.007	0.014	0	0	0

Source: Estimations based on country case studies.
a. Costs are distributed across other functions, included mainly in determination of eligibility.

Notes

1. See also Caldes, Coady, and Maluccio (2006) for a discussion of the factors influencing the CTR.

2. This fact may further imply that the targeting costs depend on other activities such as information and awareness campaigns, which may lower the targeting costs because fewer noneligible applicants will apply.

3. Mexico's PROGRESA, created in 1997, has been known as *Oportunidades* since 2002.

References

Caldes, N., D. Coady, and J. Maluccio. 2006. "The Cost of Poverty Alleviation Transfer Programs: A Comparative Analysis of Three Programs in Latin America." *World Development* 34 (5): 818–37.

Grosh, M., C. del Ninno, E. Tesliuc, and A. Ouerghi. 2008. *For Protection and Promotion: The Design and Implementation of Effective Safety Nets.* Washington, DC: World Bank.

Harutyunyan, L. 2005. "Poverty Family Benefit—Program Implementation Matters for Targeting Performance: Evidence and Lessons from Armenia." Paper prepared for the seminar, "Program Implementation Matters for Targeting Performance: Evidence and Lessons from Eastern and Central Europe," Bucharest, June 6–7.

Hodges, A., P. White, and M. Greenslade. 2011. *Guidance for DFID Country Offices on Measuring and Maximising Value for Money in Cash Transfer Programmes. Toolkit and Explanatory Text.* Unpublished report, U.K. Department for International Development, London.

Kolpeja, V. 2005. "Ndihma Ekonomike—Program Implementation Matters for Targeting Performance: Evidence and Lessons from Albania." Paper prepared for the seminar, "Program Implementation Matters for Targeting Performance: Evidence and Lessons from Eastern and Central Europe," Bucharest, June 6–7.

Kyrgyzstan Center for Social and Economic Research. 2005. "The Unified Monthly Benefit—Program Implementation Matters for Targeting Performance: Evidence and Lessons from Kyrgyzstan." Paper prepared for the seminar, "Program Implementation Matters for Targeting Performance: Evidence and Lessons from Eastern and Central Europe," Bucharest, June 6–7.

Lindert, K., A. Linder, J. Hobbs, and B. de la Brière. 2007. "The Nuts and Bolts of Brazil's Bolsa Família Program: Implementing Conditional Cash Transfers in a Decentralized Context." Social Protection Discussion Paper 0709, World Bank, Washington, DC.

Pop, L. 2005. "Means-Tested Programs in Romania—Program Implementation Matters for Targeting Performance: Evidence and Lessons from Romania." Paper prepared for the seminar, "Program Implementation Matters for Targeting Performance: Evidence and Lessons from Eastern and Central Europe," Bucharest, June 6–7.

CHAPTER 8

Summary and Conclusions

The experiences of last-resort income support (LRIS) programs in Eastern Europe and Central Asia have demonstrated the technical feasibility of highly efficient poverty-targeted programs in the region. This chapter highlights some of the lessons that stand out from the report as a whole.

The Role of LRIS in Wider Social Assistance and Social Protection Systems in Eastern Europe and Central Asia

The authors argue that the capacity to identify the poor and vulnerable at moderate costs is an institutional asset, important to maintain and improve. It may become increasingly important in the future. LRIS programs must not be allowed to further wither and, in some places, must be enlarged for their core role as last-resort programs today and for their ability to serve as a nexus to other parts of social policy, to ready them for crisis response, and to be on call as social policy changes shape the future. We see several forces that may increase the need for, or importance of, LRIS programs in coming years.

Over the short term, many countries in Eastern Europe and Central Asia need to roll back the deficits incurred during the 2008–10 global crisis. The average decline in fiscal position during the crisis was 3.1 percent of gross domestic product, although it reached more than 5.0 percent in some cases (much less in the hydrocarbon-producing countries). Lacking strong economic growth, some countries may have to resort to expenditure cuts and streamlining of their social protection systems, which are usually extensive, expensive, and fragmented. Even though two-thirds of the region's population is covered by some type of social protection system, the poor and those most in need have access to little assistance, and many remain excluded. Increasing the role of LRIS within a reduced social protection budget will help protect the poor in such a consolidation:

- Countries in Eastern Europe and Central Asia, as in any region of the world, remain at risk of another recession or stagnation and need instruments of crisis response that are as efficient as possible. People facing deprivation and poverty on a chronic basis or as a result of household-specific shocks (such as the illness or death of an income earner, an accident or disability, or the loss of a job) will remain numerous in the region, especially in the context of protracted job crisis and volatility. Experience around the world and in Eastern Europe and Central Asia shows that without timely, adequate assistance, people can be forced into detrimental actions such as selling their most productive assets, postponing health care, or reducing investment in their children as human capital (World Bank 2012). This risk will make it harder for them or their children to escape destitution. Responsive and well-functioning, well-targeted social assistance can break these cycles of poverty and, by protecting against downside risks, allow people to take a more active stance in the labor market.

• LRIS programs may become increasingly linked to other programs of social policy for multiple reasons. First, countries that operate more than one income- or means-tested program could obviously reduce the administrative and client costs and reduce the scope of error and fraud by harmonizing the rules of procedures for these programs or by merging them into a larger, streamlined program. This approach could draw LRIS programs together into a more coordinated package with other poverty-targeted programs—heating or housing subsidies, means-tested child allowance, means-tested access to health insurance subsidies, and so on. Second, especially where the income guarantee design predominates and where eligibility thresholds and benefits are relatively high, links to activation programs will become important to counter disincentives to work.

• With the region undergoing marked aging of the population, the cost of pensions, health care, and elderly care systems will increase. To create the fiscal space required, countries would need to be more selective with their spending. They could use the know-how accumulated with LRIS programs to supplement old age support, to provide a more efficient targeted means to support the needy, or to rationalize a larger set of public expenditures. Moreover, to support the growing number of elderly, countries need to invest in the human capital of all children and adults, including the poor, who often lag the rest of the population in terms of skills, employability, productivity, or earning capacity. Everybody, the poor included, counts. LRIS programs are an important tool to ensure priority access for the poor to a number of government services and cash transfers that can help close the human capital gap.

Strengthening LRIS Programs in Eastern Europe and Central Asia

Despite the successes of LRIS programs, there is an active agenda for policy action with respect to them in Eastern Europe and Central Asia. Nearly every program has one or more dimensions in which it seeks improvement.

Some common issues exist across a number of programs, for which solutions can be drawn from experience in the region or beyond.

Coverage is low, sometimes very low (3–38 percent of the poorest quintile in most countries; see chapters 2 and 4). To address this challenge, programs can do the following:

- In many cases, implementing straightforward increases in eligibility thresholds and budgets will be needed to improve coverage.
- Updating eligibility and benefit formulas will be needed. At a minimum, this means indexing them rather than allowing their real value to erode over time. Indexing to the value of real wages rather than to inflation will help a program keep a constant place in social policy, avoiding the near policy irrelevance into which some LRIS programs have fallen. Alternatively, LRIS programs may need to shift to relative poverty concepts, aiming to cover, for example, the poorest 5 percent of the population, or those whose incomes are below one-third or one-half of the median income.
- Removing or recalibrating multiple asset filters may reduce errors of exclusion.
- Improving information and outreach and lowering transaction costs to potential claimants will be important in some countries.

Improving the incidence or progressivity of LRIS programs is never a completely finished agenda and thus a pertinent if not prominent issue everywhere. However, it is the most important issue in a few countries whose targeting results are well below the regional average:

- For countries and programs where incidence needs to be improved, solutions may be possible by strengthening imputations for hard-to-verify incomes; employing cost-efficient documentation and verification of reported information; and, where warranted, complementing income testing with asset testing or other targeting methods.
- All countries could improve both targeting efficiency of LRIS programs and program compliance by investing in appropriate controls to prevent, detect, and deter error and fraud and to ensure a stronger oversight and control framework.

Administration in decentralized settings is a matter of setting the right checks and balances (see chapters 3 and 6):

- To address the typical principal–agent dilemma characteristic of national programs implemented by local governments—a feature that is largely present in Eastern Europe and Central Asia—policy makers should consider introducing performance incentives in LRIS programs. Levels of supervision and accountability will need to be higher where local levels of government are granted higher orders of discretion.

- The development of program procedure manuals or service standards for program administrators is an essential element for effective implementation, especially in the context of decentralized or complex implementation arrangements. This element was omitted in many countries in Eastern Europe and Central Asia.

- Another area that has great potential for improvement is the use of program information systems for planning, budgeting, oversight, monitoring, and evaluation. For countries that still operate paper-and-pencil information systems, the first step is to develop management information systems (MISs) using modern information and communication technology. For those countries that have MISs, the challenge is to put this information to work to improve program performance, as outlined in chapter 6.

- Countries should reflect on or reform the fundamental design of guaranteed minimum income (GMI; see chapters 4, 5, and 7): At present, GMI formulas predominate in the determination of benefits. Countries with larger informal sectors would probably be better off choosing simpler benefit formulas. This approach would reduce administrative costs, reduce fraud and error, and help redress grievances, as well as reduce work disincentives.

- Countries with smaller informal sectors and higher administrative capacities could experiment with more complex formulas that would offer protection against poverty while preserving incentives to work, by decreasing the implicit marginal tax rate on earnings below 100 percent.

- The first goal of LRIS programs is to provide simple income support, but in some countries the programs also carry requirements or services to help poor households improve their livelihoods or build the human capital of their children and adults. In most countries in Eastern Europe and Central Asia, this agenda is in its infancy, but is a growing activity.

Lessons for Other Regions

The experiences of LRIS programs in Eastern Europe and Central Asia add to the growing body of international evidence that successful social assistance programs are possible in countries across a range of income and degrees of informality. A few issues are of particular note:

- *Means testing* is often thought too difficult and inaccurate for use in economies with significant informal sectors, yet it has been used with reasonable success throughout Eastern Europe and Central Asia and in a few countries in other regions. This book parses income from various sources regarding whether income is hard or easy to measure and verify, reports how countries impute income from some sources, and then documents the magnitude of the remaining unreported incomes for several countries and the way these magnitudes change across the spectrum of welfare and from urban to rural areas. Other countries that are considering whether to use a means-test or to add income variables into proxy means tests could readily adopt this analytic framework.

- This study provides one of the best conceptual treatments of administrative costs and the way to think about them, coupled with more detailed accounting for a number of programs. The empirical findings reinforce the lesson that to operate efficiently, LRIS programs need an appropriate level of administrative cost to finance all functions of the program. "Saving" on administrative costs is often not the best option for saving on overall program costs, because it may increase the targeting errors and work against improving program effectiveness. Given their inherently greater complexity, one should expect that the share of administrative costs for LRIS programs would be higher than for categorically targeted programs. However, the marginal increase in administrative costs per beneficiary associated with means testing is often compensated many times over by the targeting effect of limiting the scope of the project to a smaller beneficiary group.

- Many programs in the region use a GMI formula designed to cover the gap between current family income and a defined threshold. This approach offers the potential benefit of wringing the greatest impact on poverty out of every dollar spent on programs but carries greater complexity in gathering information, room for fraud and error, difficulty in communicating benefits to families, and so on. It also carries a significant theoretical disincentive to work, which is then mitigated through more complex formulas to reduce the de facto marginal tax rate on earnings, keeping benefits low and then adding additional benefits for those who are not expected to work, or introducing work, job search, or other "activation requirements." On the whole, the complexity does not seem worthwhile, and the authors recommend that other countries do not emulate the GMI formula.

- The experience in low-income countries of Eastern Europe and Central Asia adds evidence that relatively well-functioning poverty-targeted programs are possible in low-income countries elsewhere. The programs also testify to the possibilities of minimum administrative capacity being feasible in these settings and demonstrate that basic program functions can be done with paper-and-pencil record keeping.

- In Eastern Europe and Central Asia, service delivery—eligibility determination, benefit award, enrollment, registration in the databases, recertification, and payrolls—is in most cases the responsibility of the lowest administrative level of elected government (municipalities, cities, towns, *rayons*, wards, or communes), usually with staff from specialized departments to run the programs. It is less common for program implementation at the local level to be decentralized to regional or local departments of the line ministry of social protection. The experience of decentralization includes several examples of financing that are left to local governments, which in each case resulted in a decline in program budgets and a deterioration of horizontal equity that often resulted in a recentralization of financing. Combining centralized financing of the program with strong oversight and control over decentralized frontline units seems the best institutional arrangement for these programs.

Reference

World Bank. 2012. "Safety Nets Work: During Crisis and Prosperity." Paper prepared for the Development Committee Meeting, World Bank, Washington, DC, April 11.